MY INSTITUTE VERSUS ME

JACOB MBUA NGEVE

MY INSTITUTE VERSUS ME

iUniverse books may be ordered through booksellers or by contacting:

iUniverse
1663 Liberty Drive
Bloomington, IN 47403
www.iuniverse.com
844-349-9409

ISBN: 978-1-6632-2808-6 (sc)
ISBN: 978-1-6632-2809-3 (e)

Library of Congress Control Number: 2021921376

Print information available on the last page.

iUniverse rev. date: 03/03/2022

To Yaya Sarah Etonde Mosoke
Who gave me the foundation to succeed and who
taught me the patience to withstand stress

DEDICATION

I want to thank my late sister, Christiana Enanga Monjowa Ngeve, who gave me the opportunity to go to school. Monjowa, wherever you may be, know that forever I will have you deeply in my heart. I love you for making me great. My elder sister Sophie Nduma Ngeve made me know what life was all about. I will forever remember you for that first pair of shoes I wore during Christmas. Mbamba Mataene, Mola Charles Eko, Daniel Ngale, Rose Enanga and Mola Lucas Kake Mosoke are not here to share in this joy, but I remember you fondly for bringing me up and taking me through the early stages of my life.

My younger sister, Rebecca Efosi Ngeve, gave me comfort and support in my journey to the summit of science. I sincerely thank you for the many things you did to keep me going.

My younger brother, Emmanuel Ngeve, and his family took care of me during the time I was sick. I have forgotten that you could be that useful, but you showed me that blood was thicker than water all the time I was in the hospital. It will take forever to complete the digestion of that food and care.

Dr Grace Enanga Mbonde, my younger sister and family doctor brought me back to life at a time when all hopes were shattered and when I knew I was on my way to the world beyond. Thank you immensely Grace for being there for me.

Several doctors brought me back to life after my ankle injury. I remember fondly Dr Luigi Pascarella, vascular surgeon, and Morgan Wamblo, a wonderful and innovative wound nurse who performed miracles to save my leg. Drs Alex Keagy and Kelly Sluss managed my post-surgical care for the one year of my convalescence. My heartful thanks go to them for doing all they could to bring me back to life.

Dr Simon Lyonga and Dr Jacques Eckebil mentored me faithfully in my journey to become a scientist and Mola Mafany Musonge was there for me when I was building up my finances and at the time when I was undergoing stress at the workplace. Hannah, my wife was there when things were good and when they went sour. Thank you all for the support, for the encouragement and for making me able to gather the ashes when all hopes were gone.

Finally, my family especially Francis Mokomba, David Ikome, Celestine Etonde, Magdalene Namondo, Eugene Ngale, Franklin Ngenye, Lovett Eko, Sally Joso, Smith Molua, Ryan-Einstein Ndive, Teddy-Faith Mafany, Herschel Nyoki, Hansel Nalionge, Bridgette Sophie Nduma, Christiana Enanga Monjowa, Dyphna Efosi, Elizabeth Efeti Njie, Vivian Limunga Enoru, Rose Enanga Betang, Emmanuel Yumu, Conrad Ngeve, my late niece, Serah Etonde Bissong, my late namesake Jacob Mbua Njie Efome, Patience Ndobe and Genevieve Nnam who provided me with the much needed comfort during the difficult and lonely times I had in the hospital and during the post-hospital interventions. I thank you all for giving me the support I needed at that crucial period of my life. May God bless you all.

Jacob Mbua Ngeve recounts in a vivid way the story of himself, a research scientist of the Tropicana Rural Development Institute (TDRI), who spends a long career characterized by a plethora of stresses of various types in that institute. Stressors he faces were with:

• Heads of research structures in the Institute,
• His promotion to higher research grades,
• His administrative nominations at the workplace,
• Frustration resulting from cancellation of international events for which he was chief organizer,
• Stresses from a greedy CEO who he met at TRDI,
• Stress from the perennial problem of shortage of research funds, and
• Slanders and sabotage from his adversaries in the institute.

And when he worked his way up to becoming the CEO of TRDI, a King's appointee, the stresses did not end. He lived a difficult life since then:

• Being stressed by the intrigues of a greedy CFO he met in the Institute,
• He had difficult relations with project heads and
• He had bad dealings with some members of the King's Cabinet

He shows how he tried to get over these hurdles for thirty-five years, and cautions young people coming after him that the path to becoming successful in an environment and a system like that of Tropicana is a long, lonely and frustrating one, but that success can be achieved if the growing scientist is hardworking, industrious and tactful because where there is a will there is a way.

Now, in his own little way, Jacob Mbua Ngeve provides the underlying facts on how he started as a research technician, worked his way to becoming a full research professor respected by many in the region, impacting research management and research output under extremely difficult conditions of stresses from colleagues who he had so much confidence in to bosses who felt they could enrich themselves with funds from the institution he was heading.

He shows how, from an unknown minor tribe in the Federal Republic of Tropicana, he was able to unify his adversaries and get the best out of them to succeed as top manager of his research institute which became an exemplary institution in the region. He concludes that he was finally fired as CEO of TRDI not because of failure in his duties but because of a failing system of the Kingdom of Tropicana. He left the place very satisfied with his accomplishments and was glad to continue his activities in the region which ended up being even more impactful in the continent than he had expected.

CONTENTS

INTRODUCTION

A scientist faces several challenges as he grows up through the various rungs of the research ladder. In addition to the perennial problem of shortage of funds, there is competition and rivalry between colleagues in the Research, as they all strive to attain higher grades and positions in the Institute. A hard-working researcher may also be thought of as being a rival of the CEO for his position as Director General, even if he is just doing his work of a researcher. In a multi-ethnic society like Tropicana, other tribes, especially the large ones may just develop hatred for you simply because you are getting to the limelight and getting near to being considered for appointment to higher positions. In such a country, every Institute has cliques of people each camp preparing candidates, irrespective of competence or talent, for higher administrative positions in the Institute.

That was the case with the Tropicana Rural Development Institute (TRDI). The TRDI was the largest research institute carrying out investigations in rural development in the region. It was a major technology developer. Results from TRDI research were being disseminated not only to growers and agro-industrial complexes in the country but also to neighbouring countries in the region.

I was lucky that through an international fellowship, the Federal Republic of Tropicana had selected me for graduate training abroad. It was a rare event because I was sponsored to do degree programs for the BSc and the MSc in rural development in any institution of my choice. I had chosen Jimmy Carter's country for my studies. At the time I was chosen to go abroad I was a field research technician with the rank of agricultural technical officer, working in the Tropicana Rural Development Institute, one of the research institutes under the technical supervisory authority of the Ministry of Rural Development Investigations. The Supervisory authorities of that Institute were the Ministry-Secretary of the Treasury and the Ministry-Secretary of Rural Development Investigations. Their roles were different. The Secretary of the Treasury was responsible for supervising financial management in the Institute, while the Secretary of Rural Development Investigations was in charge of supervising technical matters in the Institute. In principle the technical supervision needed to be handled by a renowned researcher but for some reason that position for quite some time was relegated to people with no technical knowledge of rural development. The excuse was just that there were technical directors in the Ministry to handle technical matters, and that the Secretary was just there to handle political issues. Therefore, any person could be named to head that Ministry. The King of Tropicana argued that he could name anybody to occupy that post because of his interest in respecting regionalism. It was not a policy that the Secretary had to defend his position in front of Congress to show his or her competence in the field. For the time I was in the Institute prior to leaving for higher studies, the Minister-Secretary of Rural Development Investigations was a well-educated professor known as Henry Mboko. Later, after my training, a lady was sent there in the name of Lena BigStuff, a lady who initially had received professional training in pharmaceutical sciences but who had not succeeded in that field, and instead jumped into politics, an area where she had been supported to be appointed by one of the King's friends, an elite in her ethnic group.

The CEO of the Rural Development Institute was a gentleman called Dr Ma'ama Ma Mbazi. His Chief Financial Officer was Andrew Mebane, a young religious guy who became very close to him. The person who the board had named accountant was a gentleman called Satin. He was quite experienced because he had worked with several expatriates as accountant. But after several years there was a re-organization in the country and the Minister-Secretary of the Treasury became the one mandated to name a person from his ministry to serve as accountant in the Institute. That is how Rhodanny Moliza Molondo was named accountant of TRDI. The Financial auditor was also named by the Minister-Secretary of the Treasury. The person named to that position was Johnson Igbe Vezenga.

The Heads of Projects were proposed by the CEO but appointed by the board. The name of the leader of seed systems was a researcher Conrad Moliki. I, Mwayé mo Wonduka, from a minority tribe in the country, became somehow sandwiched between these people all from major tribes in the Federal Republic of Tropicana. To grow as a researcher I was forced to survive under six types of stressors. The first was from the Secretary of Rural Development Investigations. The second was from the Chief Executive of the Institute. The third stressor was from the Chief Financial Officer of the Institute, while the fourth stressor was from the Chiefs of the Research Centers under whom I was working. My problems did not end there. I had to face the intrigues of the Chief of Projects who had formed a tribal network with the Minister-Secretary by virtue of the fact that they came from the same tribe. To crown these all, I was faced with the problem of shortage of funds to carry out the research I was called up to investigate, as well as the usual workplace slandering of colleagues who considered me a rival for administrative positions that could come up, especially that of CEO which was already vacant; Dr Ma'ama Ma Mbazi was just there in the Institute awaiting the King's decree to replace him.

The book is about stresses in the work environment. In this book, Jacob Mbua Ngeve from the Bantu African country of Tropicana recounts the story of his experiences. He works very hard to make it to the top as a rural development researcher and to becoming the chief executive officer of the largest institution conducting rural development investigations in the Bantu region. He shows that there are many hurdles in growing up as a scientist in a developing country. At an advanced stage of his career he lists the kinds of stresses and temptations which he went through, first as a scientist and then as a chief executive, insisting that it takes a strong will power and the ability to withstand temptations to be able to make a young man in his position survive in a terribly competitive and corrupt atmosphere.

He recounts the long lecture which a medical colleague working in a large medical facility near him, gave him when he told him that he was going through a lot of stress in the TRDI workplace.

There are several kinds of stresses which I had to undergo to survive in this country. Some were emotional, others behavioural whereas other stresses were simply physical. In this book I give advice to young people who are growing and aspiring to develop to high places that the challenges they would face are many. According to a medical doctor who was close to me and who started following me up when I started running into trouble at my workplace there is a clear distinction between stress and stressor, stress being a bodily reaction and a feeling of emotional or physical tension, whereas stressor was the actual cause of the stress. He cautioned that although stress itself was necessary for survival, too much stress had to be avoided because it could be detrimental. At the end of my stay in the Tropicana Rural Development Institute I summarized what, according to him, were the different types of stress and their possible causes. These stresses affected me in different degrees and made life really uncomfortable for me in my working life, in spite of the fact that I loved my job as a research scientist and even when I served as chief executive.

Of the three main types of stress (acute, episodic acute and chronic stress) the doctor showed that each had its own characteristics, symptoms, duration and treatment approaches. He went on to use another classification of stress to show that time stress, anticipatory stress, situational stress and encounter stress could step in when the individual was frustrated.

I was then able to identify three main causes of stress in the TRDI workplace: money, work pressure and health. I could compare the work-related stress with the good health I had enjoyed when I was growing up. I found out that these stressors could be worsened by other events such as death of a loved one, separation and divorce of your partner, loss of a job and the problems created by marriage, and moving to a new home, none of which had much to do with me in making me as stressed as I had become.

According to the experiences I have had, emotional stress involves the experience of negative effects such as anxiety, fear, anger and sadness which are all day to day responses that occurred to anybody. Emotional or psychological stress could stay around for some time. It had been shown to weaken the immune system and cause fatigue, depression, shortness of breath and anxiety. Emotional stress could even lead to high blood pressure, resentments, fears, frustration, sadness, grief and bereavement. With these many effects on the human body, it was necessary to do everything to avoid stress in the workplace.

I recommend that to cope with the situation it is important to reduce the triggers of stress, examine your values and live by them. It is also very important to study and practice relaxation techniques that could help you cope with the stressors.

The doctor also described what he called cognitive stress. This was often caused by information overload, accelerated sense of time, worry, guilt, shame, jealousy, resistance, attachments, self criticism, unworkable perfectionism, panic attacks and anxiety. When people are stressed they get sick and cannot handle even simple ailments like colds because the immune system often becomes too weak to fight the virus.

Behavioral stress, on the other hand, he continued, led to procrastinating and avoiding responsibilities –Symptoms of this kind of stress were the avoidance of tasks, sleep problems, difficulties in completing work assignments, fidgeting, tremors, strained face, clenching fists, crying, changes in drinking, eating and smoking, at the same time exhibiting more nervous behaviors such as nail biting fidgeting and pacing, as well as over eating, undereating, drug or alcohol misuse, and tobacco use. You could experience other symptoms of behavioural stress such as constant worry, problems with your memory or concentration, making bad decisions when serious circumstances occurred, feeling overwhelmed, unmotivated or unfocused, constant worry, depression and anxiety. Most of these symptoms occurred to me at some times of my stay in TRDI but I hardly knew they were because of the stress I was going through in the Institute.

For most people stress was commonly caused by lack of money, work pressure and poor health. But for many individuals proper exercise could help relieve those kinds of stress. For instance jogging, running, brisk walking, swimming, cycling, dancing, boxing or simply workouts, could relieve the stress.

My physician advised that it was important to manage stress by continuously doing exercise such as relaxing your muscles, deep breathing, eating well, slowing down, taking a break, making time for hobbies, talking about your problems to close people, rebalancing your work at home, building in a regular exercise schedule, carving out hobby time, sleeping enough, and taking anti-anxiety medications. Heavy drinkers should stop using alcohol; heavy smokers could stop using nicotine products, and give themselves self confidence. Also, it could be important to set for yourself realistic goals and expectations and you could reduce those things that could trigger stress such as examining your values and living by them. You could also study and practice relaxation techniques, and assert yourself.

The most stressful situation is when in a meeting with my Minister she said she would use everything including her *female self* to get rid of me. I had never heard that kind of rhetoric from a high-profile personality like a Minister, and did not expect that to come from the mouth of a cabinet member who was supposed to be leading intellectuals like the scientists of TRDI. That is when I really knew that the criteria for choosing members of cabinet had really changed in Tropicana. It used to be that a Minister had to have a successful marital life to be named a Minister. But naming Lena to that position showed that things were no longer the way they had been, and that the system was definitely breaking down.

The medical doctor told me about the long-term effects of stress: The consistent and ongoing increase in heart rate, and the elevated levels of stress hormones and of blood pressure, could take a toll in the body. This long-term ongoing stress could increase the risk for hypertension, heart attack or stroke. However, stress could go away when the stressor went away.

Then he mentioned physical stress. Examples of acute injury were pulling a muscle, slipping, fracturing your risk, pains from dislocating a shoulder, skiing, breaking a limb and spraining a ligament. These could lead to infections and all kinds of pain including headaches. This is when I remembered the physical stress I had when I sustained a slipped disc from the continued use of pick-ups on bad roads. The human body naturally reacts to stress by releasing hormones which make your brain more alert, cause your muscles to be tense and increase your pulse. In a way, these reactions are good in the short term because they can help you handle the situation causing the stress. This is your body's way of protecting itself.

Stressors are the things that create stress. For instance, financial crises and an unpleasant or uncomfortable work environment could cause emotional stress. These sometimes lead to unhealthy coping behaviours which occur in order to escape the pain, especially when the situation seems hopeless. Stressors could be a chemical or biological agent, environmental condition, external stimulus or an event seen as causing stress to an organism. Stressors cause a state of strain or tension. Psychologically speaking, stressors could be events or environments that individuals might consider demanding, challenging and threatening to the safety of the individual. Stressors could be any stimuli which produce mental or physical stress. We are exposed to certain things which may be what we experience internally, things that tell us that something is happening that will require us to do something difficult. We respond to and deal with stressors in many different ways. Also, some events are stressors for some people but not for others. In severe cases stressors impact on an individual's daily life. In such cases the individual reacts negatively and unhealthily to the stressors. It is certain that at one time or another we all do experience stress because life is never static but often continuous. Because some people behave in ways different from others, stressors are sometimes not easily perceived by many. Thus stressors may be considered a part of human life. We continually learn ways of handling stress and their stressors. When a stressor occurs, it triggers the body's nervous system to send a signal to the body which triggers a flight response in the body. The body then shifts to focus on the threatening situation.

After the entire lecture given by the doctor, I realized that I had been suffering from several stresses of different types and of different levels at various stages of my career in TRDI. Some stresses which had bothered me much were caused by interaction with colleagues Others were caused by the heads of the research structures under which I had been working. Others still were caused by my bosses such as his CEO and cabinet members who had something to do with scientific investigations. I also realized that at some times I had unknowingly developed different techniques that helped me cope with various stressors. With all these stresses, I was able to survive and even pursue studies for a PhD rising through the various rungs of the research ladder to reach the summit, and even become a CEO as an appointee of the King, the highest authority in the country. I have since been very active in counselling scientists and those managing research and investigations in institutions I visited during my frequent travels in the region.

It was when I had just finished my Masters program abroad that I started having problems with adapting to the work environment as a young researcher. During this time I tried to build friends but I failed. When I went back abroad to pursue my doctoral studies it was during the first year of my PhD that I started to realize that things weren't quite right. I was unhappy because at school I was working very hard on my courses all the time: I occupied myself nearly every hour of the day. At night I was barely sleeping. The courses I was taking were many, the teachers were different in their approaches to their subject matter. My family was not with me to give me comfort. My little boy and my niece who could have kept me company were not there with me. I was crying nearly every day. The phone lines were bad and I could not get connected to speak to my family. My research was moving with difficulty because there was so much to do given the four years I had been given by my sponsors to get a PhD. Somehow, I managed to push on with my PhD work, because I was determined to be a successful academic, not only so as to have a better life at home but also to rub shoulders with the guys who already had PhDs. As a civil servant who needed to grow as a researcher I was driven to make scientific publications on my work which I left at home when I was away. I was also required to do conference presentations so as to be known in the country and in the region. I also aimed to win awards, and accomplish these all in a timely fashion within the four years. But it seemed that no matter how much work I did, or how hard I tried, it was never good enough for my supervisors who felt I should do more so as to benefit from the fellowship the government of Tropicana had given me. All along, they had insisted that I do more than what was expected from other graduate students because I would never have the scientific support back home which typical American graduates had in their country when they started working.

Our country had oil and so paying my fees was not really a problem; I did not have to wash dishes in restaurants to survive. All that was required of me to continue having my fees paid was hard work and passing my courses. The university which I attended was required to send transcripts of my performance every semester which required that I work myself to death to attain the best grades. I felt the pressure to do more and more. I was sometimes disappointed with myself for my apparent inability to handle the heavy work in the university and at the same time keeping my research as a researcher at home going because, as a civil servant, I was allowed to maintain my salary while I went to school. Things got worse quicker than they got better. In the fourth year of my PhD program, my supervisor paid me a surprise visit at 4:00 am one morning. He realized I was busy churning out lots of data with my desk-top computer I had just bought to treat my data. The way he saw me it was as if he thought I was almost loosing the will to continue on. I had lost several pounds in just four months. He was ready to come to my rescue. He told me to go home and have some rest fearing that if I continued at that pace I was going to die. He assured me that he could extend my stay in the university for an additional semester with funds from one of his research grants, just to enable me to complete my program without the kind of strain I was going through. But I preferred to continue at that pace and reach the end. Although it took me several months to realize it, I was actually suffering from academic stress.

The racial problems I was facing at some point did not help but worsen the situation. The few friends I was able to make in the department and the teachers who knew how to deal with international students helped relieve me from the stress I was going through.

Administratively, I was not happy the way some of my bosses were treating me at home, and telegrams and phone calls I received only aggravated my frustration. At some stage I wanted to return home and relax, but one mind told me to forge ahead, after all I was almost at the end of the tunnel.

Eventually, at some stage in my stay in Maryland I went to see a nearby doctor, who diagnosed me with anxiety and severe depression and put me on antidepressants. I'll never forget the empathetic sigh my doctor gave when I told him of my problems. They were many, and he could not help me much but counsel me to take it easy and reduce the pace at which I was going just to complete a PhD. He warned me that if I died in the process of working too hard, the PhD, even if it was awarded post-mortem, would not mean anything to my family and the institution for which I was working.

It was like he knew all too well the pile of problems that were awaiting me back home, especially how difficult it was for me to climb the ladder to reach the final grade of Chief Research Officer which I badly wanted to attain as a researcher. With time, medication and thoughtful action to help me deal with my stress, anxiety and depression, I got better. The few manuscripts which I had submitted to journals during the four years of my PhD were gradually being accepted. The first manuscript had been really difficult to prepare and to get accepted. Then I was still a learner. I had not yet known the techniques of scientific writing at the time. But the later manuscripts benefited from the experience I had acquired with reviewers and editors, so they were a lot easier to get accepted.

I desperately wanted to be a successful scientist, one who would be admired and consulted in the region. With two scientific papers published from my Master's thesis and four from my PhD research I thought I was on my way to becoming the successful scientist I wanted to be. However, as a young researcher I realized that the underlying causes of my depression and anxiety were never going to go away unless things changed with my life forever.

Over the last few years, I had seen similar symptoms in other young researchers and even senior researchers. It became clear that depression and anxiety were widespread, and not just something I alone was suffering from. While an aspiring researcher, I was experiencing depression and other forms of stress, just like many others. I came to understand that what was probably more important was that I made all efforts to identify all the causes of stress and to try to find solutions to them as had been suggested by the doctor. Some colleagues who did not have the chance to study abroad and who registered in home universities joined me in experiencing more stress than I had expected. The prevalence of psychological distress was even much higher among doctoral students registered in home institutions. The simple reason for this was a result of intrigues from some home professors. Many who supervised them felt that the terminal degree was associated with pride and increased recognition in the society. Others felt they would be in the limelight for the eventual nomination into higher positions in the administration. So they made things really difficult for them.

In Tropicana Rural Development Institute, I realized that very close to half of all growing researchers were more prone to depression because firstly they were finding it difficult to get promoted to higher grades, a situation which they blamed on members of advancement commissions, but which actually just required the extra hard work to conduct high quality research work which could enable them to publish their work in reputable journals. At the same time because of limited financial resources they were often forced to do other things which took a lot of their time just to make ends meet. The low salaries, coupled with their inability to educate their children in the kinds of private prestigious schools which they would have liked added to their stress as researchers. This led to unnecessary animosity among research colleagues in the institute. The unfortunate thing was that those unable to publish kept blaming their frustration on those who were prolific. Hence, furthering their education to get higher and terminal degrees and making their way through the four grades of scientific development tended to become breeding grounds for anxiety and depression. This needed a lot of support from the environment in which they found themselves.

In Tropicana, lack of adequate funds from government to support research made it impossible for many researchers, who could not attract external grants to grow. This brought frustration in a country where other agencies like industries using scientific knowledge did not fund the research whose results they needed to develop their industries. A friend of mine was working on cocoyams (*Xanthosoma sagittifolium* and *Colocasia esculenta*) but could hardly find external funding for his investigations because external funding agencies did not find it impactful to finance research on orphan crops like cocoyams which were not very important in the region. He was so stressed that he gave up the idea of growing in the institute, and retired in the grade of research officer, just the second grade in the research hierarchy. Many colleagues who felt that just having a PhD was what was going to enable them grow, still had this terminal degree but were frustrated because they remained stagnant in lower grades; they then realized that the terminal doctorate was not an end in itself; they then knew they had to work hard to defend that degree when they went to the field. For most of them it was already too late. This added to their frustration either because they were working in areas that could not attract funding or they themselves did not have the competence in attracting external grants.

Some researchers also had weak backgrounds. Many studied in institutions where they were not required to do coursework. So even if they did good research, they lacked the competence to analyze their data. Even if they were able to identify colleagues to help them with data analysis, they lacked humility to request that kind of assistance. Others simply lacked the competence to interpret their data and identify trends in them to produce publishable articles. This added to their stress because they found themselves just unable to grow in the science environment in which they found themselves. As a result some colleagues resorted to spend their time engaging in other activities which could at least enable them to feed their families well and send their children to schools.

Finally, I realized that despite the great number of stressors creating depression and other stresses in my career, it was extremely important to be able to detect stressors and identify stresses which I was undergoing early enough so as to receive the right treatment and counseling. This meant also that it was useful to know stress symptoms for me to get the various treatment options available from my healthcare provider early before things went really wrong.

I was wondering why a colleague of mine in high school suddenly got depressed to the point of behaving like a mad man. He had been on marijuana for quite some time in school, and would hide in nearby farms and smoke. But after quite some time without treatment he became mad. One day as he was climbing into a building from the back the night watchman mistook him for a thief. He shot him and my friend lost his life. So stress can lead to madness, and this could lead you into doing things which are abnormal and which can cost you your life.

From the many things that I observed, I tried to identify the many stressors that were making me unhappy and sought assistance in dealing with them. I realized that if I was constantly feeling sad, empty and anxious about a situation, or if I felt like I was lacking emotions, and was unable to get out of the situation by myself then I was having symptoms indicative of stress. I would talk over things with a friend or relative but eventually consult a healthcare provider if the situation persisted.

One colleague in the research center walked up to my office one afternoon and told me he was feeling worthless and that he felt he was not in the right job; the work of a researcher was not yielding the satisfaction he wanted. He could better be a trader and make quick money. He told me he regretted having spent so much time going to school. He continued telling me he had a feeling of hopelessness and guilt because his parents had expected him to grow fast scientifically and financially, yet he was far behind in their expectation. From what I had heard and read and what my healthcare provider had told me I knew he was being stressed. I gave him all the consolation I could and told him he was not alone.

A few days later another colleague met me as we were having coffee in the coffee room and recounted me his life in the institute. He said he was often frustrated each time after he harvested his trials because he always had negative results, very far from what he expected. I told him that negative results were just as good. Those were not his fault; results could be positive or negative. I was wondering why he felt that was a problem. Some results just turned out to be negative and had to be reported like that.

I loved playing around with computers, doing videography, especially converting cassette videos into compact discs. I could spend an entire Saturday doing just that. But I later lost the interest in those hobbies. It took me a while to realize that the heavy work load as well as the pressure to report progress in the work of my zone of activity was causing me to be stressed. I had to find time to explain to my coordinator that I was doing my best but only that my zone of operation was large, and my research sites were very distant from each other so I was driving all the time on bad roads. I was already developing back aches because of that. I later realized that the nature of work could frustrate me and make me get stressed so I had to make a balance between distractions and the research work I was doing. One of the first pieces of advice young researchers need to be reminded of is the need to find something that they enjoy doing outside of the labs and fields and fit this into their daily or weekly routine. Regardless of how much work I had to cover, I now knew I had to make time to remove myself from research and the pile of field notebooks from my research and have some distraction from my hobbies and interact more socially with friends.

One time, I had difficulties having a good sleep. I would go to bed, sleep for just one hour and get up, stirring at the ceiling for some three hours or so before falling asleep again. Sometimes I would struggle in vain to go back to sleep. I thought it was because of fatigue but it was not. My doctor told me that in such situations there was something really worrying me which was responsible for the stress. Other times I lost my memory and could not remember a few things which I thought were necessary to include in my publication. It would take me days before remembering what I had forgotten.

The doctor cautioned that although depression could leave me feeling fatigued and completely drained, it could also disturb sleep, making me even more tired the next day to perform my routine tasks. I realized that disturbed sleep could eventually lead to decreased energy and an increase in fatigue. I would have difficulty concentrating on my data, remembering things and making decisions. Inadequate sleep (sleeping less than five hours a night) could lead to restlessness and irritability, making it impossible to complete the tasks I had set to complete on that day.

Detecting stress symptoms was not as easy as you could think because sometimes the symptoms came up very slowly. My supervisor at work was in a remote station and understood the stress I was going through covering a wide area alone; I was doing work in different disciplines of root crops research because I was alone. He could give me time off from my work, but the work would be waiting for me because there was no assistant to help me while I was away.

I also noticed that many times I would even lose the appetite to eat my favorite meals. I would think to myself that each time that happened it was merely because I came home tired after a long trip but I was told by my caregiver that the loss of my appetite and the resulting weight loss were symptoms of stress so I had to be careful to take things easy. He advised me that I should discuss with my wife that I had to make time for my meals, eating at regular periods, and avoiding skipping meals because I was too busy to eat. I would lose energy, lose weight and fail to accomplish my duties at work at a time when so much was expected from me. He make me know that if I was in the habit of consuming alcohol or other stimulants in an attempt to stay awake and accomplish tasks that was only going to help in the short run and could only make symptoms worse in the long run, and if I opted to tell lies that I was taking these substances, that was not going to help; it was just going to aggravate the situation which would be detrimental to me.

One day as my driver was going to accompany me to the airport to make an international trip, I glanced to the right side of the road. I saw something which was hanging like a scarecrow on a mango tree. I told the driver to stop. Since we were close to the airport and we had time, we walked closer to the mango tree and found that what we were seeing was actually a military man who had hanged himself. A note that the police found on the ground below him read, "It was too much, I loved my wife but my wife did not love me enough." We were sympathetic but could not do anything to help the situation: he was already gone. We continued our trip. When I was in the aircraft, I thought how stress could take away the life of someone. Throughout the flight I thought to myself never to let a stressor take control of myself to the point of taking my life away. I made it a point of duty to always confide in someone about any issue that was worrying me very much and constantly. Many of such issues would come throughout my working and social lives but I made up my mind that at the very least I would let a family member, or close friend who I trusted to know that a situation was making me feeling that way.

PART ONE

STRESSES AS A SCIENTIST

CHAPTER 1

Dealing with heads of research structures

. . . .

IN THE TROPICANA RURAL DEVELOPMENT INSTITUTE THERE WERE FIVE research centers corresponding to the five agro-ecological zones. Each of the Centers was headed by a chief of center. Within a research center there were research stations, each headed by a chief of station. In each research station there were substations and research sites.

After I graduated as a technical officer from the National College of Agriculture I was posted to Njombe Research Center, a remote research center about two hours of driving away from my area of origin. I did not like the place initially because I had heard that the town had a hot climate and that it was infested with mosquitoes. I could easily catch malaria from time to time which was a debilitating disease in the country. The acting Chief of that Center was also my coordinator for root crops research. I had expected that he, being an acquaintance, would influence my posting and get me posted to Ekona which was near home. But he did not see things the way I saw them. For him, he did not want to send me to a place near my village in which case family was going to disturb me every now and then. He wanted me to grow, and one way to achieve this was to let me work away from home, especially in a zone where people did not know me. When I reached there to start work, I was given pleasant working conditions which made me start liking the place just after a month of stay there. The first attraction was the 2-bedroom house I was given. It had a nice kitchen, a full bath and a nice veranda, in addition to the two bedrooms. Behind the house was a large grapefruit orchard belonging to the center from which I could collect fruits at will. Moreso, every Friday I was supplied with a large bag of fruits from the weekly harvest. I also had a nightwatchman to guard me. That house had been built for intermediate level workers like me. That alone was

1

quite attractive to me. I could not speak French well at the time but language was not much of a barrier to effective communication because nearly every person there spoke and understood *pidgin* (a hodgepodge of English, French and German) which was used casually in the town and which was a trading language in the big towns of the country.

Barely four months after starting work I was sent for a short training course to Nigeria. My coordinator had made that promise that he was going to send me to the International Institute of Tropical Agriculture (IITA) at Ibadan in Nigeria at the start of my career to get *baptized* in root crops research, whatever that meant at the time.

I did well in the 3-month course in IITA and was given an extension of nine months to conduct independent research under a Sierra Leonean phytopathologist, Dr Eugene Terry, who was working in the root and tuber crops program there in IITA. I conducted research on insect transmission of sweet potato virus disease agents in Nigeria. At the end I made a report and submitted it to IITA. I was issued another certificate for the specialized training I had had. That was good.

On my return to the country I was transferred to another station, Nkolbisson, to assist an expatriate scientist, Hermann Joseph Pfeiffer, in his field work. He had worked very hard to convince my coordinator of root crops research, Dr Simon Lyonga, to have me transferred out of Njombe. Hermann must have made some promises as to how well I was going to be accommodated in the new place. Anyway, the result was that I was transferred. I had bought food which was going to last me for at least three months and packed it in the Peugeot 404 pickup which I was given to take me to Nkolbisson. But when I reached there I did not have a house. As in all other research stations of the Institute, all workers were being lodged by the administration. The living quarters were also highly stratified. There were quarters for scientists, then quarters for intermediate workers (technicians and lab assistants) and a workers' camp for general labour and drivers.

I felt bad and frustrated when I found out that in spite of the fact that I had been promised one, I was told that there was no house for me. The story that I had been told by Hermann before I left Njombe was that someone, a technician like me, was leaving a house to enter his personal house which he had built in town and so his house would be vacant. But when I reached there his house had been given to another worker. I did not know anything about the town of Nkolbisson to which I had been posted neither did I know the habits of the people around. So I could not get a comfortable accommodation to rent while waiting for another house to become vacant.

I booked an appointment to see the chief of station. On that day I went up to his office and met him talking on the phone, with his legs stretched on his work table, files and documents on both sides of his legs. I waited until he finished talking. Then I presented my problem. He became angry. He turned to me and told me in a rather rough tone, "You are bothering me for a house when you are just a mere technician." I quietly left his office when I realized that he could not solve my problem. But I was very frustrated and that made me determine to have higher education so that I would not just be considered a *mere* technician. It is interesting to know that when I came back from higher training abroad and was posted to the same station, I met this fellow who was still there but he had lost the position of head of station and he consulted me to help him solve a scientific problem. I helped him with his problem but I knew he had forgotten the way he had received me in his office so many years back when I was still a *mere* technician.

Hermann, embarrassed by the situation, and seeing that the food I had brought with me was getting perished, decided to give me an outside room in his house. That was better than nothing. But the inconvenience I had was that I did not have a restroom because he told me that I could not share the inside baths with him. He had a pit toilet dug for me and covered its sides with palm fronds. I had to manage it that way.

Another experience I had about housing was when the fellow who replaced Mr Flower Stone, Mr Joe Whiteman, gave me the option of accepting an accommodation in the workers camp. The workers camp was meant for laborers, drivers and field recorders. No technician was there. I could not feel comfortable living in the crowded workers camp. So I did not accept the room and parlour accommodation he had proposed to me.

Some four months after working with Hermann, I was sent to the USA for higher studies. When I came back from training, the Institute decided that I should replace Hermann as head of root crops research in that same station. He had been sent to open a new research station in the Adamaoua region of the country. I was given the large house he had been occupying. It was wonderful that I did not have to go through that stressful situation again. Stresses come and go, and that is the piece of advice I had to give to young guys who came after me.

CHAPTER 2

Promotions to higher research grades

. . . .

WHEN I RETURNED TO THE COUNTRY WITH MY MASTERS DEGREE THE first thing I did was to apply to be recruited as a researcher. In TRDI there were four research grades: Assistant Research Officer, Research Officer, Senior Research Officer and Chief Research Officer. In a document produced by the then Delegate General for Scientific and Technical Research, criteria had been established for promotion of scientists to higher grades. These were academic qualification, longevity in one grade and number of scientific publications in peer reviewed journals. These criteria were straightforward in the promotion into the first three grades. However, to ascend to the final grade of chief research officer could be tricky because it became subjective in some instances. More hidden criteria were added from time to time depending on who was Minister-Secretary of Rural Development Investigations. That made promotion into that grade difficult and frustrating.

To be recruited to the first grade of Assistant Research Officer, the individual needed to possess a specialization degree and ought to have worked for two years in the Institute. For promotion from Assistant Research Officer to Research Officer, the scientist needed a terminal degree (PhD), two years of longevity as Assistant Research Officer, and two scientific articles published in refereed journals. To get promoted from Research Officer to Senior Research Officer, the candidate needed to have a PhD degree, and four years of longevity in the grade of research officer and needed to have published at least six peer-reviewed articles in the grade of research officer. To be admitted to the final grade of Chief Research Officer, the scientist had to have a PhD degree, longevity of eight years in the grade of senior research officer and ought to have published at least ten articles in the grade of senior research officer.

But when the time came for me to apply for that final grade, three more criteria had been added: Postulating candidates had to show two letters of recommendation from peers in the region to document his contribution in the region, the candidate had to show proof that he had been supervising younger researchers, and had to give evidence that he had been attracting research funding for the institute. As could be seen, the last three criteria were quite subjective in some way and candidates could easily be refused promotion because of them. That was stressful.

Two commissions had to sit to evaluate and promote researchers. Of the two commissions, the technical commission (also called the *evaluation commission*) was held in the Institute by members (top scientists and university professors) appointed by a decision of the Minister-Secretary. The role of this commission was to evaluate the scientific worth of the candidates. That commission would then make recommendations to the Minister-Secretary for Rural Development Investigations. In the second commission (known as the *promotion commission*) the Minister-Secretary would then make another decision comprising top university professors, top scientists, and representatives of the King's Palace, Prime Minister's Office, the Ministry of the Public Service, the Ministry of Rural Development, the Ministry of Livestock and the Ministry of the Treasury. The role of this commission was to validate the results of the advancement commission and *promote* the successful candidates to higher grades. The Minister of Rural Development Investigations then officially published the list of successful candidates as those who had been promoted, and sent a report with the list to the Minister of the Treasury for adjustment of salaries.

Research scientists in Tropicana were supposed to engage in scholarly and creative research appropriate to their fields of specialization. There were twenty-two research programs in TRDI and researchers had to adhere to the missions of their particular units or programs. In their daily routine work, they were expected to investigate new ideas, to reinterpret established ideas, and to disseminate results of their research through field days, and through media (journals and conferences) appropriate to their disciplines. Those researchers who were in a hurry to have their results published could rush and publish in small, unknown journals.

Others who were wise enough would do high-quality work and select high-quality journals also to publish their results in them. In many instances, wise evaluators, concerned with scientific promotions or recruitments, would prefer a few sound scientific articles published in reputed journals than a large quantity of hodgepodge articles published in low-grade journals. Journal reputation became picky especially in the final grade of chief research officer.

Normally, in a well functioning system, researchers have the potential to establish a research program and obtain independent research grants for their research activities. Researchers could also be involved in university teaching activities especially from their work in the research, and could also offer services to agro-industries as well as in the extension service of the Ministry of Rural Development. They could also play administrative roles as officers in their institutes as well as officers in the Ministry of Rural Development Investigations.

I was a researcher in the root crops program. I had received the right training to enable me do impactful research which could allow me to grow in the research institute. The expertise and contributions of my research results ought to be of substantial impact on growers and the agro-industries in the country. The contributions in my fields of specializations had to be impactful to the development of farming output in the country. They also had to contribute to improving the quality and quantity of products developed by the various industries. My activities were also expected to beef up the scientific literature in the region through published articles and through presentations in scientific conferences. These would benefit farmers, other scientists in the country and in the region and enable me grow as a researcher.

But my first few years as a researcher in the Institute of Rural Development Investigations were miserable; I was lonely most of the time, and stressed part of the time. I would sit in my office and ask myself if the situation was going to remain like that during my entire life as a scientist. My mind now started straying back to my family in the village. I missed them so much. I started thinking about a French novel which our French teacher had treated with us in secondary school. I was now like Haouna, the protagonist of Olympe Bhelin-Quenum's *Un piege sans fin*, a novel which had been translated in English as *Snares without end*. Snares without end (*Un piège sans fin*) is a novel, and a philosophical tale in which destiny entraps the innocent protagonist and holds him fast. The man's life is ruined when he is unjustly accused of adultery.

Although overshadowed by more prominent African post-colonial writers like Chinua Achebe, Mongo Beti, Cyprian Ekwensi, Camara Laye, James Ngugi, Ferdinand Oyono, and Wole Soyinka, in this novel, "Snares Without End" the Sorbonne-trained Olympe Bhely-Quenum, a writer from the former French colony of Dahomey (now Benin), some years after its independence in 1960 gives the impression in the introduction to the book that suggests that the author was ignored in the '60s because he wasn't anti-colonialist enough. Finally, the book published in 1960 was discovered and became impactful in African literature at a time when people mostly knew of those other prominent writers. The novel became a major comforter to Kwado, a foreign student abroad who was suffering from nostalgia because he had left his family and country for long.

For me, the main stressors I had were when I started postulating for higher grades in the research. There were a lot of intrigues in the promotion of researchers. False accusations and slander contributed in preventing me from ascending to the grade of chief research officer.

Like his main character (Kwado) in this novel I was stressed for a large part of my career as a researcher until I became a chief research officer, and even after that, the intrigues of the system continued to play a negative role on my system, eventually making me develop health problems which disabled me for quite some time. Throughout this time I survived only through the comfort of my mother and my wife. I had developed the habit of singing my stress song *Je suis fier d'etre Tropicanien*, which a French teacher had taught us in secondary school. "Au sein d'une palmerai je trouvais le jour. Ma mere était digne de tous son amour. Depuis ma naissance elle m'a nourrit, en reconnaissance mon coeur la cherit." My mother needs all my love. Since my birth she has fed me, in recognition my heart cherishes her.

Promotion procedures and promotion criteria kept changing from time to time according to circumstances, the candidates involved, and how well the CEO lobbied to hold down his potential rivals so that he could stay in power. The consideration of timely promotion had to be encouraged both to recognize and reward accomplishments, to develop productive research scientists and to promote career advancement for the benefit of the individual and the Institute. But sometimes this was delayed unnecessarily adding more stress among scientists.

Sometimes there could be conflicts of interest among members of any of the two commissions. These could include commission members who had an intimate relationship with the postulating candidate. But it did not matter much because even there the recommendation of the commission to promote a candidate ought to be based upon a simple majority vote of the participating eligible members. Often, the votes of the representatives of the Prime Minister and the King's Palace carried a stronger weight than those of the other members. Usually, the Permanent Secretary of the Ministry of Rural Development Investigations served as the rapporteur of the final promotion committee and he or she was the one to prepare and forward the minutes to the Minister of RDI for publication in the media, radio and a copy sent to the Minister-Secretary of the Public Service for finalization of remuneration into the new grades.

Before my return from the USA with the Masters degree, I had heard that the Minister was about to issue a new decision for the promotion of candidate researchers to higher grades in Tropicana Rural Development Institute (TRDI). Each new candidate who wanted to be considered as researcher in the TRDI had first to be recruited in the first grade of assistant research officer irrespective of whether the candidate had a specialization degree or not. Before then it was just automatic: you were directly given that first rank on the basis of your *Ingenieur Agronome*, MSc, MPhil, DEA, without any presentation of a file. Hence, there were now four research grades – assistant research officer, research officer, senior research officer and chief research officer. To be considered for recruitment in the first grade of assistant research officer, the candidate was expected to have a research degree – master, DEA or doctorate.

When I came back from higher studies I was still considered by the Tropicana Public Service as a research technician, so I could not be recruited in the first grade of assistant research officer. I had to wait for two years for the paper work to go through before I was *reclassified* into the grade of *Ingénieur d'Agriculture*. That was my first level of frustration. Now as *Ingénieur d'Agriculture*, I then presented my Masters degree and applied to be recruited as assistant research officer.

To get to the second grade of research officer, I had to submit two scientific publications, stay in the grade of assistant research officer for two years and present a file showing that I had a graduate degree. I had published two articles from my Masters' thesis so that was not a problem. I was easily promoted to the grade of research officer. As research officer I had more responsibilities but still I had to work under a supervisor. But because I was in a different research station from him, I was more or less independent to carry out research in the wide area which had been placed under my care.

The next grade was senior research officer. The criteria were a terminal degree (PhD or *Doctorat d'Etat*), six articles in the grade of research officer, and longevity of six years in the grade of research officer. The assumption was that if the candidate was hardworking he ought to be able to publish at least one article per year. I submitted my file and the evaluation commission considered it favourably and I was promoted. A friend of mine who thought he was very hardworking was rejected. He went to the Ministry and protested that his work was visible – one could see his products being used by people in the countryside, so that needed to be taken into consideration and have him promoted. Unfortunately, he was told that it was very difficult to evaluate him on the basis of the use of his products in the countryside. He needed to put that in writing – that was what was going to remain with posterity. The following year, he managed to develop a strategy: he made good relations with junior scientists to *tag* his name on their publications. This gave him the required six papers to get promoted to the grade of senior research officer. He was very happy. But he went on retirement at that level. What a pity!

The final grade was that of chief research officer. For this grade the criteria were now more stringent: a terminal degree (PhD or the

French *Doctorat d'Etat*), eight publications in the preceding grade of senior research officer and longevity of eight years in that grade. Three additional criteria had been added: the postulating candidate had to show two letters of recommendations from eminent scientists in the region indicating that his work had made a *significant* contribution in the region, and he had to show proof that he had brought in funds to his research institute. Finally, he had to show that he had mentored younger researchers. The last three criteria were certainly subjective and difficult to evaluate but commission members hung on those to hold down candidates they did not want to see promoted. First, it was difficult to prove what they meant by *significant* contribution. How significant did that have to be? Was that going to be through scientific publications or through conference presentations? Even with the matter of bringing in funds to the Institute, could they consider the bringing of regional, institutional project funds or grant funds in which students had worked very hard to procure? And about mentoring young researchers, did that mean having your name tagged on a young researcher's publication or his name appearing in your publication? The three criteria were not easy to judge and determine.

I submitted my promotion file to that final grade when I thought I had met all the criteria. But I was not promoted. I was unhappy and stressed. When I carried out an investigation I found out that during the evaluation commission, the assistant to the CEO of TRDI who was presenting the files of the candidates had removed some publications from my file and left only three, disqualifying me from being promoted. I was really stressed for the one year following the next evaluation commission. The worst part of the story was that I had no one to whom to complain. The results had already been validated by the Minister-Secretary of Rural Development Investigations. I gathered myself together, and waited for the next commission.

The following year, a new strategy had been developed which I did not know. My CEO sent me to a meeting in the economic capital. In that meeting I was to represent him in the signing of an international convention in my area of competence. That morning I packed my bag, got into my vehicle and drove for the next three hours to the meeting place. The meeting went well. I signed the documents, jotted some points to constitute my trip report which I was going to submit to my CEO to give him information about the meeting. I got into my car and returned to my base in Nkolbisson.

When I reached the campus of the institute, it was already 5:00 pm. Just a few minutes to my house, I turned my head to the right and saw a parish of vehicles around the conference center of the institute. There were people having snacks as if they had had a long day of work. I did not pay any special attention to them or what they could have been doing, and went home to get the comfort of my family. Late that night my house phone rang. I picked it and that was my mentor calling. When I picked the phone and started talking to him, he gave me a piece of information which pierced into my flesh: how are you doing? We just finished the evaluation commission but you were not promoted to the grade of chief research officer for two reasons – inadequate scientific output and questions about an article you published in an international journal in which you were an editor. That was terrible! I thought to myself that some games were going on. I could not have applied for promotion if I knew I did not meet all of the criteria.

The next morning, I met my mentor in his hotel room and showed him my duplicate promotion file and he saw the fourteen papers I had submitted. They were asking for just eight papers. He went immediately and saw the CEO who, guilty of the situation, sent a letter to the Minister complaining that an error had been made in the evaluation of my file. The Minister did not reply. Later when I carried out a little investigation I was told that the same CEO phoned the Minister immediately after he had written the letter and told him to ignore it, stating that he had sent it under pressure; he had been pressured to write it by my mentor. This frustrated me very much. I had to wait for another year again.

The evaluation and promotion commissions were delayed for the next four years because of candidates like me who the CEO and his assistant did not want to see promoted. The many researchers who were looking forward to climbing to various higher grades like me were frustrated. They had every reason to be.

Then, a commission was announced and we prepared and presented our promotion files again. My file went through at the level of the

Institute but was blocked at the level of the Ministry. A guy who attended the validation promotion commission in the Ministry confidentially contacted me to use all resources at my disposal to fight that. He said, "boy, this time your file was not just examined. Use all acquaintances in power to make sure your file is examined."

Luckily, a new minister had been named by the King. When he was inaugurated in his functions he got the information that some injustices had been done in earlier advancement commissions in his Ministry. That is how my case was brought up to his attention. He ordered that a special commission be created to evaluate my file. That commission met three times, the first time to examine the original publications I had submitted, the second time to examine the originals of book chapters which I had presented; for these I had to produce the books in which my contributing chapters were found (not photocopies), and finally to verify the authenticity of the letters of recommendation which senior colleagues in the region had sent to support my candidature. The hidden agenda from these commissions was that they had been contacted by those who considered me to be a rival to do everything to find faults that could hold me down. Finally, no faults could be found and I was promoted to the grade of chief research officer. That night I went home and told my mother and my wife, "I have finally been promoted." I retreated in my home office and prayed to God for he had worked his regular miracles again. I was now a research professor.

Promotion of individuals within the Research is not just encouraged but it is mandatory. However, guidelines for promotion criteria should be strictly followed so consideration is given to the main criteria of longevity, terminal degree and scientific output measured by the number of scientific publications within the grade. But when promotion has to be based on subjective criteria on top of the main criteria, it becomes suspicious that something is going on wrong. That leads to stress in many circumstances. In our Institute researchers were bound to move to higher grades or face demotion to the grades they occupied before. It hardly happened but that punishment was there, and could be executed if some strong members of the advancement commission hated you and did not like you to stay in the Institute.

I can still remember the morning that the news was announced to me that the final promotion commission was going to finish its deliberations on that day if only I produced the originals of all the documents I had presented. My mother who was living with me at the time was surprised to see me so busy that morning packing book after book and article after article to the point that she had to ask me if something was wrong. But the story was too long to narrate to her. I barely told her that my Minister wanted to see those documents. That final commission, after seeing all what they had requested, promoted me to the final grade of chief research officer. The permanent secretary in the ministry who had presided over the advancement commission sent for me. When I entered his office, he heartily congratulated me, not once but thrice, but cautioned me that I had several enemies in the Institute and in the Ministry and that I should watch out not to go too close to some of the members. He added that there were two ethnic groups which naturally and normally ran in parallel lines, but that, for once, because they had a common enemy (*me*) they were converging to fight that enemy. I took his advice. I never went close to them until I became CEO. I was already their boss and had to do everything to be friendly with them so as to get the best out of them.

CHAPTER 3

Administrative nominations

. . . .

IN MANY COUNTRIES ADMINISTRATIVE POSITIONS WERE FILLED BY necessity and qualification. If a position is vacant, the job would be advertised to allow people to compete. A short-list of three well qualified candidates is then established. Interviews are conducted and the best candidate on the short-list is selected. The panel doing the selection is supposed to be objective, although in some instances networking and connections also could influence the outcome. In Tropicana, it was rarely like that. The CEO could name any person he liked in his administration. If the position he wants to fill is at the level of director, he would make his proposal and submit it to the board of administration and have the board deliberate on it and make the appointment.

To be eligible for a high administrative appointment of the level of director in the Research, the research scientist was required to have the terminal degree in most cases awarded in one's discipline and in the area of the position being filled. This requirement could be waived for individuals with outstanding experience and achievement coming from an ethnic group which was not well represented in the institution. Usually, appointments to and promotion within the Research Scientist series also included consideration of longevity (years in the grade), levels of administrative experience and accomplishments, degree of independence, evidence of trajectory toward national and international recognition, and the impact that the scientist had made within his discipline. Prior service at other institutions or other related professional activities could qualify the individual for consideration in meeting the requirement for longevity.

Since the Assistant Research Officer rank is primarily an entry-level research position analogous to the Assistant Professor rank in the University, the individual at this level is generally not considered for administrative appointments, because that could load him with administrative duties and prevent him from carrying out research to enable him grow in the institution. A minimum number of years in a lower rank are required however in the event the individual's ethnic group of origin is inadequately represented in the institution before consideration can be made to get him into a high administrative position. For him to be eligible for appointment to this rank, however, he should in addition possess strong potential for creative and productive research showing clear potential for obtaining independent research grants that could enable him to conduct impactful work in his discipline.

Those research scientists in the grade of senior research officer which is analogous to the rank of Associate Professor in the University, under normal circumstances, must have had at least four years of longevity and experience as research officer either in the research or in the university and must have demonstrated consistency and direction in his or her research department and must have achieved a substantial measure of accomplishment or creative contributions in the field of specialization. But again, ethnic considerations could make him or her appointed into a high position if their tribe or region was not well represented in the institution.

A scientist in the grade of chief research officer (analogous to the grade of Full Professor in the university) was already considered independent. He should have achieved strong national and international recognition in the field enough for any high position in his discipline and was already in the eyes of the King to name in a position such as CEO or a Minister.

So you see that in Tropicana, appointment in the research grade was tightly tied to research grade, and a candidate's rivals could do anything and lobby to the highest level to prevent him or her from attaining the grade of chief research officer. Just as research scientist ranks conveyed privileges to candidates, so also were privileges accorded for promotions to administrative positions. The specific privileges normally varied with the administrative rank.

Thus, the rank of CEO (although analogous to a Deputy-Secretary) carried the greatest number of privileges, many times even higher than those of his Minister, the reason some supervisory ministers tended to be jealous of the CEOs under them. The privileges were well defined in the Public Service manual of appointments the reason candidates fought so hard for the positions. For instance, in the Tropicana Rural Development Institute, the CEO had his normal monthly salary in the Public Service commensurate with his grade in the Public Service, but in addition the many privileges as CEO: cash allowances of up to six thousand dollars a month, four guards in his office to screen and register visitors, determine which visitors could see the CEO, and a house staff of two guards during the day, two during the night, a cook, a driver and a washer-man whose only job was to ensure that the clothing of his boss (the CEO) was intact and presentable.

Sometimes consideration for higher administrative appointments was given to research scientists involved in university teaching and student supervision. It was felt that such scientists with the ability to guide and mentor students should be considered for that additional effort, but that carried a light weight in the evaluation of candidates for high appointments.

For the CEO position, research scientists were also given consideration if they had had considerable management or administrative responsibilities in other institutions, if they had the ability to perform as a manager, if they showed the ability to organize and manage groups of people effectively, and if they demonstrated proper grant budget management and reporting. Any marketing skills such as speaking well in conferences as well as preparing leaflets and fliers to promote the mission of their institute were an advantage and were supposed to be viewed positively, especially if there was clear indication of successful contributions of how those services were provided and testimonies of how effective those services had been to clients.

I suffered a lot of stresses as I was being nominated to administrative positions in the research. There were four major kinds of administrative positions in the Tropicana Rural Development Institute. The lowest was the chief of bureau, the second was the chief of service. The third was the sub-director, and the highest was the post of director. All these positions, except the last were filled by the CEO; the post of director was filled by the board of directors, because that post had political implications. In that position the CEO of the Institute submitted his recommendations to the board in a regular board session which made the appointment and notified the candidate of the outcome of the board meeting.

With regard to day-to-day function the chief of bureau prepared files for the chief of service and sub-directors, who assembled them for the directors. The directors then validated the information in the files, appended their visas on them and then sent them to the CEO for signature. Normally, by the time the CEO saw the visa of the director, he did not have much reason to question the authenticity of information in the file. He just signed it.

Project heads were given the rank of sub-directors, but some, because they were controlling big budgets, were very powerful and occasionally would see the Minister directly to discuss their problems, a situation which was embarrassing to the CEO who was their direct boss.

My first position was that of the head of the research service. That position was the most powerful service head position because I was the technical adviser of the CEO, preparing files of research operations, planning the training of scientists of the Institute and preparing nearly every other file except financial files for the signature of the CEO. I held that position for four years. The CEO relied on me and because I was good at manipulating the computer he was happy that I saved the Institute money by preparing letter-heads of the Institute in the computer and just fitting in information into them. He found that fascinating, and would have liked to keep me there for as long as possible.

But I had a power stressor in that position. The deputy CEO realized that I was getting too close to the CEO and was growing too fast and felt that I could easily be considered to head the Institute some day, a position he was aiming to keep for himself. So he started to develop a strategy to prevent me from getting to the limelight. One day the Institute had a board meeting which at the same time would also nominate officers in the Institute. The deputy CEO managed to convince the CEO that the meeting should hold in one of the remote stations. In that meeting I was dropped from the post of chief of the research service. Many colleagues in the Institute were surprised that, in spite of my hard work and the fact that many considered me indispensable to the CEO, I was now an ordinary researcher. Some colleagues even came to ask me what I thought could have happened. Others openly told me that it must have been the result of a conspiracy from scientists who considered me to be a rival. Those who had been judging me to be very hardworking in the position of chief of service in the Institute came and consoled me. One told me that if something is yours it will eventually come to you. I was very frustrated when the news of my removal reached me. For another three years I was not in research administration. I spent my time doing my routine work on food crops, and whenever the situation availed itself I would occupy myself with a consultancy with an international organization to make some money and regional popularity for myself.

I had been in that situation for three years when I was nominated as chief of the cooperation service of the Institute. In that capacity I was called up to prepare files that had to do with the relations of the Institute with international organizations which had activities with our Institute. It was a small but good job because it made me known by many organizations abroad. I remember one day how the CEO wanted me to attend the consultation meeting with CIRAD, a French national agricultural research center. Many officers in the Institute felt that only officers of the rank of sub-directors and above had to make the international trip. But the circumstances were such that I would be one of the most useful persons in the meeting because I mastered the many files between that research center and our institute. The heads of projects were definitely important to attend because they would have to present the cooperation projects with the French center, since they had been working with the French expatriate scientists on projects. In the end the debate favoured me and I attended the meeting. It was a nice experience for me because that gave me an opportunity to know France. It was the first time I was visiting that country.

After the meeting in France I was dropped again. Then I knew that the fight against me was continuing. I felt really stressed because I thought I was doing my best. It took another two years before I was nominated again, this time as director of outreach and development support in the Institute. In this capacity I was the one responsible for the transfer of research results from the Institute to agro-industrial companies in the country, as well as evaluating how the technologies the research had developed and transferred to the private sector and farming communities were being used. My role in that position was also to bring any problems with our research technologies back to the Institute for refinement, if need be.

It took me another three years in that position when I was kicked out again. This time I was given the same position in outreach but one funded by a regional project in the Institute. That had been done because they wanted to free a position in a remote station, and to do that they had to give the researcher who was heading that structure another position in the headquarters of the Institute.

I had barely done two years in that position when I was appointed director of food crops. In this new position I was required to supervise research activities of all food crops – cereal crops, grain legumes, root crops, and annual industrial crops in the Institute. That was the largest department in the institute. It was a good position. It was from there that the King of Tropicana identified me and named me CEO of TRDI when he realized that the position had become vacant.

My major task in my new position as CEO was to unify the many tribes among 1200 workers and get the best out of them by working with them successfully. It was a crucial moment in my life. As King David made a covenant with the 10 tribes of Israel so also did I have to make agreements with the major tribes in my Institute and those who were forced to work with me. I needed to have humility (not pride) by uniting my subjects and subordinates; I had to pass all the tribal differences in my Institute. I did this with the help of God.

I remember the Call to Worship one time in our Durham Hope Valley Baptist Church. It had been taken from Psalms 123: "I lift up my eyes to you, to you whose throne is in Heaven. As the eyes of slaves look to the hand of their master, as the eyes of the maid look to the hand of the mistress, so our eyes look to the Lord our God till he shows us his mercy. Have mercy on us, O Lord, have mercy on us, for we have endured much contempt. We have endured much ridicule from the proud, much contempt from the arrogant."

In my meditation I said to myself, "Lord Jesus, you have been enthroned with power. As the eyes of servants look to the hand of their master, as the eyes of a maid looks up to the hand of her mistress, so my eyes look up to you my Lord. Over the years I have kept weeping and looking up to you to solve my problems. I have kept seeing you as the one to sail me back to the shore. You hear me continuously crying for your help in the eye of the storm. You hear me lamenting because I have had more than enough of contempt; my soul has had more than its fill of the scorn of those who are at ease, and of the contempt of the proud. Now you have finally heard my cry and you have had mercy upon me."

I read Bible passages and remembered 2 Samuel 5:1-4 and 2 Samuel 5:10: All the tribes of Israel came to David at Hebron and said, "We are your own flesh and blood. In the past, while Saul was king over us you were the one who led Israel on their military campaigns. And the Lord said to you. 'You will shepherd my people Israel, and you will become their ruler.'"

When the elders of Israel had come to King David at Hebron, the king made a compact with them at Hebron before the Lord, and they anointed David king over Israel.

David was thirty years old when he became king, and he reigned over Judah seven years and six months, and in Jerusalem he reigned over all Israel and Judah thirty-three years. He became more and more powerful because the Lord was with him.

I remembered the counsel that Dr Wade Reeves had given me when I was leaving Africa for the USA. Boy, Let people know about you not by talking about yourself but by the way you pay attention to your goals, both short-term and long-term.

After reading the Bible passage I retired to a quiet corner after people who had come to greet me had gone and I sang the song: *Heavens came down*. "Oh what a wonderful, wonderful day. Day I shall never forget. After I've wondered in darkness away Jesus my Saviour I met. Oh what a tender compassionate friend, he met the needs of my heart, Shadow dispelling with joy, I am telling, he made all the darkness depart. Heavens came down and glory filled my soul. While at the cross my Saviour made me whole. My sins were washed away and my nights were turned to day, when, Heavens came down and glory filled my soul. While at the cross my Saviour made me whole."

Yes, all my problems were now over, my nights had been turned to day. Heavens had come down, my Saviour had filled my soul with glory and made me whole.

It is at this moment that I confirmed that largely because of appointments, tribal cliques had formed in the Institute, each projecting a candidate for succeeding the CEO. The cliques monitored on a daily basis when the CEO of the research institute would reach retirement age for the King to replace him. I had not believed the matter well when I was told of the competition that was taking place. I was now able to understand why so many members of the advancement commission had been doing everything to prevent me from ascending to the final grade of chief research officer.

I had gone through a lot of stress and frustration because of this instability in my appointments; I would be named a director of a department today and in the next board meeting after barely serving for two years or so, I would be dropped from my post. That stress would continue for some years before the Institute realized that I was useful to be used in another capacity and naming me into it.

The cliques which had formed against me knew the rules of the game. They would work hard to prevent my name coming up for consideration for appointments of directors; they would lobby among members of the board. They would go the extra mile to tarnish my image and prevent me from coming to the limelight to be considered by the King of Tropicana. There was a continuous system of lobbying and intrigues at all levels to prevent some potential rivals from getting to high positions in the Institute. To add fuel to the flames ethnic considerations were quite prominent in making appointments, especially if you came from a minor tribe and did not have any person to lobby for you. Other times an individual was chosen just because there was no other person to put in that position. The instability in appointments coupled with the length of time spent in a position affected the smooth running of research administration in the Institute. But that did not seem to mean much to the policy makers, who were just contented doing their politics.

Till today what I criticize most in the Federal Republic of Tropicana is that positions were never advertised for candidates to be invited to compete, as it is done in other countries. A candidate's file had to be defended by a member of the commission who was strong enough to influence decisions on such a position. This made the situation very stressful for scientists, especially those who felt they were qualified for positions.

Ethnicity was certainly a problem. Instead of generating diversity in the system, it promoted nepotism. The major tribes tended to be favoured largely because they had many people lobbying for them. Those from minority tribes like us had to work too hard without motivation and could be considered for appointments only when a candidate could not be identified from a major tribe. That was the country. There was nothing to do about it.

CHAPTER 4

Re-location of ISTRC-AB Symposium

· ·

A RESEARCH CENTER SUCH AS THE TROPICANA RURAL DEVELOPMENT Institute was a center of excellence for many reasons. Because the country enjoyed some kind of political stability over a long period of time, and because the country was bilingual in English and French, many organizations selected it for international conferences especially in the central African region. Also, compared with other countries in the region, the road network was not as bad as it is today. The infrastructure of conference centers, hotels and restaurants also made Tropicana ideal for bringing people together in meetings.

I had a major issue that frustrated me as a scientist in the Institute. The matter was the holding of an international event – the triennial symposium of the International Society for Tropical Root Crops – Africa Branch. That Symposium was a scientific meeting for research professionals which held every three years in some venue in Africa. The one-week meeting usually took place on four working days. The fifth day was devoted to visits to fields and places of cultural interest. That last evening was when the business meetings took place. In the business meeting, there was election of new officers and planning for the next meeting of the Society. The symposium was usually an occasion for researchers to gather and share projects, discuss ideas, and network in a professional setting. The scientific meeting was only open to scientific professionals to speak and network amongst peers. Families of host participants, although not scientific professionals, could join delegates during cultural events that crowned the meeting.

For the ISTRC-AB selecting a host for the symposium involved crucial considerations. The Society had to consider the importance of root crops work carried out in the country. They had to consider the contribution of the scientists in the region. They also had to be sure of the political stability of the country to ensure that delegates were protected when they came to the country. That is how the Federal Republic of Tropicana was selected to host the ISTRC-AB symposium the second time.

The triennial symposia of the ISTRC-AB had become a critical meeting point, a melting pot of ideas, and a catalyst of energy for the root crops community. The Society always sought to ensure that with each symposium it added new dimensions to fostering its mission and its engagements as a scientific society. The value placed on those symposia by the Society and the root crops community could be seen in the growing interest of people who attended them, and by the numbers of abstracts of papers and posters presented. The Society learnt each time the symposium was holding from past experience in terms of the process of selecting Symposium host organizations, and in the way the Symposium was being planned and managed. The Society officers were committed to transparency in decision-making processes for host selection of symposia, although there was some amount of lobbying that took place as well.

The selection of host countries followed a certain logic. Firstly, the Society launched an open call which was announced to all research institutes with activities on root crops. Interested bidders were now required to submit a concept note and give a tentative budget for hosting the symposium. Through a process of clarification, engagement and more detailed specifications the Society eventually considered several different bids against a range of pre-determined criteria and the final decision was then made by the General Assembly of the Society which usually held during the business meeting on the last day of every symposium.

Organizing the ISTRC-AB Symposium is a significant undertaking that has particular demands because of its intentions and scale. As a society, the Symposium is one way of reaching out to the global membership of the root crops Society. Although that is the responsibility of the hosting country, the Society ensures that a successful hosting bid is led by a local organizing team comprising members with strong enough credentials and expertise who can bring their own regional flavor and interests into the organization of the event.

The scale and reach of the Symposium then demands that in selecting a host city the Society requires the host country to think carefully about a range of logistical issues, and the Society must ensure that these are met. These include visa requirements, travel options enabling reasonably easy access to the host country, accommodation and security of participants as well as the size of the conference venue itself, which must allow for the range of Symposium activities including space for concurrent sessions (holding at the same time throughout the Symposium), halls for plenary sessions and rooms for special sessions. Special sessions are often sponsored by one or more of Society Sections and presentations are given in different locations that are occurring at the same time. Other logistical issues include the availability of audio-visual equipment, translation, and other services, which are important in assuring equity in access to the Symposium across language barriers. The massive effort that had been made by Tropicana in the training of batches of bilingual translators and interpreters in specialized centers of bilingual studies made the country ideal for conferences which required those services.

And finally, the Society needs to examine bidders' costs and budgets, and the fundraising needs of the Symposium, such as basic costs of the venue, catering, and the costs of simply managing an event of this scale. The Society also thrives to generate enough revenue through sponsorship, registration and fundraising to fully cover the costs of the event, including scholarships for attendance of delegates from other countries. Tax exemptions are often given to the Symposium by the host country administration but the Society must ensure that the country has given that authorization. Overall, the Society must aim to ensure that the financial health of the Society and its ability to support thematic working groups and other activities outside the Symposium is not jeopardized by host selection.

After the decision in the choice of host country and the exact venue is made, the real work begins. First, the focus of the Symposium is developed. Then the program is elaborated. Over the whole three-year period between Symposia, various groups would be working hard to reflect on past experience, develop the theme, think through the overall shape and size of the program, add new activities and engagements, raise funding, reach out to new audiences and communities, review abstracts, build the program itself, and manage the logistics.

One morning as I was lolling in my seat in my office, the messenger knocked on my door and stepped into my office. He told me the CEO wanted to see me urgently. I stopped the punching of field data on an Excel spreadsheet to analyze the data later with SAS and went immediately to his office. His Chief of Cabinet went in to see him to announce my presence. He let me in. Then, opening a letter which had reached him the previous day, he announced, apparently happily, in a soft and assuring voice, "the Federal Republic of Tropicana has been selected by the International Society for Tropical Root Crops-Africa Branch, to host the triennial symposium of the Society. Since you are a member of the Society and that is your area of expertise, and the fact that you have been hard-working on root crops matters, I have decided that you should be the chief organizer of the Symposium." He added that consequently he was calling me to constitute a strong team and set it to work for the organization of the meeting.

I was happy and elated. It was a great honour for me. I was still a senior research officer, still waiting to meet the longevity requirement to apply for the grade of chief research officer. We were twelve researchers working in the root crops program and anyone could lead the organizing committee. I figured that he found me most qualified and better talented to do the job. He handed the entire file from the International Society to me. I thanked him and promised that I would do my best to ensure that we had a successful symposium. I left his office and went back to my office. When I was settled in my office, the first thing I did was to make an outline of the work we were going to do and which subcommittees were going to carry out the various tasks.

The second thing I had to do was to prepare a letter which the CEO was going to sign informing all root crops scientists of the national root crops improvement program about the selection of our country to host the Symposium. After I had constituted the work teams, I assigned responsibilities to individuals, giving them delays for executing their tasks and requesting them to propose budgets for the individual activities of the organization entrusted in their hands.

The next thing I did was to inform the King through the Minister about the selection of the country to host the Symposium. The letter of information had to be accompanied by the formal request for funding for which a budget had to be elaborated, a justification of the benefits that such an event would bring to the country, and the benefits that country researchers were going to have from the hosting of the symposium in our country. Although the letter had to contain only the outline of these issues I prepared a brochure with the symposium details for anyone in the Ministry and in the King's Palace who wanted to and had time to read more about the event.

From past Symposia which I had attended I had learnt that it was important for countries to communicate with each other whenever there is an event of such magnitude because international relations are key for ensuring a safe world. Without effective communication, small misunderstandings could occur which could have serious consequences for the organization. I had made an inventory of all countries with active root crops programs. I knew the root crops workers in those countries and the crops they were working on. I also knew their specialties. I prepared a catalogue showing all these to make it easy for the Society to prepare invitations of participants.

I had learnt that as the nations grew in their memberships in the Society over time, international relations often become important for forging beneficial relationships among countries. Countries needed to communicate in order for them to survive. For Tropicana national events like this Symposium connected us as a people of a nation and even connected citizens to important moments of a nation's history. Usually in a country with already highly developed infrastructure of the basic requirements for hosting a Symposium of that nature, the country would automatically cut down the costs for hosting the event, leaving tourist development to be the next economic impact that the host country would have with the holding of such a major international event.

There are several benefits that a symposium brings to the hosting country. A symposium usually has one day, usually a day before departure of participants for exploiting the cultural attributes of a country. These are an expressive way to celebrate glorious heritage, culture and traditions. They are meant to rejoice special moments and emotions in the lives of the people of that country with loved ones from other countries. They play an important role to add structure to our social lives during the time foreigners spend in that country. They provide a distraction from the hectic days of the scientific presentations and debate, exhausting routines of scientific life as well as give delegates some inspiration to remember the important things and moments in life. The cultural attributes are also meant to pass the legends, knowledge and traditions onto the next generation of delegates.

One major benefit of hosting an international event is the acquisition of tourist income that will be received by the hosting country. Revenue generation is a major gain from an international symposium. On top of all the other benefits offered by the Symposium, they can be great revenue generators for groups and associations. The revenue generated by a successful Symposium could help fund other activities undertaken by the Society and the country's root crops program such as promotions, advocacy and lobbying.

Another benefit is long term investment for the country (such as the refurbishing of the international convention center. Another benefit is legacy benefits which also raise the profile of the city in which the event is taking place. There is certainly a lot of impact and stories that the event leaves behind after the event is over.

The Symposium, although a scientific event, is cultural in one way or another. In that sense it is a way to bring happiness to the delegates' lives, and strengthen their sense of community and camaraderie. They connect country participants as a people of a nation or a region, connecting people to important moments of a nation's history (such as the founding day of a nation or the independence day of the country), and help to solidify the spirit of patriotism in the society.

Hosting a Symposium also benefits the scientists of a country. The great benefits for scientists who attend international symposia include first the opportunity for presenting a paper from his or her research work. Presenting a paper is one of the main objectives of a research scientist who participates in a symposium. The presenter will have the chance to present a paper in front of colleagues of the same or similar fields of study. They will be able to receive positive feedback and constructive criticism about the research they are conducting. The exchange of ideas on fields of interests may provide the links for future collaborations across the world, some participants developing research projects together and even writing papers together. With all of the hurdles on getting papers accepted by journals symposia are an essential part of scientific life. Although the stress of presenting a talk can sometimes feel like an overwhelming or even scary experience, being able to present papers in a symposium can be a big learning experience for the scientist. However, scientists have countless other reasons to attend a symposium. These are some of the ways that scientific symposia could change the life of a scientist.

The article presented in a Symposium publication proceedings is always a good way to have your research published and indexed. You will also have the opportunity to publish your research later in a journal of the Society because only selected papers are published in the Society journal or the proceedings. Although in TRDI, symposia papers (whether they have gone through thorough editorial review or not) were unfortunately given one-third of the weight of a peer-reviewed journal article, were a good place to start.

One important reason to present a paper in a Symposium is to get feedback on an early version of your latest work. It is vital to find out what's new in your field of study to survive in an academic discipline. Another major reason why a scientist should attend an academic symposium is that it would keep you updated on new findings that have taken place in your research area. Also, there is added research value in a symposium presentation since it could help to make research on a particular subject easier for students and scientists. They provide access to various research activities related to a particular subject with current findings and developments anticipated from them.

The foundation of any good symposium is a good program. Having interesting and qualified speakers and workshops on hand for your delegates can help promote new ideas and best practices in your field. For instance, I benefited a lot from statistical packages such as AMMI and regression models used and clearly explained by other scientists in symposia I attended in various parts of the world. These made my scientific life better and our research industry as a whole function better. When one attends a scientific symposium he or she is sure to meet people of his or her same stature, mindset and goals. This is a motivational factor as one aspires to overcome presentation fears and achieve one's dreams of speaking successfully in science.

Some scientists find that presenting a paper at a symposium could be nerve-wracking. This might be true. You might even be tempted to fall back on the same presentation that you always give because you know that it is safe. But if you do this, you'll be missing out on one great benefit of symposia: the chance to get feedback from experts on early versions of your work. You can use your presentation time to talk about preliminary results from your most recent experiment, and the feedback you get from your audience can help you to improve your publication and anticipate reviewers' comments when you try to get it published in a scientific journal. Alternatively, you could present your well-established work, and then at the end, you could throw out some ideas you have for future experiments and get feedback on these.

A Symposium presents the chance to see a whole room full of world experts in your particular field, so there's no better chance to get your work in front of these people and have them candidly discuss its strengths and weaknesses. These would help you have the paper accepted later when you submit it for publication in a peer-reviewed journal. I remember several times when, after attending a symposium, I threw out sections out of a manuscript I was preparing for publication just on the basis of the criticisms and ideas I had received from the symposium.

Another reason for attending a symposium is to get to know other people in your field. It is actually one of the biggest benefits of attending a scientific symposium, and getting to know other people in your field broadens your network of collaborators. A scientific symposium like a Society symposium is a key opportunity for networking which is very important for job hunting. Obviously having a big network benefits the scientist in other ways too such as getting advice from an expert in another field, or asking someone to come and give a talk at your institution. These are easier when you have a network to reach out to. Networking also helps you to get support from people who are at a similar stage in their careers like you and can empathize with the problems and struggles which you go through in your institution. It is possible for the delegates to develop networking for future collaborations. When a scientist attends a scientific symposium he has an opportunity to build networks with other academics and experts in the same or similar field of studies all around the world and to share thoughts on recent advances and technological breakthroughs. It is an opportunity to expand the knowledge that one has and upgrade performance in accomplishing institutional objectives. Symposia bring together people who share a common discipline from different parts of the world, bringing different forms of ideas which build into something greater in later life. As you keep attending symposia you build a network of people who can raise your caliber of work to greater heights as you achieve shared objectives in your field.

When one attends a scientific conference he or she is sure to meet people of his or her same stature, mindset and goals. This is a motivational factor as one aspires to overcome fears and achieve one's dreams. Furthering networking in a scientific conference is easy because it brings together a large collection of people from within your field as well as from peripheral and related industries. This offers great opportunities to expand your network both within your own sector as well as others that are connected to your own. As is the case with networking, you can never tell when these new connections could prove productive. Country delegates in a Symposium gain from relationships developed in their respective disciplines. Also, having speakers with varied scientific understandings in various disciplines and domains can help provide to them a better understanding of their topics. Diversity in speakers in a Symposium could bring in new ideas and new ways of looking at research and issues that country participants encounter.

The researcher can also hear about the latest research. If a researcher wants to know about the very latest findings in their field before the results are even published in journals, then a symposium is the place to be. Many researchers will present in a symposium preliminary findings of their work which has not yet been published. However, this is a great chance to get an idea of what other people are working on which can be a source of inspiration for your own research.

Symposia can also improve the presentation and communication skills of the researcher: Soft skills are important for every career, and in the research your skills in presentation and communication are even particularly important. Fortunately, symposia give you the chance to practice these skills. Rehearsing and giving your talk or poster presentation will make you more comfortable in front of an audience, and you will learn things like the speed at which you should talk and the amount of detail which you need to include in your explanations. Also, answering questions after your presentation and chatting with other participants will help to boost your communications skills.

Attending a Symposium is a chance to visit a new place and have fun. Many scientists are excited about going to a Symposium in a country where they have not been before just to get that fun. Travelling to a new place is a big part of the pleasures you get from a Symposium, because you get to see a different city, eat new food, and see some local cultural landmarks or tourist attractions. That aspect should not be overlooked because it is enriching. Although it is unequivocally a scientific work event more than a leisure one, it can still be enjoyable. You might even try out learning a little bit of the new language of the place. It also gives you the chance to attend social functions as part of a conference, such as dinners, trips, or parties. Sometimes these events can be formal or dull, but very often they are relaxing and friendly. With the opportunity to meet other academics with similar interests to you, you can enjoy the company of others and you might even make some good friends, sometimes life-long friends. Many friends I met in triennial symposia in Ghana, Benin, Togo, Democratic Republic of Congo and Malawi have remained very good friends till today. I was able to perfect my capacity to speak French as well as learn some regional languages like *lingala*, a language spoken in the Republic of Congo and the Democratic Republic of Congo. I was able to learn some words and phrases in another regional language like *Swahili* just because I had the opportunity to visit Kenya, Uganda and Tanzania.

A Symposium could be a great way to have a "break" from your academic responsibilities at the research institute or university. It enables you to relax and discover different cities of the world and the way things are done there. After the Symposium you will generally feel refreshed when you return to your institution. Socialization and the culture factors should never be neglected because meeting new people with different cultures and dispositions enlightens your way of thinking in your field of study. You will witness some of the many different aspects and solutions which exist on the same issues. You could also have the chance to socialize with your colleagues at coffee breaks, lunches and social activities. A Symposium without socializing or learning more about other people's cultural tradition could be extremely boring because people from different parts of the world have uniqueness in their ways of living which you are often surprised to learn from when you meet in a Symposium.

One major benefit I have had is that Symposia give me the opportunity to meet my scientific heroes: If there's a researcher whose work you admire, it can be both inspiring and educational to meet them and to talk to them directly. My attendance in a Symposium in England gave me the opportunity to speak to the experts on quantitative trait loci, which I had only encountered in the literature. So also was the experience of meeting key speakers on regression analysis who clarified the concepts more than I had picked up from the literature. In one Symposium I had the chance to learn new statistical software, the Additive Main Effects and Multiplicative Interaction Model which became a program I used several times in my data analysis of genotype x environment interactions back in my home country.

If one of your academic heroes is speaking at a Symposium, this could be the perfect chance for you to meet them there. This could even lead to future collaboration and funding for some aspects of your research. Country scientists gain enormously especially if some time has been taken to look at the quality of scientists invited in various fields and that the organizing committee and the Society have not overlooked someone who would be a valuable asset in the symposium. This is usually successful when efforts have been made to consider the diversity and backgrounds of speakers participating in the event. Positive impacts of prior symposia of the Society sometimes cause an excitement among the participants, and energize them in the way they look at various topics during the event.

Symposia give the country scientists access to influence makers because this is one of the largest collections of individuals from your industry in one place at one time. I remember meeting a prominent member of the Cameroon Academy of Science in a Symposium. After my presentation in the meeting, he called me to the side and told me how impressed he was with my presentation. He promised sending me the application file to membership into the academy. I did not know before then that he was the dean of the college of biological sciences of the academy. That is how I eventually became a fellow of the academy after I had submitted the file along with all the publications that were required.

There are few better opportunities to offer to politicians and senior bureaucrats to connect with you and your colleagues. This is a two-way street, and will offer your institution the opportunity to present them with your ideas and concerns around policy, legislation and funding. Some of those politicians may have heard of you but the fact that they are meeting you physically for the first time creates a different impression about you in their minds. I remember a senior scientist who later worked as an administrator in the Ministry advocating for my good work one time when others wanted to hold me down in my promotion as chief research officer.

In a symposium a researcher may have the chance to engage in high-level debates and refine their ideas. Listening to and participating in lively discussions in a scientific conference can give you new ideas, help refine your existing concepts, and may even change your mind about some key issues in your field, especially if you, the researcher, are humble and receptive.

Attending a symposium may also go on a researcher's CV, especially if they have given a talk or poster presentation. It shows potential employers or grant-awarding bodies that the scientist is engaged with his field and is taking an active part in communicating with other scientists, important criteria which donors use to give grants.

A Symposium could be a great opportunity to showcase your institute and expand the reach of your organization and to others in your field, to peripheral sectors as well as to the public. Increased exposure will help promote your organization and its members. A successful conference will garner attention on social media, traditional media and with those connected to your institute who haven't previously been involved with the organization of the meeting.

Finally, in today's fast changing world, attending a scientific conference has become a "must" to survive in an academic discipline. Many academics and scientists have become aware of this fact as the number of scientific conferences and participants from various countries increase dramatically, and because they want to strive in science, they make every effort to participate.

There are certainly also some disadvantages in the hosting of international events. The first disadvantage is the enormous cost of the investment especially as there is short-term use of the facilities for which the investment for refurbishing has been done. There may be higher taxes to pay for the costs especially if things are done in a hurry. There are serious security concerns as many organs of national security such as the police and the military are mobilized to ensure that delegates are well protected during their stay in the country. I dared not mention these disadvantages that the Symposia could bring when I was preparing the document for the King.

In TRDI, although symposia were happy events, sometimes they were a source of frustration. One thing which was stressful in our institute was the way some international events were handled. Several officers who were chosen to treat files for the event would put in a lot of effort only if they had financial gain for themselves for the event. If they did not find their own interest in it or did not like the person who was responsible for it, they sat on it and paid little attention to it. Sometimes they even worked to make it fail. I had my own stresses and frustration the way I was treated when I was chosen to be chief organizer of the Symposium of the International Society for Tropical Root Crops Africa-Branch. The holding of an international meeting as this needed the support of several people in the Ministry and in the King's Palace, because it was a big honour for the country and so everything had to be done for it to be successful. If there was any blockage at any step of the process, either in the research institute, in the Ministry or in the King's Palace, things would not work and the organization would fail. I was fortunate that the documents I prepared on the symposium passed through at the level of the CEO without any problem. That was the first successful step. As a second step, the CEO forwarded the file to the Minister for approval and onward transmission to the King's Palace. Unfortunately, the file entered wrong hands at the level of the Ministry. The Minister gave the file to a person who had been nursing a *ngevephobia* for some time. I had provided sufficient information to guide the officer treating the file at the Ministry and to enable him prepare the transmission letter to the King's Palace. Unfortunately, as I later found out the officer at the Ministry treating the file was abhorrent to me; he did not like me to have the honour of succeeding in the organization of such a Symposium. He even thought I would receive some benefit and personal gain from it. I had made the file to be explicit. A modest budget had been elaborated. Delegates who were to be invited from the various countries had been selected. I had gone through the difficult process of inviting the Prime Minister to be the main speaker in the opening ceremony. I had given enough justification for the holding of the meeting as well as the benefits which the country and its scientists would have in hosting such a meeting. The only thing that was left was for the Minister to transmit the file to the King's Palace. But for one year that was left, no word was received from the King's Palace. After making a tracer to find out where the file was stuck, we realized that it had not been transmitted to the King. Further information revealed that the file had simply fallen in bad hands. The officer in the Ministry who was treating the file had decided on his own that I would not have the pride of succeeding in the organization. In fact, he had worked hard to convince the Minister that the Symposium was not worth the effort for the amount of money that we had requested from the King for the event.

I felt really stressed as I moved from place to place begging and lobbying to get funding for the symposium. I had anticipated that things could be slow, the reason I had started early with the arrangements. But as funds were not forth coming, and official authorization had not been received from the King's Palace, I did not know what again to do to proceed. I convinced myself that I had done everything to be sure that the King had been properly informed. As a young researcher just returning from higher studies in the USA, the thought of successfully organizing a symposium was daunting. But this was me now, although being given that responsibility and the huge tasks that came with it I was failing. I had assembled all the ideas for a successful symposium from previous symposia I had attended. I had chosen a captivating theme: *The role of root crops in local food industries in a developing economy.* Initially I was worried that the theme I had chosen for the symposium could be rejected, but my mentor encouraged me to pursue it and it was accepted by the Society. I needed to get a creative title that would appear in banners that would stand out and be also descriptive, one that provided a clear aim or goals for the symposium. This was the opportunity to summarize ideas and advocate for why the symposium should hold, and if the symposium we were organizing represented the diversity of work being done on the topic. I had done that and it too had been accepted.

I had also done the task of having a diverse group of presenters, in addition to the Prime Minister in the opening of the symposium, including those who were selected from typically underrepresented groups and who could have been overlooked in the Institute, Ministry, other institutions and the Universities in the country. In our complex society of 256 ethnic groups, I wanted to watch out to include speakers with diverse backgrounds (gender, ethnicity, career stage, etc.) who could bring unique perspectives and deepen the impact of the symposium. I thought to myself that I had to be brave to invite non-root crops senior workers in the Ministry of Rural Development and those in the Ministry of Livestock and Fisheries to come and share ideas in their work.

Finding out that we had the support of higher authorities for the symposium could always be exciting. I then had to contact speakers and start thinking about the story they wanted to tell in their presentations during the Symposium. I made every effort to reconnect early with speakers to confirm their participation. If they had a conflict with the date of the symposium or had a change in their situation, they could ask if they could send a potential substitute speaker. I would have to contact those speakers in time to have them to provide titles and abstracts for their talks.

I took time to search for additional speakers in areas where it was necessary to do so. I realized that sometimes between the time I first started researching speakers and the time the Symposium had been scheduled to hold, new research on the topic could have come out. I would take time to look at the scientists in that field and make sure we had not overlooked someone who would be a valuable asset to the Symposium. Again, I kept reminding myself that considering the diversity of speakers and their backgrounds could bring in new ideas and new ways of looking at research and issues that were encountered.

In the last minute when funds could not be obtained for the event, the International Society for Tropical Root Crops took the fast decision to move the hosting of the Symposium to the IITA campus in Nigeria. That was how the Symposium was held in IITA Ibadan in Nigeria. I felt so disappointed with the way things were done in my country.

It was extremely frustrating to me. For one full month I could hardly eat. I did not know where to keep the shame. It was also very stressful to me because so much work had gone into the organization. The theme of the meeting had been chosen. The topics to be presented had been selected. The members of the local organizing committee had given the best of themselves in providing whatever input they could give. We had chosen the speakers in the opening of the meeting. We had known that having important speakers interested in talking in the opening of the symposium would help support the importance of the symposium. I had been given by the Society useful tips that could be useful for inviting speakers, and had succeeded in convincing the Prime Minister to do the final opening. I had also invited the Minister-Secretary of Rural Development Investigations to be present in the first day of the symposium, and to make a presentation as one of the speakers in the opening ceremony. I had also struggled to get a prominent root crops scientist like the retired coordinator of the root crops program to make an important opening presentation. Although I had initially been somewhat afraid to reach out to some personalities to invite them to participate, I had come to realize that some were even happy to participate and speak.

Now with the Symposium not holding in our country, I had to deal with the disappointment of the re-location of our Symposium to Ibadan, Nigeria. I felt very frustrated. That is when I knew that disappointment could be one of life's most uncomfortable feelings, There is enormous difficulty in cancelling plans – remaking flight bookings, abandoning the printed material which had taken quite some money and effort to produce, and the feeling of dealing with your disappointment as well as the guilt of disappointing other colleagues who had made plans to attend just because they had heard of the football country and wanted to be there. Feelings could be extremely complex. There are emotions like anger, hurt, sadness, and probably many others too subtle to identify. I realized that disappointment could leave one feeling unsettled, and unresolved.

I then realized that I had to deal with two kinds of disappointments when our Symposium could not hold in the country: the disappointment I felt when our Ministry let me down and the feelings that came when the other members of the International Society felt, and how disappointed they were in us from our country for letting them down, the so-called "vaporous guilt that clings to people when they let other people down."

The whole disappointment experience sent me looking for some comfort even after I was informed that a different location had been chosen as a matter of urgency to host the symposium. I noticed that there were four steps I had to go through to deal with that disappointment. In the first place, I needed to let it out. For this I noticed that one of the hardest things to do in a world where everything appears immediate is to just let oneself experience a feeling. Allow yourself to feel what you are feeling without any agenda of speeding up the process. Whatever you are feeling is fine. I had to take some time to just sit with my emotion and experience it without moving to fix or change it. I came to realize that genuinely experiencing emotions, no matter how painful, is one of the beauties of life. I did not have to shy away from these moments but be present in them.

The second thing in dealing with the stress was to get some perspective, a kind of point of view. I needed to develop a particular attitude toward a way of regarding and dealing with it. Once I had allowed myself the space I needed to experience my feelings of disappointment, I was able to give the situation more room to breathe. I realized that giving myself the space to be, I was prepared to allow the same for other colleagues and members of the society.

The third thing I did was to make every attempt to know my own heart. Disappointment could ripple through to the core of who I was. I reminded myself that if I did not know what my core values were, I would not have a framework to support myself when I experienced negative emotions. One of my core values was open heartedness. I had to keep an open heart and had to be ready to share love and kindness with others, regardless of how they could behave. I went to the Ministry several times and even met the people who could have been assigned to treat our file, and I appeared cheerful and friendly, as usual to them as if nothing had happened. They were surprised with my behavior. Some even started to excuse themselves that they had not taken part in the process of treating the file and sending it to the Palace and even claimed not to know that the famous file had not been sent to the King.

Finally, I decided to practice acceptance of what had happened. I realized that this step was crucial and a lifelong challenge, and was fundamental in dealing with my disappointment. I consoled myself that disappointment was an integral part of life, part of being human and would no doubt happen at various points throughout the rest of one's life. I had to learn to say: I will be disappointed, you will be disappointed, and life would be disappointing, but that will come to pass. And it came to pass.

As I started my journey to IITA Ibadan, I pondered on my seat in the 737 aircraft of Cameroon Airlines. The crew members were good and polite, the food they served was nice and appetizing but my mind was not there. I just kept thinking about the shame I was going to have in front of my other colleagues from other countries who had hoped to have fun in the Federal Republic of Tropicana.

The saddest moment I had was when after the two-our trip from Lagos to Ibadan, the van wheeled into the entry gate that brought us to the IITA campus. As we drove past the Security gate, I saw the large banner: *The Role of Root Crops in Local Food Industries in a Developing Economy.* Tears flowed down my cheeks and I felt empty since then.

Looking at it now, the way things happened was as if the Society had a Plan B. IITA was immediately chosen to host the symposium just two weeks before the holding of the event. The main challenge the Society had was how, in such a short time, it was going to communicate to the various delegates from different countries the new venue for the meeting, and the new air tickets and reservations they had to issue for them to attend. I am sure the Society learnt one lesson that it had to be prepared and had to be flexible in future, and be ready to make changes to the venue of a Symposium if that happened again. By using preparation and flexibility, cancelling a symposium would probably be a major inconvenience but certainly not a tragedy.

CHAPTER 5

Shortage of research funds

∙∙

IN THE FEDERAL REPUBLIC OF TROPICANA, THERE IS BROAD AGREEMENT among scientists that a lack of funding currently represents the biggest impediment to conducting high-quality scientific research. Nearly half of the scientists in the Institute, when interviewed indicate that a lack of funding for their basic research is a very serious impediment in achieving their research goals of carrying their research activities to the end and getting good results. Generally, research scientists who primarily address basic knowledge questions are more likely than applied researchers to describe a lack of funding as a very serious obstacle to scientific research. Still, overwhelming majorities in both groups of scientists see a lack of funding as at least a serious impediment.

A few other scientists see other factors as presenting serious obstacles to high-quality research. In plant science, there is decreasing funding for research, because of non-availability, but also because the population has the feeling that food availability in markets is not because scientists worked hard to develop high-yielding varieties and improved farming technologies but because farmers worked hard that year. I find it difficult to wipe this out of the minds of people, even those who are educated enough to understand. Meanwhile, science spending is increasing in other countries, leading to notable achievements. For instance, the European Space Agency landed the first spacecraft on a comet, and Chinese researchers unveiled the world's fastest supercomputer. These developments are largely because of substantial funding to research. Also, without investment to support the development of new vaccines and antibiotics the threat to US public health a decade from now may well look very challenging. Reduced research funds have always had detrimental effects on developing countries like Tropicana which need these funds most.

In the Federal Republic of Tropicana, about 90% of the country's research is funded by the government, but in many instances, reduced funding is not only a matter of affordability but also one of lack of support and priority. While large sums are spent each year for national defense and public health, only a small portion of the national budget is spent on scientific research. To make matters worse, some of the people appointed to head scientific research who could have made strong advocacy for increased funding are people whose major interest is to amass wealth for themselves.

Many scientists in the Federal Republic of Tropicana have been stressed for most of their careers. We just console ourselves that stress is a part of everyday life, but if most of us had our way, it wouldn't even exist. Stress negatively impacts our minds, bodies, and performance. Our stress is caused by stressors and we have convinced ourselves that learning more about those stressors could help set us on the path to reducing our exposure and negative reactions to them.

There are indications that some fields of research, in spite of having great national importance are suffering owing to a lack of sufficient funding. The time I was doing active research in Tropicana, there was no funding at all for cocoyam research. Yet cocoyam flour could easily replace wheat flour and reduce imports of wheat flour from abroad. Government could not fund the crop because it was considered to be in the low category of speculations requiring funding. The food industry could not support cocoyam research because the industries did not have the habit of doing so. International organizations reserved their funding for high priority crops which were grown in several countries in the region. Hence funding research proposals on cocoyams submitted to those international donors was hardly ever received positively because the crop was regarded as one with only local interest. I was surprised to see that underfunding was not only common in developing countries. It occurred even in the USA. For instance, underfunded areas in the USA included neurodegenerative disease, such as Alzheimer's, cybersecurity, infectious disease, and robotics, but their agricultural industries supported food production research to some extent, the reason their silos are bursting with food like maize and soybean.

In Tropicana, there was hardly any privately funded research, simply because the will of the food industry and private companies to release funds for research was not there. In other countries there may be some ethical concerns with privately funded research where a profit is at risk. For instance in the pharmaceutical industry there are rigorous requirements in the United States regarding pharmaceutical trials and the process can take up to ten years. Of course funding bias can be completely eliminated by only allowing research grant funding to come from the public sector, but again money matters, and the public sector does not have enough money to support all the research that needs to take place.

Most of my research work was funded by grants obtained either from international organizations or from regional research networks. Also, what I sometimes used to do as a researcher was to create allies with colleagues in international research centers. They had funds for some lines of research. I had ideas that could foster research. We would carry out some research activities together, collect data together and publish our results together also. I had a good friend in the name of Dr Alfred Dixon, a cassava scientist, who came to my rescue several times in this regard. He made me survive in peak periods of frustration. This was one way to take away the stress we as national scientists used to have in not having funds for research. The fact that I kept myself busy working at times when several colleagues were stressed because of lack of research funds, caused enormous jealousy from other colleagues who did not have research projects or research partners that could assist in funding their research.

Some researchers of perennial stimulant crops research in our institute benefited from externally funded research conducted by expatriate scientists in various research programs in the institute, although in some cases the results from such experimentation was published without national scientists even knowing, and therefore not being as contributors in the resulting publications. That frustrated a good number of them.

Many times the stress I had came also from my bosses. They would engage themselves in activities which could not be covered by research money and insist that I defray the costs from my project funds. This caused a lot of frustration because I found myself between horns of a dilemma – if I financially settled those activities I would have hard time accounting for the funds. If I refused to do it, I would be in the bad books of my bosses. The frustration here was that it was difficult to strike a balance between doing and not doing.

With time I came to realize that not only developing countries face the problem of lack of research funding. For instance, lack of research funding is currently hunting the American Dream. In many developed countries such as the USA challenges to the traditional promise of opportunity born from hard work and determination stem from a troubling lack of investment in basic scientific research that supports the health and economic prosperity of the countries. The case has recently been made that in order for the USA, for example, to remain globally competitive, the three sectors of academia, government and business need to form stronger partnerships to support research. People also feel that the federal government of the USA needs to increase its investment in basic and applied research as well as development in all aspects especially in agriculture and health. Congress has probably taken it for granted that America's leadership will continue as it has for a couple of centuries. The sky seems to be the limit to what Americans could do, if the will is there. For instance, NASA made pioneering efforts to launch the Apollo flights to the moon, and even after that they have broken through the sky. The success has certainly continued in some respects, enough to make members of Congress complacent, thinking that all has been done to make the USA the technology leader in the world. But more has to be done in the area of investments in research funding. The statistics show that the USA currently ranks 10th among the nations of the Organisation for Economic Co-operation and Development (OECD) in overall research and development investments, behind even smaller countries like Israel, Korea, Finland, Sweden and Germany. During the last two decades, America's investment has been about 3 percent of GDP, but other countries, such as China, have increased investments by as much as 8 percent per year.

The unavailability of money for research caused some researchers in our institute to just give up looking for research money. They spent their time engaging in commercial activities like operating cold stores, small provision shops and hardware stores to supplement their incomes and make ends meet.

With the perennial problem of lack of funding the question that has always come to my mind is this: Is the general lack of research funding in science a reflection of a low demand for new discoveries and technology, or something else? I have found it difficult to get a good answer.

Funding has ever been scarce. From stories which have been handed down to us there was no system of funding until after the second world war, at least not in the way we think of it today. Now, the government (in whatever country you are in) funds most scientific research. In Tropicana research is funded through a research ministry and its research institutes. There are no dedicated science funding agencies with defined degrees of oversight and funding levels.

The second question that keeps lingering in my mind is: What is the right way to think about science funding? The government pays for roads, and companies get to use those roads for free to ship their goods across the country. Similarly, the government pays for science and companies get to use all of that science for much less than it would cost to develop it themselves. This seems good in the competitive business market. It is good for consumers because anything discovered is *everyone's*. When I discover something, any company gets to use my results, and those results then get embedded into products. If the government didn't fund science, companies would have to - in which case they would insist on patenting even more than science is already patented. Imagine if someone discovers a cure for a disease like Alzheimer's disease but that a drug company has patented both the cure *and* the knowledge of how that cure works that cure might never be found, because maybe it relies on proprietary knowledge held by a different drug company.

What puzzles me is: *Is science funding decreasing?* By some measures, it is. By other measures, no. *Do local industries want science?* Yes. *Do industries want to pay for it?* No, why would they? After all they do not randomly pay for roads when they feel they don't have to? *Why might science funding be scarcer now than in the past?* Maybe for the same reason that we aren't investing in fixing our bridges and roads the way we should.

Researchers everywhere feel there has never been a time when funding for their activities had been abundant and that is why research funding is hugely competitive. But things have changed a lot in the past thirty years or so. This is not because the need for funding has lessened, nor that the need for research has decreased. But this is because government, the major funding source, has come to the belief that they should be funding nothing at all. Some donors argue that in many research proposals, researchers hardly tell them the donors (or those reviewing proposals for them) what they actually want to do with the money, or what the probable benefits of the research will be. However, the fact that graduate students especially at the doctorate level and even many young scientists are continuously grilled in the writing of proposals it is because research generates knowledge, whether that knowledge is useful in the short term or in the long term. And if the researcher cannot prove that new knowledge will be created from the research for which a proposal is submitted, then such a research proposal does not need to be funded.

Some research areas may be attractive whereas others may not be. For instance a research group working on tropical diseases in a tropical country, can easily get funding for its research when compared with another working on a dry, and apparently purely academic area like astrophysics whose results may not easily be useful to the wider community. In many cases, research funding has to be justified. No donor is ready to dish out money to researchers to enjoy their time and come up with insignificant results, unless the donor is extremely rich and would like to see further progress in that field of research.

In our research institute chemical companies would use our facilities to test for the chemical products which their industries were producing, in a way to encourage the marketing of their products in developing countries. I remember vividly why some expatriates from some European countries spent huge resources working on diseases like black pod of cocoa or coffee berry disease, and their research was mainly on chemical efficacy to control those diseases, and not on integrated pest management strategies which emphasized disease resistance, for the control of these diseases. In fact, a colleague of mine, a geneticist, was working on cocoa breeding. The Institute felt he should look at generating cocoa varieties resistant to the black pod of cocoa. But he did not have any financial support for his research and government funding was not coming regularly. The expatriate scientists could not use him because breeding for disease resistance was not their line of research. The guy became very frustrated and left the institute and looked for an administrative position in one of the Ministries in town.

In some countries like the USA in recent years there have been some highly visible attacks on American scientific research, the biggest threat to science funding being quietly occurring under the radar, even though it could be changing the very foundation of American innovation. The threat has always been money, specifically, the decline of government support for science and the growing dominance of private spending over American research. In 1965, the US federal government financed more than 60 percent of all Research and Development (R&D) projects. By 2006, the balance had flipped, with 65 percent of R&D in the USA being funded by private interests. According to the American Association for the Advancement of Science, several of the nation's science-driven agencies like the Environmental Protection Agency (EPA), the Department of Agriculture, the Department of the Interior, and NASA, have been losing funding, leading to more "outsourcing" of what were once governmental science functions. It is said that the government is clearly increasing its reliance on industry and forming 'joint ventures' to accomplish research that it is unable to afford on its own anymore. I often wish that such partnerships ought to develop in developing countries as well.

Research universities, too, are rapidly privatizing. Both public and private institutions now receive only a small portion of their overall research funds from government sources. They are looking instead to private industry and other commercial activities to supplement their funding. Many wonder if all this is truly harmful or beneficial to science. Some experts argue that corporate support is actually beneficial because it provides enhanced funding for R&D. It speeds the transfer of new knowledge to industry, and boosts economic growth. It isn't enough to create new knowledge. That knowledge needs to be transferred for the betterment of society.

Many industry leaders worry that the current mix of private and public funding is out of balance. Some people have noted that market pressures have compelled industry to put nearly all its investment into applied research, not the riskier basic science that produces results 10 to 15 years later. Others fear that if the balance tips too far, the "public interest" side of the science system—known for its commitment to independence and objectivity—will atrophy. In many areas of scientific research the needs of industry have become paramount, turning science into "a contested terrain" where facts are increasingly contingent on who is funding the research. The entire scientific revolution is threatened when science is commercialized. People now ask the question if private funding has become a boon or a bane for American science. The answer requires looking carefully at how the phenomenon is playing out in the real world. In developing countries the situation will be worse simply because the implication of industry is not just in the culture of the society.

Some industries intentionally conceal negative data that concerns them, making it risky to depend wholly on the private sector to fund research in some areas. Experiences like these have bolstered the position that the independent research system needs to be protected and preserved. The rise in academic patenting and licensing also gives universities and their professors growing financial ties to outside companies, not to mention growing investments in their own research (including patent rights, stockholdings, and royalty shares). What academic institutions always argue is that they have sufficient safeguards in place to protect against any influences on the academic research.

In my evaluation I see that private industry has become increasingly sophisticated about how it uses "science" to achieve its commercial objectives. Positive research gets published; negative research doesn't. The sponsor's drug is given at a higher dosage than the competitor's drug. In many cases, the sponsors control study design, access to data, and statistical analysis and even ghostwrite articles and pay prominent academics to sign on as "authors." But since many professors are so desperate to find research money for their experiments, a lot of them are naive to challenge the potential for industry influence on the results they would eventually generate. That was the situation in our institute where some scientists were forced by expatriate colleagues to work in areas which were not really in their interest or not in the interest of the country but because doing such research kept them occupied and gave them some financial profit which they badly needed to supplement their incomes.

CHAPTER 6

Slandering in the workplace

· ·

SLANDERING, MAKING FALSE AND DAMAGING STATEMENTS ABOUT SOME colleagues was a common feature of the life of researchers in the Tropicana Rural Development Institute. I do not know why that was so prominent, but I guess it was because many scientists spent a good bit of their time aspiring for high administrative positions. One way to achieve their objectives was to tarnish the images of those researchers who they considered to be rivals. Appointments into higher administrative positions were achieved mostly from recommendations of people in high places. That ought to be by merit. In developed countries, a search committee would be created when an administrative position became vacant. The position would then be advertised and people who felt they were qualified for the position would apply. A short list would be made of potential candidates and interviews conducted among those short-listed candidates. The best in the interviews was selected and given the post.

That was not the case in the Federal Republic of Tropicana. Most of the appointments were done through lobbying. The major ethnic groups had *big* people in all spheres of influence in the Kingdom. They thus formed strong lobby groups and projected a candidate for each high-level appointment that could surface up in the country. If that position finally became vacant, the members of that ethnic group would make the necessary contacts and lobby strongly among the people that mattered, projecting their candidate and proposing him for the position. They would do whatever was necessary to do to show that their candidate was the best person for the job. In practice, therefore, the most qualified people from the minority ethnic groups did not just have a chance, mainly because they did not have strong people to lobby for them. There were a few cases when qualified people came to the limelight and were nominated to high places, but such cases were not common. The candidates who knew they were being proposed for those high positions would resort to slandering so as to tarnish the images of their rivals; that way dirty information would be available to have them rejected. The basic idea behind slandering was therefore to dirty the person with any false statement or any wrong accusation which could damage that individual's reputation or their career in the workplace.

Workplace slander should have no place at work, because everyone is supposed to pay attention to their work, doing it efficiently to gain the admiration and subsequent recommendation of their bosses if the time came for them to postulate for higher positions. Since slandering was so rampant in Tropicana, it was important that employees understand how to protect themselves from workplace slander claims when those went beyond gossips or claims that could hurt their attitudes, feelings or happiness.

Workplace slander (or libel) happens in most workplaces but the individual needs to tackle it and not let it destroy their life both personally and professionally. A senior colleague who was aware of our struggles and rivalry in Tropicana gave me a few tips on how to deal with workplace slander. He told me that the first thing to do to avoid workplace slander was to stay silent. If you wanted to stay away from any kind of workplace slandering you could mention to colleagues that you wanted complete silence and did not want to interact with others, especially when it came to ongoing gossips on issues in the workplace. He cautioned that if I acted in this way they could stay away from any kind of offensive behavior or slander going on in the workplace because even if they had the information they would not have others to tell it to.

The second thing to do in a place where individuals were used to slandering was to keep calm in the workplace, and not bother much about colleagues from different backgrounds and different ethnic groups. Whatever may be going on in the workplace, whether it's any kind of false remarks or accusations about the individual himself or any other employee in the workplace known to the person, you should always stay calm in the workplace and outside so that you do not lose your mind over it and have difficulties in both your personal and professional life.

He cautioned me that I should make it a habit to avoid any kind of interactions or conversations with co-workers which are unnecessary. Gossips in the workplace would drive you into conversations which would lead to issues concerning other people and even your bosses and these would be transmitted to those bosses as if you were the one who originated the nasty issues. If you adapt yourself to this method you are likely to surely stay away from office gossips but you will also not have employees talking to you for a very long time.

Usually, gossiping easily turns into slandering. Office gossip is a natural thing that happens in the workplace on an everyday basis and it cannot be stopped. Having intimate conversations with colleagues and talking about other people in the institution will make colleagues know that you are accessible for stray talk and would get information from you, twist it to become attractive to others and turn out to be slandering against you. Though gossips happened on a daily basis it was necessary that no kind of trouble caused or any misunderstandings happen as these small gossips could turn into slandering which could damage your reputation. So, you must not let this happen.

You must pay attention all the time. If you want to know whether the conversations going on in your institution involve slandering, then you should start paying attention to what is spreading in the office, who is talking about it and whether that person gossiping has any kind of history when it comes to behaving this way in the past. Such a person should be avoided altogether but he is likely to get you in trouble.

This may appear contradictory but if you notice that any kind of slandering is going on in the workplace about you or someone else and if you want to put an end to it quickly, you should avoid the gossip at all times. If you entertain gossips, they are likely to be done on you, and even provide negative information about you which will turn out to be slandering. While those conversations are taking place, you should also let them know indirectly that any kind of slandering can get you to lose your job. Those doing the gossiping could notice it and put a stop to it completely. It does not mean you should not talk to colleagues. Whenever you have to talk to them be brief and give only information on a specific topic and stop. Do not digress; especially recounting things about others who you think do not like the person you are talking to.

That made me remember a friend who at one time I considered intimate. We would discuss science most of the time. He had been interested in occupying the position of chief of our center. When that position became vacant, he started shifting our conversations into appointments; he would talk to me about how the present chief of center was not qualified to occupy that post and how he had been appointed to it in those days simply because there weren't qualified people to occupy it. He would say that the time had come when there are several well qualified people with higher degrees like *us* who needed to be given those positions. But he had just left an international organization where he had been fortunate to have a year of sabbatical. Back home the older scientists, especially those occupying higher positions would frown at those who left the institute and went and pursued greener pastures elsewhere. The old *stalwacks,* who felt they had stayed around with the low salaries, would do everything to suppress people like that who had enjoyed better conditions outside and now returned to take their places.

I learnt to have effective communication at work. It's always known that if the communication is effective enough in the workplace then there will be no kind of slandering about any employee or the employer as they can approach them without any fear and tell them their problems. If this does not happen then you will go towards other unwanted measures which quickly may turn into slandering the employee or the employer. When you communicate well on work-related (not social) affairs, you will be considered to be minding your business. You will from then be seen like one who is too busy to be involved in gossip or slander.

Any employee in the workplace needs to identify negative people at work and the negative gossip in the workplace and stay away from it if they wish to be away from any kind of slandering about any individual. If you can identify such people stay away from them. This will help you to not involve yourself in talks or chats among the negative crowd in the workplace and carry on your life in harmony, and not have your life affected negatively. You can easily identify a negative person in the workplace. Such a person will leave work and come and see you in your office, and will then engage in an issue which concerns other people in the institution.

In our institute, one of the issues which colleagues constantly gossiped about centered on the ability to publish articles regularly, the interest that researchers had to get appointed to higher administrative positions, how over-represented some tribes were in the administration, and how some scientists published prolifically but people did not see the work they were doing. A colleague who entered your office and started a discussion on any of such topics was likely to be a slanderer. You would have to find a way to get him out of your office.

This makes me think of two CEOs I met in the Institute. One of them was my mentor. I respected him very much and I liked his personality. Some researchers felt they could get favors from the CEO by gossiping and telling him what he would like to hear. If a researcher came to his office and told him something that another researcher had said about him, he would listen very attentively till he finished talking what he had come to talk. He would say nothing in response. The next day, he would call the gossiping researcher and the accused researcher to his office and would ask the gossiping scientist what he had said the day before about the accused scientist. Ashamed, the gossiper would not be able to repeat what he had said just a day before. This made researchers stop coming and gossiping to him about others.

The second CEO behaved in a directly opposite manner than the one just mentioned above. He loved gossips. Researchers, knowing that, would come to his office or in his home and manufacture a story and tell him. He would offer the gossiper a drink to hear more and would start hating the accused researcher from then on. He was interested in keeping his position as CEO forever, and so became very sensitive to any thing he heard about another person wanting his position. So most of the gossips that came to him centered about how one researcher was lobbying among his relatives in high places to get him out of his position and put someone else in his place. Because of this he had many enemies in the institute. Strangely, he would be welcoming to and would smile whenever he saw the researcher who had been accused of wanting to take his place.

He counseled me that I should never start a negative conversation with another colleague in the workplace. Also, whenever a person was talking to me or other employees of the workplace, that person must never begin any kind of conversation or gossip negatively and initiate the conversation in that sense. Such an individual was likely going to be a slanderer. If the person initiated the conversation negatively, he or she might say something which could reach the wrong ears with the blame of it entirely coming upon that individual, which could then turn into slandering against an employee. You should avoid further contact with that person once you heard him or her start with negativity against another employee.

He advised that I should never stay alone with a co-worker and only chat with that person. This advice actually referred to that person who wished to stay away from any kind of negative behavior in the office. He or she shouldn't spend any time with any one employee in the workplace and be chatting with that lone person. For instance, if it was lunchtime and you wanted to eat your lunch, you should try as much as you can to stay alone in your office and eat your lunch at your desk rather than interacting with other employees in the restaurant in a corner where there are a few colleagues eating lunch at the same time. This could lead to gossips among all of them.

This makes me think of the situation we had in our research center. There were snacks very close to the campus. Workers would go there for lunch and eat a meal and take a drink. During that period, employees would chat on all kinds of topics. Some would gossip the boss, others would slander their colleagues about the kind of worthless research they were doing, and others would slander their colleagues on social matters relating to going out with married women and so on. I decided to stay out of these interactions. After all, my house was just a 3-minute drive from the office; I could go there for lunch and come back to the office after I had taken my meal.

If you suspected someone was a gossip, one way of avoiding any kind of office gossip was that you could approach your boss and ask him to hand more work to that person so that the individual would stay busy concentrating on the work in hand. If the boss asked you why you were asking that they should be given so much work then you could respond by mentioning ongoing problems in the workplace in general but not necessarily pointing out anyone in particular. I realized that this approach was good only as long as the boss himself was not interested in gossips. Because of the multiple ethnicities in the workplace, tribal alliances were common, and gossips would be much entertained as one tribesman talked about others to his tribesperson who was in a high position. That is how scientists even went directly to see the Minister who was from the same tribe as him or her, and gossiped about their CEO or another employee in the institute.

He advised that I should never believe rumors. So many accusations in the workplace are rumors. If there had been ongoing gossip regarding a particular individual, not knowing the entire situation or reality could lead it to be an ongoing office rumor that someone had started. It would be necessary to stay away from it. Do not believe in this completely if you were sure you did not know the whole story. Also ignore it so that you were not affected by it in your life. I had several experiences with rumors. When I became CEO of the Institute, my Minister did not like me because she thought I was claiming to be *clean* the reason I was not yielding to nasty requests she was making. My assistant, who was eagerly looking for my position as CEO, would *manufacture* rumors and go and dish them out to the Minister. I would just notice that the Minister was becoming increasingly hostile to me with time. A friend in the Minister had told me that my assistant was certainly doing something fishy with the Minister and that that could concern me. But I took it lightly. But later on, I came to understand that the rumors he was making were really the cause of the animosity.

I came to know from the advice of my friend that if the slandering going on in the workplace was about an employee and I came to know about the best I could do to put an end to it was to take necessary steps so that this did not happen again. It depended on how serious the gossiping was and how fast it was spreading. So at first just knowing all the necessary facts and tackling all these problems individually was recommended to every individual.

It was often important to understand the situation. When you understood the situation completely you could realize that the problem was not as big as you were expecting it to be. The situation could be small, just involving a smaller group. In that case it was recommended that you forget about it and not let the situation affect your personal life, or your happiness in your personal life. So it was very essential to see how big or small the situation was in the workplace. The situation could be small yet repeated over time. Then it became significant. If a researcher from a majority ethnic group started a gossip with one of his tribesmen, that gossip could spread to other kinsmen of that tribe and become significant enough to affect my personal life. One topic which made gossips very palatable was the prolificacy in scientific publications. If one researcher was churning out papers in renowned journals, he became hated by his colleagues who could not write.

It was wise to know the history with the individual. The person who slandered or gossiped negatively in the workplace ought to have some kind of history. So you ought to realize that the person could try and harm your personal feelings. You should act accordingly towards that whether to ignore it as you weren't bothered by it or take some necessary action regarding it. It was quite difficult to know the gossiping history of a colleague. I remember a colleague of mine who had been quite intimate to me when we were both senior research officer. We always discussed science together. Immediately I was promoted to chief research officer and he was not I became his enemy. The relationship was never mended from then on till we both left the institute.

The senior colleague who was counselling me advised that it could be useful to try to communicate with the employee. If you realized that you did not have any kind of history with one another then you both could start up a conversation about the comments passed but in private so that you could understand how he or she felt about it. If it was passed up unknowingly by the person then you could understand that you had hurt the feelings of the person and could issue an apology regarding the comments passed and could also improve the relations between you for the future.

You should try to stay positive at all times at work. Whenever you got involved in office gossip or got to know some rumors regarding colleagues then you would tend to lose the positive mind that you had and you tended to become a bit more negative towards your professional life giving less interest to your job. This could even affect your behavior whenever you were around your family as a result of stress.

You also had to gather concrete evidence about the situation. Before taking any kind of necessary action, you could gather all kinds of the necessary information and entire package of evidence before you took any further action regarding the situation going on. If the person did not wish to take it publicly then you could personally write a letter to the employee.

Also it was wise to gather people as witnesses. To further support the claim of the false accusations done by the person, you could gather several people who had witnessed such conversations and use them as a proof present over there at the time when the conversation happened. Even at the time when the letter written to the employee was presented as proof, these people could be presented so that they could back you up whatever the situation could be.

There were times when an informant about a gossip was from a lower social class and would not like to be seen as a witness. It would be impossible to use that kind of individual as a witness in a matter of slander. I remember getting information one day from a friend, an electrician in the institute. He told me confidentially what a research colleague of mine had recounted about the rapid rate I was *pretending* to show with regard to my scientific papers. I just stayed quiet with the information and did not let it bother me because I could not just say who had told me. I would be betraying my electrician friend.

My counselor friend indicated that one thing I could do was look at the Employee handbook. At first, if the person wasn't changing their behavior regarding the ongoing situation in the workplace then for a first-hand reference to solve the problem you could refer to the manual or the employee handbook of the institute or look over the contract with the institute which the person had. It would give you and the person a better understanding of how this situation had to be dealt with and how to tackle any kind of gossips going on in the workplace. One day I took time to consult the Employee handbook of the Institute, but I found out that it was quite vague in the way it treated the matter. Then I knew that I had to follow other options in such situations.

When everything was going over the limit, it could then be necessary to talk to the boss. He cautioned that I could consider using this option only if in doing so, I could calmly present the case in front of the boss and be sure I had at hand all the facts that needed to give him light on the situation. I also had to let the boss know what efforts I had carried out so that the boss understood how bad the situation had become and how I had tried to solve it. He added that I had to be ready to present all the evidence to the boss. When presenting the case in front of the boss I always had to remember that all the evidence that I had collected before concluding should be available for presentation and given to the boss, so that the boss could get a better understanding of the situation. It was necessary to know all the efforts I had made to solve the problem on my part so that a solution could be presented to the individual as soon as possible. This was certainly a good option but with ethnicity playing such a crucial role in our society, I could only consult my boss if he was not of the same ethnic group as the gossiper, or if he himself was not the type who liked to accommodate gossips.

The last thing that could be done in a case of workplace slander was to get higher management involved. If writing a letter or talking to the person and the boss hadn't made any difference then I could take a step further and approach the management or the department of Human Resources of the Institute. I had to let them know about the ongoing situation about the individual in the office and see if they would try and provide a solution to the problem as soon as they could, so that everything would once again start functioning in harmony.

So, one must know how to deal with slander in the workplace, because, slander is a very harmful and painful act towards an employee. It happens to cause not only a physical but also a mental problem in their life as colleagues. If such a thing happens you should always keep your calm so that you can try and find a solution to the problem as quickly as you can. It is usually necessary to approach higher officials if this situation is going out of hand. He concluded that these problems were quite common in the workplace so I had to ensure that slander wasn't affecting me, because that would further delay bringing in the solution to the problem. Therefore it was crucial to think smartly at as early as possible to get a long-lasting solution to solve the problem.

PART II
STESSORS AS AN ADMINISTRATOR

CHAPTER 7

Dealing with project heads

· ·

ADMINISTRATORS DEAL WITH EMPLOYEES AND BUDGETS. AN administrator is any person who is responsible for running a business or an organization. An administrator in a research Institute is one who performs administrative maintenance, compliance, review, or oversight for a sponsored project. A research administrator facilitates the link between research activities and research outcomes, promoting the use of best practices in administration. He is responsible for building an infrastructure that will support research administration within a Ministerial department or unit. Having the ability to connect with people and getting along with everyone makes you an approachable person, which is an absolute quality for a research administrator. A research administrator will have a 'can do' attitude and always attempt to achieve a win/win situation; he must show that he has three basic personal skills – technical skills, human skills and conceptual skills. One other important skill a research administrator must possess is communication abilities.

An administrator must have personality because the personnel he manages need to know they can trust you to be the face and voice of other employees and even the institution. People who want to be really good administrators are those who feel they are highly organized and meticulous. Some feel they need to be in that supportive role that allows them to work with lots of people. Others believe that there is always a way to learn in administration which makes them feel like they are constantly developing their skill set. Administrative skills are required to complete actions related to the management and running of their businesses. This could mean duties such as meeting high-profile visitors, stakeholders, answering telephone enquiries politely and tactfully, as well as appropriately filing of personnel and research information, inputting data, compiling documents and making intelligent presentations on the activities of the Institute.

In Tropicana Rural Development Institute (TRDI), 90% of the funds for running the Institute came from the government. A budget would be submitted by the board of administration of the Institute through the Minister-Secretary of Rural Development Investigations who would forward it to the National Assembly. The National Assembly would then deliberate, vote and adopt the research budget for the year. Once the budget was voted, it would be forwarded to the Treasury for execution. At the Treasury, each parastatal organization operated an account. The budget would simply be credited to the Treasury account of the Institute by the director of the central treasury and liquidity dished out to the institute in instalments.

The running cost would first be disbursed to the Institute (by crediting its account in the Treasury) in six instalments. The infrastructure budget (the so-called investment budget) would be sent directly to the Institute account in the Treasury and be disbursed straight to the contractors by the director of the Treasury himself as infrastructure expenses were made. That was the normal procedure. Sometimes there would be big delays in making payments because the Treasury could only pay bills from what had come in as earnings of the State.

All the research funds were also given by the State. But most of the time disbursements were erratic, the research often considered of low priority when compared with sectors such as the military, public health and education. Hence most of the time, the TRDI functioned through research funds received from its participation in regional networks, projects funded from its collaboration with expatriate researchers and international donors.

As a matter of principle, the researcher who wrote a grant and brought in funds from regional research networks was made the head of that project in the Institute. This was because that researcher was the specialist in the research domain and would be the most appropriate person to execute the project in the field, attend coordination meetings, collect the data from lab and field trials, and prepare the technical report of activities to present to the network. He was also the individual to prepare the financial report and represent the Institute in the presentation of both technical and financial reports to the network.

When I was a researcher in the TRDI, I attracted a good number of projects in various networks, some short-lived and others long-lived. Those that lasted for more than one year were the On-farm Adaptive Research Project (OFAR), the Regional Research Project for Maize and Cassava (RRPMC) and the Ecoregional Program for the Humid and Sub-humid Tropics of Sub-Saharan Africa (EPHTA). I was the project leader of the three projects. I had a lot on my plate. They kept me busy and provided a good bit of funding for my research in the years when the projects were in execution. Those projects also made me quite known by the many colleagues heading the projects in their respective countries in the region.

Heading projects came with several stresses I had in the execution of the projects. Firstly, the OFAR trials were in farmers' fields which were very distant away. Land preparation, planting, field maintenance and data collection in the field were not easy to achieve because of the distances separating trials, and because of differences among farmers participating in the different trials, no matter the amount of effort I made to try to uniformize the trials. The roads to the trial sites were bad and lateritic most of the way. I would be driving for a long distance and would have a flat tyre on a narrow unpaved road which was busy and being plied by other vehicles. It would be a tedious task to change the tyre on the narrow road. It would also be risky at the same time because I would run the risk of being knocked down by passing vehicles.

The most difficult thing in executing regional network projects was interference from the research administration in the management of the funds. Since the funds were managed by the Institute and its accountant (networks do not send money directly to researchers or project heads because legally, according to the conventions signed between the network coordination and the research institutes, they could not be held accountable if funds were misused, mismanaged or not properly accounted for). But the greatest embarrassment was that many times some expenses, not eligible for funding by project funds would be engaged by the CEO of the Institute and just presented to the project head (like me) for settlement. If the expenditure was small, that would be fairly easy to account for. But if the expenditure was large, that would create a serious problem for me to settle. If it was an expenditure such as paying an electricity bill, I could manage and justify that kind of expenditure by saying that there was an electricity outage and I had to settle the bill because I could not do the analysis of my data, the reason I paid the electricity bill to have electricity to be re-installed. Large bills, which were difficult to account for stressed me the most. That is what happened one time when my CEO sent me a phone bill to settle. It was 15,000 US dollars. I did not just know what to do about it. I went to see him and explained that it would be impossible to settle that bill because phone bill settlement was not among the budgetary lines authorized by the project. He scolded at me, and instructed me to go ahead and settle it. The assumption was that I had been making my own financial gain from the project funds and yet did not want him to make small benefit from them.

I reluctantly called the network coordinator in the international center, gave a lot of explanation to convince him to get a special dispensation to pay the bill. That was how that matter was settled. But it was really stressful whenever the time came to prepare financial reports of network-funded project funds.

Funds obtained from collaboration with expatriate researchers were a lot easier, because such funds did not pass through the Institute; they were small and the accounting and the financial reporting were done by the expatriate scientists themselves. I would easily account for the small bits given to me by the scientist. I had a couple of such projects on yams and cassava. I needed to bother only about the technical implementation and reporting of the trials. That could sometimes be frustrating but not as stressful as if I had to do financial reporting of the entire project.

Funds from international donors were usually small and were often given to the researcher directly and accounted for directly to the donors. This was easy because the funds were given piecemeal and accounting for them had to be done as soon as the expenditures were made. That was the case with some maize projects which investigated soil acidity and aluminium toxicity. Although there had been so much research that had been conducted on maize in the country, soil acidity and aluminium toxicity were perennial problems facing maize production especially in the humid forest region. Grant funds were often available for research in those areas. My colleague who was in charge of that project would get funds directly, hire personnel as the need arose and fire any worker at will. Another colleague who was working on maize entomology was addressing the problem of stem borers (*Buseola fusca*). She too got funds from the French and worked almost independently in the institute. The funds came to her directly and had no stress dealing with the Institute administration.

A large project another colleague was managing was one on maize seed multiplication and distribution. This project was funded by international funds but lodged in a special institute account. The management of the project was in the hands of a colleague, Zika Charles who was so powerful that he could hire and fire personnel working in the project. He often made the budget for expenses, got the approval of the CEO and the funds made available for him to spend as he had proposed. He had semi-autonomy in fund management. This made him sometimes abuse the powers he had.

I had been named CEO of TRDI and was now in charge of supervising all the projects under the Institute. Zika Charles had been sent on retirement and another younger colleague of his, Conrad Moliki, who had been working with him for quite a while, was named by the board to head the seed multiplication project. The young guy would propose budgets and prepare the files for expenses and submit them to me for signature. That was fine and that worked well for us.

But one day, he prepared a file for the purchase of fuel claiming it was for the Minister-Secretary, for an amount of 10,000 US dollars. When the fuel vouchers were delivered to him he went ahead and took his own share of 5,000 US dollars without telling me. He went straight to the Ministry and gave Lena, the Minister-Secretary her own share of 5,000 US dollars of fuel. Being a *budgetivorous* animal, she was enraged and scolded him, "is this all the fuel that you could give your Minister?" Lena was someone who was never satisfied with whatever she was given by the Institute. Lena who had been nursing a grudge against me thought I had instructed Conrad Moliki to give her just 5,000 US dollars worth of fuel, whereas I did not even know that the fuel he had requested had been delivered.

It was very stressful to me when Lena sent me word that I should learn to respect her, and that I could not just do anything to hurt her because she was a woman. I felt bad. This had happened because Conrad Moliki was from the same ethnic group like the Minister, and he had developed the habit of contacting her directly for many issues because of their common ethnicity. That was another problem which was caused by ethnicity in the Federal Republic of Tropicana. A subordinate would be loyal to his boss only when he needed his signature.

I called Conrad Moliki to my office after that hostile reaction from the Minister. I showed him the employee manual and let him read his responsibilities as a project leader. I had highlighted the hierarchy in the chain of command. He had no business going and seeing the Minister directly without passing through me.

The Employee manual showed the duties of a project leader as follows: the gathering and distributing information, leading, planning, coordinating, moderating and controlling the project team. His other role was to inspire a shared vision and motivate team members. A project leader could also be a project manager in a distant research station where the chief of station was far away from where the project was executed. In this case he could manage the funds directly and coordinate the activities of the project as well.

The project leader was required to have sound communication skills because those were vital in managing a project successfully. He had to be a good communicator because he needed to communicate with scientists and, to get the best out of their input he needed to be tactful in dealing with them. Another skill which the project team leader needed to have was conflict resolution, a skill which was inevitable in situations where the project team leader was introducing something new such as a new concept or changing something which the Institute was used to doing in a different way. Other common Project Leader duties included directing employees, mitigating project risks, solving standard and non-standard problems and reporting to senior management about the evolution of the project. Being able to resolve conflicts between the workers in the team was very important in carrying the project through.

The Employee manual reminded him that what makes an effective project leader is the vision he has of where to go and his or her ability to articulate that vision. A visionary project leader makes every effort to change things and being able to draw new boundaries. He should be one who lifts his team members up and gives a reason for being members of a project. He is the one who gives the vision and spirit to change things in the project. An effective project leader often has, accompanying his communication skills, integrity, enthusiasm, empathy and competence. He must be someone who has the ability to delegate tasks to other members of the team possessing team-building and problem-solving skills. He must have a cool composure when he is under pressure to deliver. The project team leader must ensure that all members of the team are contributing each to the overall objectives of the project, completing the deliverables of individual team members, providing expertise and working with users of the results as well as other international participants of the network in projects which are network-related. He must have as major objective to meet overall needs of the project, and be always ready to document the process leading to success at all times.

The project team leader had to be the front runner of the project forming a permanent liaison with other team members in generating results and in developing a positive image about the project in the network, an image which is capable of achieving the criteria for progression using proven methods in the shortest time possible without much expense.

A good project team leader also had to have the habit of being able to motivate other team members so that they would continue to be hardworking and productive, even when they weren't officially entitled to get those benefits. Such was the case with the distribution of fuel purchased by the project. If the team leader purchased fuel for use in running of project activities it would make sense to motive team members with small amounts of fuel at least to enable them come to work, go to the field or run project errands with their private vehicles. In the TRDI, the younger members of the team appeared to need motivation more than the Minister-Secretary who already had enormous benefits from her Ministry as a cabinet member.

In normal circumstances, these qualities in the Employee manual had to be considered before naming the candidate to the post, but things were rather lousy in a place where it was not habitual to consider personality, competency and numerical testing of the candidates before they could be named to a post of assistant director such as that.

After my discussion with him I warned him that his role was to lead people throughout the project. The project leader was responsible for telling people all the basic information concerning the project and how it was evolving. He had to be always there in case any trouble appeared with the project. He was the guide for the team in the tasks they had been assigned to perform. He was more concerned with the project's outcome rather than making himself close to the Minister or anything else. He had to be interested in the effects relating to the project activities, *the how, why, what for* of the project. He had to aim to make sure that he was aiming for the stars and that the project was carried out in the best way possible. He had to ensure that every detail was taken care of and that there were no understatements.

As project team leader I stressed his responsibility of having a vision for the project in which he engaged people adequately to meet the required goals. He had to give clues, ideas as well as listen to the team members. He had to take care of their needs and had to pay attention to how the employees under him felt. He had to make the atmosphere at work to be friendly and conducive so that the work was being done productively and with dedication. So ideally, he needed to have great project leadership skills. I told him that he had to know that he had people beneath him, responsible to him and was the one to give orders and control people under him and the entire project. He had to add value to the project and the team with which he was working, ensuring that their work was appreciated and was important. He had a spiritual support for the team, and as one who was concerned about meeting deadlines he had a lot in his hands to bother about making the project succeed.

He had to use a tactical approach in leading the project. He had to take care of the budget, schedule deadlines, ensure proper documentation, manage staffing, and to keep things organized to facilitate implementation. He had in addition to report the progress of the work, and was responsible for delivering updates on the progress of the project as well as any possible obstacles.

I reminded him that before naming a team leader like him it was just normal to organize at least two interviews, the first among the short-listed candidates, and the second between senior management and each project staff candidate before the final selection and the team leader was made. But in Tropicana some of those steps were omitted for ethnic reasons – one person replacing the other because they wanted someone from a certain ethnic group to lead the project, since administrative positions were filled according to tribe, not efficiency.

I reminded him of the five major steps that had to be involved in the management of any project: project identification and initiation, planning, project launching, project performance and closing. All these had been done when the seed multiplication project he was now heading had just begun. He was just a project team member then, but it was necessary to remind him of all these now with his position of project leader because putting these key steps into action had to give the project the best chance of being successful.

Conrad Moliki listened attentively to all what was said in the Employee manual and the instructions and suggestions I had made. I guess he understood that, although he had been named to head that large project, he was lacking in many of his duties. However, the way he left my office gave me the impression that the information got into a deaf's ears because he did not sound apologetic for the fuel scandal which he had caused. I guess this was because he felt, being too close to the Minister was what was more important than all that lecturing from the Employee manual. He felt that as long as she was there, no sanctions could be given to him even if he committed a similar or even more serious offence again. But I had played my role as CEO. His behaviour gave me the impression that in TRDI, the way and manner the project leader decided to function had to do with and even depended somehow on the ethnic group the Minister-Secretary of the Ministry of Rural Development Investigations came from. The team leader was not supposed to have a direct connection with the Minister without being sent by the CEO. However, for that particular case, Conrad Moliki felt secure because in his frequent visits to the Minister he also had been motivating her with project funds to keep himself in the post even though he had been named to the post by the board of administration.

There was a case in point with another colleague who was leader of another project. His name was Johnny Tougnon. He took a whole building for his project, hired his own workers and gave them office space, distributed and supervised their work and maintained an independence from the rest of the Institute largely because he knew that the CEO was helpless and could not sanction him if he did anything not authorized by the Employee manual because he knew that he was close to the Minister who was from his tribe. So, this direct connecting links between project heads and Ministers was an ethnicity problem which was quite difficult to resolve when I was CEO of TRDI.

CHAPTER 8

Relating to my Chief Financial Officer

· ·

WHEN I BECAME CEO OF TRDI, I HAD PLANNED TO WORK WITH THE Chief Financial Officer who I met there. I had no plans to change him because he had been a friend before I was named to the post. I figured that my work was going to be easy working with someone who I had known quite well before. I thought I would rely a lot on his judgment in the treating of financial files. However, I invited him right at the start of my tenure, for a frank discussion as to what I expected of him. When he entered my office, I pulled out the Employee manual (the so-called *Manuel des Procedures*) and went over the entire document with him.

I wanted to be sure he knew who a Chief Financial Officer was. According to the manual, a chief financial officer (CFO) was the senior executive responsible for managing the financial actions of the Institute. The CFO's duties include tracking cash flow. He was in charge of financial planning as well as analyzing the Institute's financial strengths and weaknesses and proposing corrective actions to the CEO. The role of a CFO was similar to that of a treasurer because he was responsible for managing the finance and accounting divisions. He had to ensure that the Institute's financial reports were accurate and completed in a timely manner. Many institutions called him Chief Management Administrator because of the vital role he played in the organization.

The Employee manual stressed that the chief financial officer of the Institute was the top-level financial controller who had to handle on a daily basis everything relating to the Institute's cash flow and financial planning so that resources were properly used and not get exhausted before the end of the financial year. He was responsible for informing the CEO on a daily basis of the financial situation of the institution.

Although the role of a CFO could be rewarding, there could also be legal considerations that had to be strictly adhered to. CFOs of TRDI had also to oversee taxation issues for the institution. The CFO was the third-highest position in the Institute after the CEO and his deputy, playing a crucial role in the Institute's strategic initiatives with regard to financial management.

The Chief Financial Officer of the Tropicana Rural Development Institute reported to the chief executive officer (CEO) but had significant input in the Institute's investments, its capital structure and, and how it managed its income and expenses. The CFO worked with other senior managers and played a key role in a company's overall success, especially in the long run. For instance if one of the technical departments wanted to launch a new campaign about a technology it had produced, the CFO could help to ensure that the campaign was feasible or could give input on the funds available for the campaign or publicity. In TRDI the CFO was certainly the most highly ranked financial position within the Institute.

The CFO was expected to assist the CEO with forecasting, cost-benefit analysis, and in obtaining funding for various initiatives. Although the CFO of TRDI had to focus on compliance and quality control he had to use much of his time in business planning and process changes. In that respect he was a strategic partner to the CEO, playing the vital role of influencing the Institute's strategy in the development and dissemination of technologies to users. The CFO had to report accurate information because many decisions which were taken by the Institute were based on the data he or she provided. The CFO was responsible for managing the financial activities of the Institute, adhering to generally accepted accounting principles set by the government, and adhering to regulations such as would make the control and audit of the Institute to be smooth and transparent in front of the Supreme State Audit Agency. These would include provisions such as fraud prevention and disclosing financial information out of the Institute.

In TRDI the CFO was the Institute's liaison between local residents of the country and elected officials on accounting and other spending matters being responsible for setting financial policy and being responsible for managing government funds put at the disposal of the Institute.

The Chief Financial Officer of TRDI was also the senior corporate executive who was responsible not only for the overall planning and management of the Institute's financial affairs but also developing the Institute's budget, communicating with the Institute's banking and insurance partners, and advising other executives on strategic matters relating to the Institute's finances as well as leading new investment initiatives, such as deciding on whether to proceed with new acquisitions and capital expenditures. This was the reason the position of CFO in TRDI was reserved for highly qualified and very experienced professionals with established track records in their field of financial management. It was expected that the individual selected to be CFO of TRDI would have professional backgrounds in fields such as accounting, investment banking, or financial analysis which would contribute in making the CFO professional the most prestigious and highly-paid position after the CEO and his deputy in the Institute.

The CFO had to be very polite and receptive in order to relate well with other senior executives such as the technical directors of the various departments of the Institute, the heads of research structures and the chief operating officers (or chiefs of programs) of the research programs who were found in the agro-ecological zones all over the country. The CFO of TRDI was typically subordinate to the CEO in the corporate hierarchy, but he was generally the foremost decision-maker on all matters within the Finance department of the Institute.

After going through what the Procedures Manual gave him as responsibilities, I warned him that, in addition, I expected a high level of loyalty in the way he executed his tasks. That would make my work easier and would certainly make us better friends. I also warned that fraud in all its forms was my enemy as CEO, reminding him that several CEO's were in jail not because they did not do their work well but because they were induced into error by their CFOs. I certainly did not want that to happen to me. I concluded by thanking him for his patience in listening to me.

I had barely done two months as CEO when two events occurred that pierced deep into my mind. I was really astonished because I believed the CFO had noted what I expected of him in the execution of his responsibilities while I was there. I was frustrated because I thought I could rely on him in his work and that this was going to make my work easy.

The first thing that happened had to do with what I would call fraud. One morning as I was studying and signing documents placed in the finance folders, I noticed an irregularity which drew my attention. At the start of my tenure, I had given myself two principles in the way I was going to work. First, I had planned that I would sign all financial documents only after 5:00 pm when I had finished receiving guests. At that time I was alone and the place was quiet and conducive for uninterrupted work. That would give me the chance to concentrate on what I was going to sign. Secondly, I would go through *three* times every document which exceeded a payment of 10,000 USD. In my mind I was telling myself that I could easily reimburse any payment which I had authorized in error for a sum less than that amount.

As I signed documents I came across a payment voucher of 100,000 USD to be paid to a contractor for the supply to the Institute of a Massey-Fergusson tractor. After studying it for some time, I thought it was regular and was ready to sign it. However, I hesitated when I realized that there was a document in the file which dated five years earlier, well before I even came there as CEO. So I pulled the document out of the folder and kept it in my drawer so that later I would make some verification about it. The next day I sent for the financial controller. The financial controller was responsible to the CFO but showed loyalty to the Minister of Treasury because he had been sent to the Institute by him, as was the case with financial controllers of other state institutions which had an autonomous budget. Government felt that it was better to have someone from outside the Institute to control the manner in which State funds were being used, than having someone in that position appointed by the CEO himself.

The financial controller came to my office and I handed him a photocopy of that document to verify if that payment had been done. He went and checked. First, the document was irregular because although it carried his signature, it did not have the composting stamp which he was using to authenticate his signature on a document which had been properly controlled. This meant that his signature had been imitated.

Secondly, the payment had been effected some five years ago, and was certainly not eligible for payment again. I took all the evidence the controller had provided and kept the entire file in my drawer for later use.

The second event that happened concerned a payment voucher which was presented two times. In the first folder, the voucher carried a payment of 120,000 USD. After I had examined it, I kept it aside, and as I continued to sign, from an entirely different folder, I saw another payment of 124,000 USD very similar to the first document; the budgetary lines were exactly the same. I pulled it out and compared it to the first document. Both had the same budgetary lines, except that the final sums were slightly different. When I did the addition I realized that in one of the documents the addition was not right. So I called the CFO to ask him why those two documents were like that. When he came he defended himself that it was an error from his chief of bureau of the office of the budget. He went out and called him. When the guy came, the CFO scolded him asking him why he had to present a document twice for the signature of the CEO. The young guy looked steadily into the eyes of the CFO as if to ask him if he had not been aware of the deal. The CFO, in front of me and the chief of bureau, withdrew one of the documents from me and shredded it.

After the chief of bureau had gone out, I asked the CFO why he was behaving like that. I reminded him how implicating that was to me. In the financial circles, that was known as embezzlement. He tried to defend himself that it had been an error from his chief of bureau and that he had just induced him in error to visa a document two times.

Then I pulled out the document for the tractor payment. He could not defend himself anymore. He went down on his knees to plead with me to forgive him. He went out of my office and brought in my chief of cabinet to assist him in pleading with me for forgiveness. I forgave him but did not forget the implications of the two acts. I made up my mind to get rid of him, much against what I had initially planned to retain my subordinates in the Institute to continue benefitting from their experience over the years.

I went and discussed the matter with my board chairman. He advised that I should get rid of him but cautioned that I could find difficulty in doing so because my predecessor had made an attempt to get rid of him but failed because it appeared as if the CFO had special ties with the Minister, Lena BigStuff, which made her always there to protect him when someone wanted to do anything to sanction him.

I prepared a short list of three candidates with the assistance of some reliable expatriate scientists who were heading various projects in the Institute, and invited them in a meeting. They ranked the three candidates on the basis of qualification and experience. I took that to the board chairman and he signed the recruitment decision of the guy who was top in the list. That is how my CFO, my closest financial collaborator, in TRDI was fired.

CHAPTER 9

Stresses from the CEO

. . . .

A CHIEF EXECUTIVE OFFICER IS ONE OF A NUMBER OF CORPORATE executives in charge of managing an organization or any legal entity or non-profit institution. The position of CEO is usually given to someone by the board of directors. However, in the Federal Republic of Tropicana, the CEO was named by the King of the country. He is at the highest position in the Institute although he is responsible to the chairman of the board of directors. Unlike in other places where a CEO can be fired by a majority vote of board members, the CEO of Tropicana cannot be fired by the board, even at the end of his contract period; he can be removed only by a decree of the King. This means that the CEO of a Tropicana institution could be left in his job for as long as the King desires. The CEO is usually given a higher salary than the board chairman in some companies. However, in Tropicana, the reverse was true, the board chairman had a higher salary.

The Chief Executive of Tropicana Rural Development Institute was a Chief Executive with a difference. He had been there for nineteen years. He had been too used to his house and office that he thought he was going to be there for ever. He would invite his tribesmen to his home on weekends and share a drink of palm wine with them, eating pepper soup made with snakes and vipers. He had given the impression to his kinsmen that he was indispensable in the Institute, the reason he had been left there for nineteen years. He had bought over the Minister by purchasing a brand new Toyota SUV for her. He had made very strong connections with some members of the King's Palace who were there to protect him any time he was in trouble. That is how he was able to stay in power for that long.

In a country with 256 ethnic groups he did everything to maintain his tribal hegemony. He favoured some researchers from his tribe and would prevent the growth of any person who he perceived as a threat or one who would stand on the way of these tribesmen. Unfortunately for him, his tribesmen in the Institute who could replace him in the event that position became vacant were not as hard working and were trailing behind low in the research hierarchy.

The Chief Executive Officer of Tropicana Rural Development Institute, wrote to the government to fire me from the Public Service for staying against government wishes in the University abroad when I was asked by the University to stay and prepare to write my candidacy exam for the PhD. The accusation was unfounded and did not warrant the kind of punishment that was inflicted. Government could not fire me because I was a tenured civil servant, and wrote back to Tropicana Rural Development Institute that I could not be fired for that reason. The procedure was this: I had first to be invited to the Disciplinary Committee of the Ministry of the Public Service which would determine what kind of punishment, if any, could be given to me for having stayed for two additional weeks. Angry with the reaction of the Tropicana Public Service, the CEO insisted and had my salary stopped by his Institute for well over eight months through a revenue recovery order (*ordre de recettes*), because personnel salaries were at the time paid locally at the level of the Institute.

He found me to be a rival and treated me like Alfred Dreyfus, a young French Jewish artillery officer who in 1894 was condemned by court marshal to a life sentence on Devil's Island for offering to sell French military secrets to the Germans. Most of the accusation was the result of anti-Semitism. Being of Jewish ancestry he was involved in a trial and conviction in 1894 on charges of treason which became one of the most controversial and polarizing political dramas in modern French history. The incident has gone down in history as the Dreyfus Affair, whose effects were felt throughout Europe and ended with Dreyfus's complete exoneration.

In this particular situation which led to the recovery order, the CEO had gone beyond his powers. Normally, his functions in the administration of research were based on responsibilities set by the organization's board of directors. As Chief Executive Officer of an independent legal entity as Tropicana Rural Development Institute, he was chief administrator typically reporting to the board of directors.

He was in charge of managing the Institute so as to achieve outcomes related to the Institute's mission, such as reducing poverty among the growers and agro-industries. His responsibilities could of course be far-reaching or quite limited and were typically enshrined in a formal delegation of authority regarding business administration. Typically, responsibilities could include being a decision maker on business strategy and other key policy issues. The CEO also represented the Institute as main communicator which involved speaking to the press and the rest of the outside world, as well as to the Institute's management and employees. His CEO role also involved the decision-making job of high-level decisions about policy and strategy.

There were several other things which could occupy him as indicated by the Public Service. As CEO of the Institute he had to report the status of the Institute to the board of directors, motivating employees, and driving change within the organization. As a manager, the CEO had to preside over the Institute's day-to-day operations, being ultimately accountable for the Institute's business decisions, including those in operations, marketing, business development, finance, human resources, and so on. As CEO he was not necessarily the owner or the head of the Institute. But, instead of doing this he deviated from these responsibilities and took major decisions even without consulting the board.

In Tropicana, it is alleged that the CEO of the Institute had a salary and allowances higher than his supervisory Secretary. The media had made several criticisms of Chief Executives that their relative salaries and allowances set by the board, which they were receiving in their positions as CEO, were relatively higher than that of the Minister whose salary was fixed by the National Assembly. The Minister of Rural Development Investigations had complained about it several times and threatened to reduce those salaries. But that was not within her competence; that was the decision of the board. Observers had always differed as to whether the salary rise was due to competition for talent or due to lack of control by compensation committees. Some years later, the taxpayers even insisted on having more say over executive pay. But this could work only if they did their protests through the board which was the competent authority to effect change. The apparent difference in salaries between the CEO and the Minister led to some form of hostility whose aggression was transferred over to innocent people like me.

Probably because of his shaky position and the fact that he was being criticized for having a higher salary, he had tried to buy over the Minister-Secretary, his supervisory authority, by purchasing for her a brand-new Toyota SUV and even making several expensive presents for her, including using Institute money to repair her house in the village and providing her with funds to contribute in traditional events in her county. But the Minister-Secretary, although appreciating these presents was still not satisfied with him because she could not easily manipulate him on some issues as he was much older than her. So the Minister-Secretary still made up her mind to get rid of him after sucking the best out from him.

So, because the CEO had the backing of the Minister-Secretary, I became a victim; I had no superior who could listen to my complaints and frustration. I would end up suffering from nearly one year without a salary because I had stayed out of the country for two weeks longer than I had initially been given permission to stay.

The story was painful when I recounted it to the Head of Judicial Affairs in the Ministry of Rural Development Investigations. He wanted more information and I took time to explain everything to him. I had been sent abroad to take courses for the PhD. The official document which allowed me to travel out of the country was a mission order which had a travelling warrant. That document stipulated when I was leaving the country and my date of return. I had successfully finished taking the courses. The purpose of the Candidacy Exam, usually given to second year PhD students and first year Combined Degree students, was for students to demonstrate preparation for PhD level research. Each Graduate Studies Committee of a PhD student had to ensure that a rigorous examination was given to that student and that the student's performance was carefully evaluated at the time of the exam. Once the student passed this exam, he or she could now begin full-time research toward the PhD. The Candidacy Examination could consist of two or more parts: a summary of all the coursework the graduate student had done throughout his university career, and a written proposal and oral defense describing plans for the thesis project. The candidacy exam was usually a very detailed and comprehensive exam. So my committee had advised me to stay in the university for an additional two weeks to do the exam. I sent a telegram to my CEO announcing the decision of my Graduate Studies Committee, and requested that my stay should be extended for two weeks. For this, I could be notified for my annual leave so that the additional two weeks would be covered by my annual leave. Ordinarily, that would have been no problem at all. The Institute did not respond, giving the impression that no news was good news. So I stayed and did my exam. Luckily I passed.

Immediately after my exam I returned to the country. The first person I went to see was my CEO to greet him and give him a summary of what had transpired during my stay in the university for that semester. His response was astonishing. "Mister, did you not want to return to the Institute?" I felt embarrassed. I replied him by telling him that I had sent him a telegram about the Candidacy Exam even proposing that he should use one of my annual leaves to make it possible for me to stay for an additional two weeks. Since I did not hear from him, I thought he was in agreement with my proposal and was letting me to stay and do the exam.

The Director of Training of Civil Servants in the Tropicana Public Service was astonished and embarrassed that such a decision to have me fired from government could be taken by my CEO after I had made all such efforts to stay out officially. He told me to go back home and continue my research work, adding that nothing would be done to me. I was glad to meet an objective person.

As if that was not enough, one day the financial officer of the Research Center called me and showed me a document, in which he had received instructions from my CEO that he should give me a revenue recovery order for having stayed in a government house five years back at a time when I was receiving a rent allowance from the Institute. He confided in me that he was not going to execute it because that was too much load on me at a time when I was having my salary slashed from another *ordre de recettes*. I was glad, because that would have reduced my salary by a further 30%. But the lesson I learnt was that I was in real trouble with my CEO. He hated me and wanted to do everything to frustrate me and make me quit the Institute.

Before he was named CEO by the King of Tropicana, he has been heading one of the research centers of the Rural Development Institute, the one very close to the headquarters of the Institute. He wanted to impress the CEO at the time so as to gain his favor in recommending him to take over him as CEO. One dirty thing he did was to show that he was strict in managing his personnel. One day, when I was out of the country taking courses in the University, he wanted to use a typewriter I had bought through one of my research projects. He drove down to my house and called my mother and asked her to get into his car. My mother was surprised. She left whatever she was doing in the kitchen and jumped into his car. He drove to the Center and led her to my office. He explained to her that he wanted to take an IBM electric typewriter which was in my office and wanted to break open my office to get it. My mother was really surprised. She watched Dr Ma'ma, break the door into my office and take the typewriter. My mother returned to the house unhappy and frustrated. She asked herself several questions: Was she a worker in the Institute? Could the Chief of Center not just send me a telegram to ask me where the keys of my office were? Why that particular typewriter? Had she not just be wrongly led to be a witness in such an action? Eventually, my mother contacted me and recounted the story. I was very surprised, but I learnt another lesson that Dr Ma'ma did not like me.

The Chief of Center was later named CEO of Tropicana Rural Development Institute, as he had anticipated, and now had full powers to do whatever he liked with his subordinates in the Institute. One evening, at about 4 pm, I had a phone call from Dr Ma'ama, now CEO. He gave me a drink, a Beaufort beer, and told me a story. He started by praising my computer skills and how he knew I could do many things with my knowledge of the computer. We had just finished the evaluation commission of scientists in the Institute. The results were being awaited by the Minister-Secretary of Rural Development Investigations to invite officers for the validation and promotion commission. But Dr Ma'ma intentionally delayed transmitting the results of the evaluation commission because he wanted me to do something for him.

He then proceeded by telling me that he wanted me to do something. He said it with all seriousness such that I had to listen attentively to hear what he was about to say. "Dr, you have just had your PhD. You have nothing to fear. I am behind you. I would like you to take the results of the evaluation commission and imitate the signatures of all the examiners and promote *your brother*, Wolo, to the grade of senior research officer." There had been eighteen examiners in the evaluation commission. They had worked so faithfully to reach the decisions they had taken about the scientists. Now, I was being asked by my *boss* to change the results and to formalize those by forging signatures of examiners. It was unethical and immoral. I knew I could not do it. I told him I could not do it because it was unethical, and more so it was against my way of doing things. I thought it was over.

Another day, he called me again to his house and asked me the same favor. I told him it was not morally correct to forge signatures of people, and that it was not right to favor some people and not others. After all, there were several other researchers who had not made it to the next grades. In that commission I had been proposed for promotion to the next grade because I met all requirements for promotion. There was no reason why some people could be promoted through intervention by our boss, on the basis of ethnicity.

The third day, he called me again, offered me a beer and made the same request. I did not say a word and returned to my house. He thought that my being quiet meant I had consented to doing it. But instead I confided in one senior financial officer in the Institute. When I finished narrating the story of the CEO's request, he told me not to do it. He added that "the CEO had all the powers when he was Minister to sit in his office and promote any person he wanted; he did not need to pass through you to promote his brother. "Do not do it because if you run into trouble tomorrow, he would deny that he gave you the authority to do it." I felt relieved. I went back home and was even too tired to discuss the matter with my wife. A week later, the CEO made the request for the fourth time. When I bluntly refused, a bone of contention was created between us. I knew the consequences of that but I also knew I had done the right thing.

I was running an international research project at the Institute. I had worked so hard to make the technical report and financial report and was ready to travel out of the country to submit and defend these documents in IITA Ibadan. By convention, the financial report had to be co-signed by the CEO of the Institute. So I moved over to his house for him to sign the financial report as I was going to catch my flight very early the following morning. When I reached his home, I met one of his house boys who went and called him. When he came he started signing the documents. Just midway in the signing, his wife came out from the sitting room to meet us in the veranda where the CEO and I were sitting. With her face seriously twisted, she looked at me with extreme disgruntleness. "What are you doing here – the person who is looking for the position of my husband? "You can look for big positions but do not spoil the name of my husband. You went to see your kinsmen in high places in government and told them to get them fire my husband and name you in his place. I was very embarrassed. I turned to her and asked her if she knew the person who was in front of her. I told her, this was me, the scientist she knows very well, and one who considered her and her husband as his parents. How on earth could I want to get the place of her husband? I told her that that was the last time I would ever come to their house again. I had been coming and even eating in that house, not knowing they had been thinking of me as one who could be the rival of her husband, the CEO. And from that day on, I never went to that house again.

I was so frustrated that as I took the one-hour flight to Nigeria, I was only thinking about what had happened to me. Could someone be jailed for not committing a crime?

One day as I was taking a drink in town I saw one of his house boys. I offered him a drink. Then he started to recount the story to me. He said that it all happened on a certain Saturday. The Secretary of the CEO (actually his chief of cabinet) came to the house to see the CEO for a discussion. She started by praising him for the efforts he made and initiative he had taken to send her to the USA for an administrative course. That without him, she would never have seen the whiteman's country. "Sir, I heard a terrible thing two days ago which I wanted to share with you. I was in the office arranging some files after work when I heard Mwayé talking. I sent my head out of the window and saw who was really talking. It was Mwayé. I heard him saying that you were already old and was sleeping all the time in meetings. The worst thing was that he added that he was going to see his kinsmen occupying big positions in government to have you fired so that they could name him in your place."

The house boy went on to say that he told the CEO and his wife after the Secretary had left that the story could not be true. He did some investigation and realized that the Assistant CEO, who had been aiming at the CEO position for quite some time, was the one who had really invented that story and had handed it over to the Secretary of the CEO to present it to the CEO.

Another story related to favoritism concerned one of his tribesmen, a researcher in the Institute. He had prepared a manuscript for publication in the Institute journal. The procedure for having a manuscript accepted for publication was clear. The manuscript would be submitted to the editorial office of the journal. The editor-in-chief would review it to determine if it met the standard and conditions for publication in the journal. Then he would select three reviewers and forward it to them for evaluation. The process could take close to a year for the back and forth from editorial office to the author until the editor-in-chief was finally satisfied it was appropriate for acceptance for publication. This peer review was mandatory. But Dr Ma'ama, did the sad thing of receiving the manuscript and accepting it for publication in his comfortable hotel room where he was attending a meeting. He forced me to accept his decision. On the basis of that, his kinsman was promoted to the higher grade.

CHAPTER 10

The dilemma of the agricultural show

. . . .

THE AGRICULTURAL SHOW WAS AN ANNUAL EVENT IN THE FEDERAL Republic of Tropicana, the country being an agricultural country. It would rotate from one agro-ecological zone to the other. The agricultural show was a public event exhibiting the equipment, crops, animals, sports and recreation associated with agriculture, forestry and animal husbandry. The largest event during the show comprised of a display of crop products, farm plots, food technology produced as well as a livestock show in which there was massive display of breeding stock produced in the country. There was also a trade fair with competitions of harvested crop products as well as animal products. The event was usually animated by entertainment of all types. As an important feast, there were music, dance and even cultural displays. The work and practices of farmers, livestock husbandmen occupied a large part of the exhibitions. The livestock part of the show was usually a whole event by itself, attracting some many spectators. In that section animals were exhibited and judged on certain phenotypical breed traits as specified by their respective breed standards. Species of livestock that were shown included pigs, cattle, sheep, horses, rabbits, guinea pigs and poultry including chickens, geese, ducks, turkeys and pigeons.

Prizes were often given by the State to the farmers with the best products. In the Federal Republic of Tropicana, since 1969, the agricultural show had provided local people with an opportunity to celebrate achievements from their fields and to enjoy a break from day-to-day routine. It is known that since the 19th century, agricultural shows had been major events for crop and livestock farmers, as well as the populations. Records show that the very first agricultural show was held in Salford Agricultural Society in Lancashire (UK), in 1768, and since then the event had become a worldwide manifestation of importance, gaining more and more importance and acceptance in those typically agricultural countries of the world. With a combination of serious competition and light entertainment, agricultural shows acknowledged and rewarded the hard work and skill of primary producers and provided a venue for rural families to socialize. The part of the event dealing with town and cultural shows which accompanied agricultural shows also provided city people with an opportunity to engage directly with rural life, cultural exchanges and food production. There were also marketing of exhibits at the end of the show.

In Tropicana it has become a tradition for agricultural shows to be more and more enlivened with competitive events, including food competitions, scientific and technical presentations, video shows of agricultural production in the country and several events. In the agricultural show which took place in Ebolowa in the Southern Region of the country, a large area was ploughed and prepared for the exhibitions. That agricultural show village, as it was called, provided ample space for crop and animal exhibits, research farm plots as well as a landing strip for the King's helicopter.

Prize-winners at agricultural shows in the Federal Republic of Tropicana were generally awarded certificates, inscribed medals, cups, rosettes or ribbons. The Ministry of Rural Development kept a rare collection of medals and certificates documenting the history of agricultural shows, their winners and rural industries across the country. Many of these awards were associated with significant individuals and organizations of agro-industrial complexes in the country.

Agricultural shows, although being events of national importance in the country, could also be sources of transmission of animal diseases to other animals and human populations. For instance diseases such as the African swine fever, coccidiosis, respiratory diseases, swine dysentery, greasy pig disease, mastitis, porcine parvovirus, parasites, lice and flies, hog cholera, foot and mouth disease and anemia could easily be transmitted. Particularly important were swine influenza which was very easily transmitted to animals and man. The viruses that cause this influenza are extremely common in pigs across various agro-ecological zones. Their subtypes (H1N1, H1H2 and H3N2, named for their specific genetic make-ups), initially reported mainly in the USA, are now common in many parts of the world. These are easily passed between pigs when proper hygiene and safety measures are not carried out prior to arrival in the event village. It is rare for the virus to spread to humans. However, genetic reassortment could lead to susceptibility among humans. Due to direct contact with infected animals or a contaminated environment, swine influenza strains could be transmitted to human populations. For instance, in 2009 the virus was transmitted from swine to humans and this caused a global pandemic which led to the deaths of some 12,000 people in the United States alone. For this reason, people who work or spend any time in close proximity with pigs are at risk for infection and must follow specific precautions to prevent the spread of swine influenza in their countries.

Certain populations at agricultural fairs particularly pregnant women are at increased risk of developing serious complications after swine influenza exposure. These viruses are extremely common in pigs across various industries, and are easily passed between pigs when proper hygiene and safety measures are not carried out. These viruses are extremely common in pigs across various industries in a country, and are easily passed between pigs when proper hygiene and safety measures are not carried out prior to coming for the show. Also, women are more susceptible than men to swine influenza and have been shown to have increased rates of swine influenza mortality relative to the general population. In like manner, adolescents, infants and those with health challenges such as diabetes and hypertension have disproportionately high rates of mortality with swine influenza. This is of great concern because many youths participate in agricultural shows and similar manifestations every year. Hence, agricultural fairs can readily lead to swine influenza infection in vulnerable populations since that event attracts many people and is frequently visited by entire families, including children and pregnant women.

The commonest cattle diseases which are easily transmitted to other animals are foot-and- mouth disease, trypanosomiasis, bovine respiratory disease, rinderpest, and bovine malignant catarrhal fever. Proper hygiene had to be exercised whenever animals were being conveyed to the sites of agricultural shows.

Rinderpest (also called cattle plague or steppe murrain) was an infectious viral disease of cattle, domestic buffalo, and many other animals including the large antelope, deer and giraffes. The disease was characterized by fever, oral erosions, diarrhea, lymphoid necrosis, and high mortality death rates during outbreaks, being usually extremely high, approaching 100% in some populations. Rinderpest was mainly transmitted by direct contact and by drinking contaminated water, although it could also be transmitted by air. After a global eradication campaign since the mid-20th century, the last confirmed case of rinderpest was diagnosed in 2001, the disease has since not been a major disease of cattle in Cameroon.

The foot-and-mouth disease is caused by a virus of which there are seven 'types', each producing the same symptoms. The seven types of virus are distinguishable only in the laboratory. Unfortunately immunity to one type does not protect an animal against other types. The interval between exposure to infection and the appearance of symptoms varies between twenty-four hours and ten days, or even longer. The average time, under natural conditions, is three to six days.

Trypanosomiases is a collection of several diseases in cows and other vertebrates caused by parasitic protozoan trypanosomes of the genus *Trypanosoma*. In humans this includes African trypanosomiasis and Chagas disease. The causal organism belongs to a different *Trypanosoma* subgenus, is transmitted by a different vector and the disease characteristics are different. Other parasite species and sub-species of the *Trypanosoma* genus are only pathogenic to animals and cause animal trypanosomiasis in wild and domestic animals.

Trypanosomiasis in domestic animals, particularly in cattle, is a major obstacle to the economic development of affected rural areas. Animals can host the human pathogen parasites; domestic and wild animals are an important reservoir so extreme care is usually exercised when humans interact with animals in events such as an agricultural show. Some breeds of cattle have however been identified that have innate resistance to trypanosomiasis and could play a valuable role in reducing the impact of the disease in these areas. However, such resistance could be lost because of poor nutrition or heavy tsetse challenge like is the case in the Federal Republic of Tropicana. The good thing is that both acquired and innate resistance to African trypanosomiasis can occur in cattle. The former raises the possibility of a vaccine against tsetse-transmitted metacyclic trypanosomes which have been shown to have a smaller repertoire of variable antigens than bloodstream parasites. The latter provides two further avenues of approach. Firstly, trypanotolerant breeds are being increasingly exploited and improved by conventional management and breeding methods including embryo transfer. Secondly, active research is being carried out into the factors associated with their innate resistance, i.e., the control of trypanosome growth, the development of effective immune responses and resistance to anemia. If the mechanisms underlying these factors are identified it might be possible by immunisation, by specific drug treatment or by transfection of appropriate genes to produce highly productive cattle resistant to trypanosomiasis.

Because of these diseases, all the veterinary doctors of the Institute were mobilized to monitor and give prophylactic treatment to animals before taking them over to the agricultural show village. In spite of the fact that I had succeeded in doing massive mobilization of scientists and technicians to the agricultural show village, I was very stressed throughout the months preceding the Southern Region agricultural show. I was supposed to manage the purchase of field equipment, the preparation of field plots and the refurbishing of houses which had to accommodate the scientists and technicians who had to participate in the event. As usual there were funds that had been allotted by the Government for the holding of the event.

For the purchase of field equipment, we needed tractors, tractor accessories (ploughs, rotary tillers or rotavators, small field tools such as hoes and machetes as well as irrigation equipment for the watering of plots. The King had instructed the Minister-Secretary of Rural Development (the chairman of the organizing committee) that the procedures for the acquisition of equipment for the agricultural show be facilitated such that acquisition of material was very simple to prevent any delays in their acquisition. But my Minister-Secretary, Lena BigStuff, went behind and signed out funds destined for our Institute, and found it difficult to account for them because the equipment had not been supplied. The Minister-Secretary of Rural Development kept firing letters to me to account for the funds even though I had not been involved in using them. I was so stressed that in the last evaluation meeting I told him that I had not signed out for those funds and could not be held responsible for their use. He understood what I was saying but he did not have the courage to expose his colleague, question her, or recommend sanctions to my Minister who he knew had consumed the money.

The second operation which took a lot of effort was the preparation of field plots where our crops were going to be planted. Here again, funds did not reach us at all, and the activities had to be done very fast. So what I did was to borrow money from friends who were doing business with us to finance the operations. I had to do that because time was running out: plant nurseries had to be installed, crops transplanted to the agricultural show village and watered profusely to sprout and germinate to a reasonable height before the show started. I did all that with my team of directors and we succeeded.

The most painful and stressful of all the operations was the refurbishing of houses to accommodate the scientists and technicians who had to participate in the event. Even more stressful was the refurbishing of the house in which the Minister-Secretary of Rural Development Investigations was going to live for the one week of the event. Rooms were added to the staff houses in our Nkoemvone research station which was the station closest to the agricultural show village; these had to lodge scientists. Other rooms were added to houses in the workers' camp to lodge technicians and field recorders. Even here, I had to ask friends from the business community to pre-finance the operations to be paid later because I did not want to fail. The most expensive part of the refurbishing was that of the house which was going to house our Minister. What made it very difficult was that she had instructed on the special kind of furniture (beds, and chairs) that *her* house was going to contain. And since she was looking for faults from me, I had to do whatever I could to satisfy her.

What I detested even more in all these were the many meetings I had to attend prior to the holding of the event. Most of these meetings were to present the state of progress of our activities, even though I had not been given the funds allotted for their execution. All of these meetings were implicating to me because the Minister-Secretary of Rural Development wanted to hear from my own mouth that my Minister was the one who had signed out all the money for the agricultural show preparations.

After all this effort of borrowing money from business people, the time came for the event. The King himself was presiding over the event. I had to be prepared with my exhibits. My plots had to be attractive for the King to realize that I was doing a good job in my Institute. The exhibits from my five technical departments – annual crops, perennial crops, forestry and environment, farming systems and livestock production and fisheries – had to be beautiful and attractive to show the King. We were ready.

Just when the King had arrived in his helicopter and had started the visits of the agricultural show village, a colleague scientist came to me and delivered a message which my Minister-Secretary had sent to me. "Tell Dr Mwayé, the CEO of TRDI that I did not want to see him handshake and embrace the King. He would be in deep trouble with me if he did that." My board chairman was standing just near to me when that message came. He came even closer to me and asked me exactly what the Minister had said. I told him. He asked me what the hell the Minister meant by that. "Is it here that she wants to shred the King's decree that appointed you?"

Luckily the director of the civil cabinet of the King, who was moving ahead of the King came and played the usual diplomacy that he exercised with cabinet members, calmed her down averting the chaos which would have happened. The King had been scheduled to visit agricultural research for forty-five minutes but he was so impressed with our work that he spent two and a half hours with us. I took him and his delegation around the entire plot introducing the various departments and their products as well as the heads of those departments. He was impressed. I was happy. The board chairman was also happy. The one person who was not happy (you could tell that from her face) was Lena BigStuff, because she felt the King had been happy with my work; that was very displeasing to her.

My Minister was now left to play all the gymnastics to account for the money she had received from the Minister of Rural Development in the name of the Tropicana Rural Development Institute.

CHAPTER 11

Dealings with the Kingdom cabinet

. . . .

THE WORST THING THAT COULD HAPPEN TO A CEO WAS HAVING problems with members of cabinet of the Kingdom. They were so powerful and had very important connections that they could get rid of any CEO under their supervision at any time.

TRDI, being a national institution, had two supervisory authorities – the Minister-Secretary of the Treasury and the Minister-Secretary of Rural Development Investigations. The Minister-Secretary of the Treasury was required to ensure the timely supply of funds to the Institute for its running costs, the development of its infrastructure, as well as supervise the way the funds were used. At the start of the financial year, the Secretary of the Treasury would credit the account of the TRDI in the national treasury after the budget had been voted by the national assembly. He would send a letter called the letter of notification (*lettre de notification*) to TRDI informing its CEO that his Institute's account in the Treasury had been credited and would indicate the amount credited. The letter would mention the budgetary lines for which the money had to be used. That letter of notification was the Bible of the CEO in the management of government funds put at his disposal. Usually one sixth of the yearly budget was sent at a time. Hence the annual credit was supplied six times. That letter of notification was always accompanying any funds received by government and had to be considered to serve as the Bible of financial management of the Institute. Any deviation in the way the money was spent was considered to be embezzlement. The Minister-Secretary of the Treasury could at any time and without notice send auditors to audit the accounts of TRDI. He could order the prosecution of a defaulting CEO. He had the powers to do so.

The Minister-Secretary of Rural Development Investigations was charged with ensuring that the Institute was well run politically and technically. That Minister had nothing to do with the finances of the Institute.

But it turned out that the Minister-Secretary of Rural Development Investigations was more interested in the management of the finances of the research institutes. After several Minister-Secretaries had come and gone, the one who was there was a tiny imposing lady with a heavy voice in the name of Lena BigStuff.

I spent thirty-four years in the Tropicana Rural Development Institute (TRDI). TRDI has always been rated as the biggest and most developed agricultural research institute in Black Africa. It had a total employee pool of 1200 workers among which there were 300 scientists with Masters and Doctorate degrees. It was the only research institute in Central Africa which had exhaustive research going on in all agro-ecological zones – Sahel, moist savanna, western highlands, forest-savanna transition, semi-humid zone, and humid forest zone. So there were active research programs on Sahelian crops such as sorghum, millet, wheat and cowpea. There were research activities on small and big livestock (cattle, poultry, pigs and goats). There was active research being carried out on starchy staples such as bananas and plantains, roots and tuber crops (cassava, yams, sweet potato, cocoyam and Irish potato). In the Institute there was also active research on humid forest perennial crops such as coffee, cocoa, rubber, oil palm), and programs on humid forest industrial annual crops such as sugarcane and tobacco.

I came there as a field technician after graduating from the National College of Rural Development as an Agricultural Technical Officer. I received my university education later while already an employee of the TRDI. For the thirty-four years of my stay in TRDI I had witnessed several changes taking place year after year in the Institute. I had also seen the Institute change its name three times, from the Institute of Agricultural and Forestry Research (IRAF), to the Institute of Agronomic Research (IRA), to the Institute of Agricultural Research for Development (IRAD). I was able to see TRDI operate under the auspices of a National Office, then a Delegation, and finally a Ministry.

Of all leaders in the offices that controlled research three stood out to be very impactful; their imprints can still be felt in the research institutes today. Unfortunately, many of them have been considered as people who were there only for political reasons, because they had nothing to show as contributions to the growth of rural development research in the country, while others have been seen as people who came there only to amass wealth for themselves in a system which all along had had no effective system of national audit. Others still did not appear to have the qualification or interest to direct research for the benefit of the country. That was Tropicana, a country with 256 ethnic groups whose king was doing all he could to satisfy ethnic distribution of positions even if the persons projected for cabinet positions from those regions were not qualified in every sense of the word.

Two of the leaders of scientific research stand out conspicuously as people who affected me negatively as I grew up as a researcher in the TRDI. The first was Prof Henry Mboko and the second was Lena BigStuff. Prof Mboko was from a major ethnic group in Tropicana. He was certainly qualified to head research but came there more for political reasons. As a member of a major ethnic group, he tended to join the clique of that tribe to groom their candidates for higher administrative positions in the various research institutes. In terms of output, scientists in the institutes openly expressed their disappointment with him and could be heard gossiping that he did not meet their expectations as a good and learned leader of scientific research. He also had a handicap in that he spent a good bit of his time there in the Ministry criticizing his predecessor for having lived a miserable life in the Ministry, not even letting water flow in the building but leaving his office and going to ease himself in the house of a neighbouring kinsman who was living just opposite his office building.

On a personal basis, I was disappointed with him in two situations – one in which he failed to transmit to the King's palace an important file regarding the holding in Tropicana of an international symposium on root crops research. In their annual assembly the International Society for Tropical Root Crops Research had selected the Federal Republic of Tropicana to host the symposium. The Federal Republic of Tropicana had three years to prepare for the hosting of the symposium. The hosting country had to do just a few things before the holding of the symposium. First, it had to choose a venue for the symposium. Secondly, the research institute hosting the symposium had to prepare a budget for the symposium and secure funding from its government. It also had to make hotel reservations and negotiate room rates for lodging and feeding of participants. It also had to identify farms and cultural areas for field visits. There was also limited support from the international society to help the host country as well as sponsor researchers from various countries to take part in the Symposium.

As contact person (chief organizer) in TRDI I prepared the necessary documents requesting a budget from the King for the symposium. I gave the transmission letter to the CEO of TRDI to sign, and after that signature, I obliged myself personally to carry the file to the Minister-Secretary for Rural Development Investigations. The file which accompanied the letter included the rationale for the financial request as well as the honor and economic benefit that the country would have for hosting the meeting. All the Minister-Secretary of Rural Development Investigations had to do was to transmit the file with a favourable recommendation to the King's palace for funding to be secured. Only the King's Palace budget could cover events of that nature. The budget of the Secretary of RDI or that of the TDRI did not have funds to finance such meetings which required heavy funding from upwards of sixty thousand dollars because such money needed to have been budgeted a priori for and approval obtained either from the board (in the case of TRDI) or the National Assembly (in the case of the Ministry. That was a long and tedious process.

But disappointingly, the Minister of RDI sent the file to be treated by some officer in the Ministry who happened not to like me, for reasons best known to him. The only intelligent guess I can make is that he saw me as a better candidate than the candidate than the candidate his tribe was projecting to take over as CEO of TRDI.

Till now I believe he did not just treat the file at all. He may have told the Minister that the Symposium for which I was requesting funding was a minor event not needing the intervention of the King.The result was that the file remained shelved in the Ministry and was never transmitted to the King's Palace. So the funding was never received by TRDI. Because the Institute had still not obtained funds three weeks before the international event, the International Society was forced to relocate the meeting to neighboring Nigeria, re-establish new air tickets for participants and withdraw their own contributions to TRDI for the hosting of the symposium. It was pathetic.

The second situation that worried me when he was Minister was when I was invited to a scientific panel in the Ministry of RDI to explain why I published an article in an international journal in which I was editor-in-chief. It was really a setup by his clansmen in the Ministry. Everything surrounding the allegation was because a clique surrounding him did not want me to get promoted to the grade of Chief Research Officer, an event that would bring me to the limelight and make me a likely candidate for the highly contested post of CEO of TRDI. That clique could not stand the idea that I would one day become CEO of the Institute. The scientific *tribunal* to which I was subjected hurt me so much that it kept me stressed for quite a good while. My disappointment in the Minister of RDI was because he, as professor, knew better than those guys who treated my file and could use his judgment to realize that some games were being played to hold me down. He needed to show that he was fair in a matter like that. But he joined his kinsmen in holding me back, contributing in supporting their tribal candidate for that CEO position.

The second Minister-Secretary of Rural Development Investigations was a lady called Lena BigStuff. She was not a scientist so many felt she did not even have the competence to direct rural development research in Tropicana. But she had been brought there by the King for political reasons, to satisfy her ethnic group which was bringing him a lot of votes during elections. The King had always had the sole prerogative to name cabinet members. She appeared to have a complex in her Ministry and in supervising the research institutes which had more qualified people. In many instances she showed how uncomfortable she was in the position and how she lacked the confidence in herself to head the institutions which she was supposed to supervise. So she resolved to enrich herself by using funds from TRDI and the other institutes. The house in her village would have a crack and she would request 50,000 dollars from TRDI to repair the crack. Her kinsmen would be enthroning their village chief and she would request 100,000 from TDRI to pay her own contribution for the event. In short, she just wanted to make as much money as possible for herself, not bothering about how those funds were going to be accounted for.

Many times I see her like a character in William Shakespeare's *Macbeth*. When Macbeth was told by his subjects that he had been made King, instead of rejoicing, he said, "*To be thus is nothing but to be safely thus. Our fears in Banquo stick deep and in his royalty of nature reigns that must be feared.*"

Lord Banquo is a character in William Shakespeare's 1606 play *Macbeth*. In the play, Banquo is at first an ally of Macbeth (both are generals in the King's army) and they meet the Three Witches together. After prophesying that Macbeth will become king, the witches tell Banquo that he will not be king himself, but that his descendants will be. Later, Macbeth in his lust for power sees Banquo as a threat and has him murdered by three hired assassins; Banquo's son, Fleance, escapes. Banquo's ghost returns in a later scene, causing Macbeth to react with alarm during a public feast, and makes a public pronouncement how unsure he is to be a safe king as long as the ghost of Banquo was still there pursuing him.

Lena hurt me in several situations. I had been named CEO of TRDI by the King of Tropicana when she was the Minister supervising rural development research. I had worked my way up to becoming the CEO, a presidential appointee. It was a big manifestation the day I was inaugurated as CEO. Even the people who had worked hard to trample on me attended the ceremony. She made a long and flowery speech praising me during the installation, calling me a square peg in a square hole, and informing the many attendees of my huge achievements as a scientist. But the glory was short-lived. After barely one month, the bomb came. A hand-carried letter came from the Minister-Secretary of Rural Development Investigation (RDI) addressed to me, not to the CEO. The letter was not deposited in my mail office, nor was it given to my Chief of Cabinet. The carrier of the letter, one Andrew Yabassi, insisted on seeing me to personally hand the letter from the Minister-Secretary of RDI to me. Hearing the name of the Minister-Secretary of RDI, my Chief of Cabinet let him in to see me. Andrew Yabassi, greeted me and handed me the letter, stating that the Minister-Secretary said that the letter was so important that it needed urgent attention from me. I read the letter twice, and could not believe what I was actually seeing. I told the guy that I would see the Minister-Secretary concerning the letter the next day. He left. After he had left, I read the letter the third time. The Secretary of RDI was ordering me to transfer 700,000 dollars from the Institute's account in the Treasury to her private account in a commercial bank indicating that the money was meant to do the humanitarian activities of the First Lady.

The next day, I went to see her. When she received me I told her that I did not have the necessary authority to effect that kind of transfer. I explained that I could transfer such an amount only from instructions by the board of administration or from the Minister-Secretary of the Treasury, the principal budget holder of the Federal Republic of Tropicana. Her answer was harsh, *"Monsieur le DG, vous voulez faire le bras-de-fer avec un membre du gouvernement?"* Translated in English she was saying, "Mr CEO you want to make resistance with a member of government, do you?" I told her I was not offering any resistance with a Member of Government but I could not do what she was asking me to do because I would be unable to account for it. In my mind I was telling myself that I could not carry out an instruction simply because a member of government had given it. In this case all I had as a cover was a small letter from the Minister-Secretary of RDI, nothing from the board chairman who was my direct boss, and nothing from the Minister of the Treasury.

I left her office and went back to the Institute. But I knew a real *cold war* had started between us. Then I remembered that it was for that same reason that my predecessor had been fired. But I was consoled by what people close to me who knew the story said, namely that nothing could be done to me because I had barely begun work in the position of CEO, and that the King did not have the habit of firing people he had just named. But it turned out to be wrong.

A senior colleague had once told me that being asked to do something unethical by a boss is stressful. A lot of thoughts and emotions fly through your mind at once. If you don't know what to do or where to turn to, you should realize that you're not alone and that you have more control over your situation than you think. Before deciding to become a whistleblower, each time you are confronted with a moral grey area do the following:

First, pause to collect yourself. It is important to pause and regain control over your emotions. Being asked to do something you don't think is right can make you feel angry. Don't let your emotions get the best of you. You want any action you take to reflect your professionalism and maturity.

Secondly, take time to understand the situation. Ask your boss for clarification or ask him or her to restate his or her request. It's best to make sure you have an accurate understanding of what you're being asked to do before you accuse someone of being unethical. I read a Bible chapter about ethics but the headway I had was that I would be wrong if I did it.

Thirdly, gather the facts. If after you've clarified your boss's request, and you still think you've been asked to do something unethical, start to gather the facts. Collect and document the information you think will support your case. Be sure to collect information in a legal manner. I assembled a folder comprising of the letters she had sent to me, a copy of my responsibilities as CEO as shown in the Employee manual, and a note she had sent to me about the justification she was making for requesting that money transfer.

Fourthly, assess your options. Seek the assistance of someone who can help you understand your options. You don't need to act immediately, but taking small steps early on is wise. I only shared the information with my wife, I did not want to make it public by discussing the matter with another person in which case I could be considered a whistleblower.

Fifthly consider potential consequences. What happens as a result of being asked to do something unethical is largely the result of how you choose to react. Consider the potential outcomes of all options before deciding what you want to do. I definitely knew that if I yielded, I would find myself eventually in jail. I also knew that if I did not satisfy her, I would be in her bad books; she would be working hard to get rid of me as she had done to my predecessor.

Sixthly, document everything. Anytime you speak to someone about your situation, make a note of what was discussed, who was present, and any other information you think will be valuable. Having this information usually comes in handy down the road as you face your situation. The matter was so frightful that I found it really difficult to discuss it with even my best friends, but they indirectly came to know about it because they could tell from stories they were hearing from other directors as to the way the Minister was insulting me in meetings.

The senior colleague advised that, in addition, I did not have to wait too long to respond to the situation. While it's a good idea to proceed with caution at a reasonable pace, taking too long to respond could make it more difficult to challenge the boss. He also advised that I did not have to share my story with everyone in the office no matter how upset I was with my boss. He repeated that I follow the channels set in place to resolve the situation at hand. If that didn't work, I could consider speaking with a legal authority or lawyer. A legal authority could help me understand my options so that I could take a stand for what is right. I made the matter known to the Minister of National Security. I gave the information to the Tropicana Bureau of Investigations. I notified the permanent secretary in the King's Palace. I thought I had made my complaint reach all those who mattered.

I had to use intentionality because I was required to accept responsibility for both my actions and my motives. At that level I knew I could not say "I didn't mean to." It required that I manage difficult emotions and continue to think clearly. I had to be clear about my own stand. I had to ask myself whether I was supposed to do unethical or illegal things. I was convinced that this was a "yes" or "no" question. Of course I also knew that by the same token, not knowing the law was not a justifiable defense if I blundered in doing the wrong thing.

Other ideas came to my mind. I could consider contacting a governmental agency like the Department of Labor, in addition to the National Security and National Intelligence. I could consider hiring a lawyer or talk over what was happening. I could talk about what was going on with someone knowledgeable about such things, a friend, or spouse to get some perspective. The last thing I thought of was to get my resume ready just in case she succeeded in kicking me out.

For two years I could feel emotions coming into play. I knew these could confuse the issue for me. First I could suffer from intimidation from her. I could fear of losing my job. I could be confused about just what was ethical and what wasn't. I could even fear authority or the anger if I refused to do what she was asking me to do. I could be tempted to do what she was asking just to avoid conflict, or I could try to rationalize to justify to my boss as being a normal person who could not do harm to me. Several ideas came to my mind. First, I had to understand that just following orders won't necessarily protect me from criminal charges. Secondly, I did not have to comply simply because my boss had given me instructions. Third, I had to make documentation in writing about the chain of events for self-protection, especially when it came to presenting the situation to higher authorities to which the matter was presented. I could of course brave the situation by reporting the matter to the National Security including the police, the Intelligence Agency and the National Bureau of Investigation of Tropicana.

Several letters followed that first letter talking about the urgency in satisfying her request. In one of the last letters she cautioned me that I would blame myself for the consequences. At the end I damned the consequences and decided not to comply, and decided to care less whether or not she registered my name in her *black book*.

One evening as I was driving on the highway from a trip I had made to one of the remote stations, my phone rang. The number was not familiar because it was not in my phonebook. I reluctantly picked it because I was driving. I realized the person calling was working in the Palace of the King. "Please come and see me urgently." I told her I was driving back to my home from a trip. She insisted that I should stop by her house before even reaching my home because the matter she wanted to discuss with me was explosive and was of extreme urgency. She directed me the way to her house, and as I approached the city I followed the instructions she had given me and found her home. She invited me in and when I was seated she went to her bedroom and brought out a letter. It was a copy of a confidential letter which my Minister-Secretary of RDI had written to the King. In the letter, she was requesting the King to fire me for *insubordination*. She listed a good number of issues which she felt were wrong with my management of the Institute: I was disobedient to hierarchy, I was managing funds poorly, I was tribalistic and I did not honor the institutions and rules of the country.

I knew I was in hot soup. I came home and recounted the story to my wife. She did all she could to console me, and told me that we should start packing our belongings from the Government house we were occupying because according to her, if my Minister-Secretary had reached the stage of reporting me to the King, there was not much I could do.

Another event involved the sale of two buildings belonging to TRDI in the economic capital of Tropicana. Exactly six months after my inauguration as CEO, I was in my office, busy with a huge pile of folders treating and signing documents, when my Chief of Cabinet came into my office and told me that there were two people, sent by the Minister, who badly wanted to see you. I told her to let them in. They came in and took the two seats I had given them. Then one of them started a long story which he claimed he also had discussed with the Minister-Secretary of RDI. "We live in Luala. We were driving around and found two buildings opposite the Governor's residence. Those buildings are in an advanced stage of depreciation. Given the strategic location in which they are found, we feel we should buy the buildings and refurbish them so that they can improve the look of that area. We have already *seen* the Minister-Secretary of RDI. She says we should also *see* you, the reason we are here. The man who was speaking opened his briefcase and pulled out a big khaki envelop and gave me. I could not even guess what was there. I opened the envelope and saw a pile of bank notes, amounting to 100,000 US dollars. I started to recount my functions as CEO, namely to protect government property which was under my care. I continued to tell them that the only administrative authority which had the authority to sell government property was the Minister-Secretary of Lands.

The two guys became uncomfortable. They stepped out of the office and concerted a bit while I continued treating my files. When they returned to the office they handed me another envelope containing 50,000 US dollars. I told them that the amount of money was not the issue. I was just not authorized to sell government property. After failing to convince me that they really needed the buildings, they left my office in anger and went away. As it turned out, they went straight to the Ministry and saw the Minister-Secretary of RDI and recounted my reaction to them when they went to *see* me. Immediately, the Minister-Secretary took her phone and called me. Her message was astonishing, "You think you are clean and have no dirt in your eyes. If I send Etame to your Institute, he will still find something you have done wrong." Etame was the Minister-Secretary heading the Supreme State Audit of Tropicana. I did not say a word until she hung up.

Nine months later, we were in a meeting in the Ministry when she announced that my predecessor, Dr Israel Ma'ama ma Mbazi, who was a good person and who had served the country faithfully needed to be given a present. She was ordering me to *hand over* to him the Toyota Crown Super Saloon sedan which he had been using while he was CEO of TRDI. Two weeks later, I finished tuning up the car and was ready to hand it over to Dr Ma'ama. All I needed was a letter of instructions from Lena indicating that she had authorized me to hand over the vehicle to Dr Ma'ama. I prepared the letter for her signature and I personally took it to her. When she saw it she refused to sign it, stating that I should just hand the vehicle to him insisting that it was an instruction that I did not have to question. But I knew that the procedure was not right. Any vehicle in TRDI which was a government vehicle could only be sold by the Minister-Secretary of Lands. In spite of the fact that the vehicle was in my custody did not give me the authority to sell it. When I contacted the Minister-Secretary of Lands on the matter, he told me that she really just wanted to put me in trouble. I avoided that.

One morning an employee of the Institute came in and brought me a copy of a newspaper article which had just come out. In it journalists of the newspaper *Mutation Moliki* were accusing me of having swindled Institute money. In the article they were accusing me of having influenced my finance service to increase my salary as CEO. The salary of the CEO was made up of two sub-salaries: a public service salary which was given according to your public service grade as civil servant, and a salary (actually called CEO allowance) accorded by the board of administration to the CEO of the Institute. I met that allowance and I had no reason to question it. In some government institutions the CEO could influence the board (through lobbying) to revise their allowances. Sometimes, that was done. Other times, they did not succeed. But when I came there, I did not want to bother myself with such maneuvers. I decided to be satisfied with what I was receiving, and concentrated on the heavy volume of work on my table. So I wondered where the information about salary increase came from.

About two months later, another issue of *Mutation Moliki* came out. There was a big article about me again. In this article I was being accused of swindling 20,000 USD to buy furniture for my house. There was even a page devoted to the decision I had made giving myself the money. The newspaper concluded by saying that I was a typical CEO abusing the powers of my office. Actually, the board of administration had decided well before I was appointed to the post that once appointed, there would be an establishment allowance to be given to the CEO which comprised funds to buy furniture, glassware for the kitchen and a small amount to receive guests. When I was appointed to the post, I was given that allowance. It became a story in *Mutation Moliki.*

About three months later, another article came out from *Mutation Moliki.* I In this article I was accused of swimming in a luxury of vehicles. It stated that I had a sedan and an SUV as service vehicles, and that I had just acquired ten new pickups for my personal use. Actually the sedan and SUV were vehicles used by my predecessor. I had merely inherited them from him. The sedan, a Nissan Avensis, was being used for in-town driving, while the SUV was for long-distance trips for supervisory trips to remote stations. The ten pickups had been budgeted by my predecessor well before I came there but they were delivered to the Institute when I had begun the job of CEO.

When I carried out an investigation I realized that *Mutation Moliki* was a private newspaper hired by the Minister of Rural Development Investigations to tarnish the image of her CEOs who were not complying with her instructions. It was a pity. That is when I was made to understand that she spent quite a good bit of money buying over several newspapers to write good about her. She would even pay the national newspaper editor to hide nasty things she was doing which she did not want people to know.

I wondered from then on why my Minister was using her time as member of cabinet just to be involved in things of this nature. She would hold meetings, invite all the CEO's of research institutes and give them an agenda for the meeting. She would first of all come about an hour late to the meeting, wasting the time of CEO's who had work piled up in their institutes to treat. But barely thirty minutes after she started talking she would digress to something else, spending some two hours or so insulting his CEOs who were not complacent.

She would warn me not to visit the research centers of my Institute, stating that I had work to occupy me rather than going out to fetch out-of-station allowances and other benefits from visits to research structures. But she would oblige me to arrange visits to research structures so that the heads of those structures would send truckloads of food items and slaughtered animals for her. I would find it extremely difficult to live with such a *budgetivorous* individual who just spent all her time acquiring things.

During my first year as CEO I had negotiated a funding with the Asian Vegetable Research and Development Center (AVRDC). Their regional office in Tanzania invited me to attend a meeting which had to concretize the project. I made a request for a mission order and travelling warrant from my board chairman. When I reached the airport, I was refused from boarding the aircraft. The authorities in the airport told me my Minister had issued a travel ban on me (*an interdiction de sortie*) so I could not travel until the ban had been lifted. I was very stressed. I could not travel. The project which was going to bring in money for the Institute was cancelled. It took the intervention of the Prime Minister to lift the ban several months later before I could make an international trip again. In the Prime Minister's letter, he stressed that the only person who could give me a travel ban was my board chairman, not the Minister. It was a big victory for the board chairman.

In the second year of my stay there as CEO, Lena BigStuff wrote to the bank and blocked the account we had there for maize seed multiplication. For several months we could not use the funds in that account to do seed multiplication and other activities funded by that account. That stressed me so much because funds were available but could not be used because the account had been blocked.

I had ordered 10 pickup vehicles for the Institute. I distributed them to various structures of the Institute. After Lena learnt of the distribution, she ordered that the vehicles all be brought back from the structures. When they arrived, she took two of the vehicles for herself and distributed the rest the way she liked. She had now taken over the functions of the CEO.

I ordered three heavy duty trucks for the Institute. When they arrived, I put the TRDI logo on them. She seized the trucks because she was angry that I had put the Institute logo on them without her permission. It was very embarrassing and frustrating to me. I could not imagine how I could do something to protect government vehicles from misuse and instead be blamed for it. When the time came to pay for the vehicles, she insisted that she would be the one to write out the check to settle the payments. When the suppliers saw her she asked to be given the envelope they had prepared for the CEO before she could release the funds. It was terrible.

There was an agricultural show in the southern region of the country. The Minister-Secretary of TRDI signed out the funds which were meant to be used by the Institute for various activities – refurbishing of houses to accommodate technicians, scientists and the Minister-Secretary, buy field equipment for preparing the plots as well as installing the field plots. The Institute strained to carry out activities successfully till the event was over. During the event, the Minister-Secretary of TRDI sent me a message that I should not attempt to shake hands with the King. It was terrible. It needed the intervention of a senior officer in the Kingdom to avert chaos during the event. There she showed open distaste for me. She had repeatedly insulted me in meetings in the Ministry. This kept me stressed to the point that my board chairman advised me never to attend her meetings any more, but send my deputy to attend in my place. In one of the meetings on seed multiplication she deviated from the topic of the meeting and spent close to one hour just insulting me and telling me that I was claiming to be clean and honest but faults could always be detected by controllers and auditors from the Kingdom.

The Kingdom of Tropicana had authorized the recruitment of scientists and support staff for TRDI because the employees were fast reducing as they were being sent on retirement. The recruitment offer was well publicized in the media and qualified candidates eventually recruited. The Secretary of RDI was angry with the recruitments and accused me of tribalism. It was a pity and really frustrating because that was a real lie. She fired the entire lot of personnel that had been recruited. It was really embarrassing because many of those who had been absolved in the recruitment wave had left other offers they had elsewhere just to take up the positions in TRDI.

As CEO of TRDI, I made it a habit of purchasing fuel for the Institute on a quarterly basis. Each quarter I would purchase fuel vouchers from an oil company for 10,000 US dollars. When the fuel vouchers arrived I would share the fuel among the Minister of RDI, the board chairman of TRDI, the CEO, the Assistant CEO, the CFO and the different service heads. I made sure everyone handling an administrative position had some fuel to run around and do their errands.This time, barely eight months in power, I purchased fuel for 10,000 US dollars, shared it. The Minister had the lion's share – 2000 US dollars – the board chairman 1,500 US dollars, and the CEO just 1000 US dollar. I went to the Minister to personally give her own share to her. When I handed the envelope to her, she opened it, saw the fuel and threw the vouchers back to me saying, "is this all the fuel you can give your Minister? Take it back, leave my office and go away." I was so embarrassed as I left her office to go back to our campus. That same evening I went to see the board chairman and after handing his own share to him, I complained about how the Minister had sent me away. He was very astonished, and comforted me by saying, "all the time I was Minister I never refused anything my subordinates gave me as a present. What I would advise you to do is go back and order fuel for 10,000 US dollars and give her. It is not the right thing to do but just do it to buy your head." I did as he had recommended and I took the fuel over to her. She appeared satisfied but she told her chief of cabinet to sign for it. I could tell she did not want to have her signature on any such document which the press could exploit, if they got hold of it, to tarnish her image as a *budgetivorous* Minister.

A colleague of mine directing one of the research institutes confided in me about funds he had received from a foreign donor to remove toxic gas from a lake in the grassland region of the country. When he wanted to start the activity, Lena asked for half the amount of the grant for her own purposes. And to keep his position he had to give her. It was so unfortunate that we had that kind of *budgetivorous* supervisory Minister-Secretary whose only job was to grab and enrich herself

Persistent lava lakes are rare on Earth and provide volcanologists with a remarkable opportunity to directly investigate magma dynamics and degassing at the open air. Lake Nyos in the north-western region of Cameroon, is one of the very few basaltic arc volcanoes displaying such an activity and voluminous gas emission. But studies had long remained hampered sometimes by challenging accessibility. The Institute of Mining and Geological Research was assigned by Government to find out where the gas came from in Lake Nyos, and to degas the lake. It was found that CO_2 was being emitted by the lake. As years passed, scientists of the Institute and their foreign partners resolved the debate about the origin of the CO_2. After measuring gas at the bottom of Lake Nyos, they found a CO_2-rich layer, where levels of the gas were rising over time, suggesting gradual leakage into the bottom of the lake.

Lake Nyos had long been quiet before it happened. Farmers and migratory herders in the West African country of Cameroon knew the lake as large, still and blue. But on the evening of Aug. 21, 1986, farmers living near the lake heard rumbling. At the same time, a frothy spray shot hundreds of feet out of the lake, and a white cloud collected over the water. From the ground, the cloud grew to 328 feet (100 meters) tall and flowed across the land. When farmers near the lake left their houses to investigate the noise, they lost consciousness. The heavy cloud sunk into a valley, which channeled it into settlements. People in the affected areas collapsed in their tracks, at home, on roads or in the field losing consciousness or dying in a few breaths. In Nyos and Kam, the first villages hit by the cloud, everyone but four inhabitants on high ground died.

The valley split, and the cloud followed, killing people up to 15.5 miles (25 kilometers) away from the lake. Over the next two days, people from surrounding areas entered the valley to find the bodies of humans and cows lying on the ground. It was so severe that some European countries came to their rescue. They provided funding for degassing of the lake, and technical expertise to assist in making sure that the event never happened again. That is how the Institute of Mining and Geological Research received those funds. But when their scientists were about to start the activity of degassing, the Minister Lena BigStuff ordered that the director of that institute transfer half the funds into her personal account before the work could start. The director wanting to avoid losing his job did the transaction. It was a big scandal especially as it involved foreign partners. But that did not bother Lena. She had been used to that kind of way of doing things.

When I look at the way things happened at the time I was there as CEO I can list so many conflicts I had with her. Everything centered around money and property. Her behavior makes me feel she wanted me to be a figurehead CEO; she wanted to be the one to rule my Institute, especially the finances. Her behaviour towards me was if I just had to stay there waiting to receive orders from her. She had actually told me a day before my inauguration that she did not expect me to carry out any new research; TRDI had enough results to disseminate to the farmers of Tropicana. Now I know she was preparing my mind to know that the funds I was receiving from government were actually meant to be transferred over to her for her political motives, including doing everything that could keep her in power. Her behaviour makes me think of some history lessons I had studied while in secondary school. The two were the Franco-Prussian War and the bravery of Mustapha Kemal Ataturk in the Turkish War of Independence.

The Franco-Prussian War or Franco-German War, often referred to in France as the War of 1870, was a conflict between the Second French Empire (later the Third French Republic) and the North German Confederation led by the Kingdom of Prussia. The conflict which lasted from 19 July 1870 to 28 January 1871, was caused primarily by France's determination to restore its dominant position in continental Europe, which it had lost following Prussia's crushing victory over Austria in 1866. It is alleged that the chancellor of Prussia, Otto von Bismarck, deliberately provoked the French into declaring war on Prussia in order to draw four independent southern German states into an alliance with the Prussian-dominated North German Confederation. It could also be that Bismarck just likely recognized the potential for new German alliances if Prussia went to war with France.

A series of swift German victories over France, led to the capture of the French Emperor, Napoleon II at Metz and Sedan decisively defeating France and effectively ending the war on 28 January 1871. What is interesting in this Franco-Prussian encounter was probably the diplomacy that was provoked by the Ems Telegram to create war between France and Prussia.

The Ems Telegram (or Ems Dispatch, as it is sometimes called) (in French: Dépêche d'Ems) was an edited report on an encounter between King William I of Prussia and the French ambassador. The Telegram was sent by Heinrich Abeken of the Prussian Foreign Office from the German city of Ems on 13 July 1870 to the Prussian Chancellor, Otto von Bismarck.

In early 1870, the German Prince Leopold had been offered the vacant throne of Spain. The French Emperor, Napoleon III, and his government were concerned over a possible Spanish alliance with the Kingdom of Prussia and protested the offer, threatening to go to war with Prussia. Following the protests by France, Leopold withdrew his acceptance on 11 July 1870. This alone was already considered a diplomatic defeat for Prussia. The French were still not satisfied and demanded further commitments, especially *a guarantee by the Prussian king* that no member of his Hohenzollern family would ever be a candidate for the Spanish throne. That guarantee was insulting.

On 13 July 1870, King Wilhelm I of Prussia, on his morning stroll in Ems, was stopped by Count Vincent Benedetti, the French ambassador to Prussia who had been instructed by his boss, the Foreign Minister, Agenor, duc de Gramont, to present the French demand that the King Wilhem I should guarantee that he would never again permit the candidacy of a German prince to the Spanish throne. Politely and in a friendly manner the king refused to bind himself to any course of action in the future relating to that.

Heinrich Abeken wrote an account of the event for Otto von Bismarck, Prussian Chancellor, in Berlin. King Wilhelm I described Benedetti as "annoyingly persistent," and asked Bismarck to release an account of the events. Bismarck, having full liberty to inform the press in a suitable way, decided not to publish Abeken's original report but to use some of Abeken's wording for his own press release. He removed King Wilhelm's conciliatory phrases and emphasized the real issue, namely that *the French had made certain demands under threat of war,* and *Wilhelm had refused them.* Certainly, Bismarck's text, released on the evening of the same day (13 July, 1870) to the media and foreign embassies, gave the impression that French Ambassador Benedetti was not just being more demanding but that the King was also exceedingly abrupt. It was designed to give the French the impression that the King had insulted Benedetti. On the other hand, the German people interpreted the modified dispatch as Benedetti had insulted the King. Bismarck, viewing the worsening relations with France, was satisfied with the effect it was going to have, namely that it would be a red rag (a matter which was inciting anger that could eventually lead to violence) on the Gallic (French) *bull.* If war had to come, then it would be better to come sooner better than later. The edited document was diplomatically then to be presented as the cause of the war.

By an overwhelming majority in the French legislative chamber, the votes favouring a war with Prussia were passed. France declared war on 19 July 1870, starting the Franco-Prussian War which France lost. Following the French defeat in 1871, the Duc de Gramont attempted to throw the blame for the failures of French diplomacy on Benedetti. Benedetti, in defence, published his own version of the events in *Ma mission en Prusse,* a book digitized from digital images created through the libraries' digitization efforts, cleaned and prepared for printing, and eventually got published. You can see the number of parties who became interested and involved diplomatically in the matter: Prince Leopold, Napoleon II, King Wilhelm I, Benedetti, Agenor, Heinrich Abeken and finally, the architect, Otto von Bismarck.

Diplomatically, Lena fought me, and continuously for close to two years, using diplomacy to gain support of the powers-that-be, including the chief of civil cabinet in the King's palace. Whereas Otto von Bismarck twisted the Ems Telegram to incite hostility in the minds of the French to the point of declaring war with Prussia, Lena twisted issues about my management in her letter to the King's palace to justify why I had to be replaced. I could not win. Our war effectively ended on 12 September 2011 when she succeeded in convincing the King of Tropicana to fire me.

Now I try to evaluate the diplomacy that she used to get rid of me. Lena had made several alliances in the Kingdom of Tropicana which supported her request to the King to fire me. I was alone in the fight, not even my kinsmen in high places in the Tropicana government could intervene; everyone felt Lena's roots were deep in the King's Palace, and they feared losing their positions in government. Lena succeeded, and I was fired.

Throughout my tenure as CEO I worked extremely hard, trying to redress the awful situation I met. I used all the experience I had acquired by visiting several countries in Africa and Europe, and working with administrators and scientists in research institutes I saw in those countries. All along I had counted on a clean Kingdom which would compensate me for my hard work. I had put all this effort in redressing the Institute because I truly felt that I was in a country where there was objectivity in the way things were done. I had relied on a supposedly understanding cabinet, headed by a competent Prime Minister. I had convinced myself that it was nice looking up to the powers-that-be to come to my rescue. I met every VIP who mattered in the Federal Republic of Tropicana. In one of my dreams during the strong fight I was saying to the PM in a telegram: "Commander, Your Majesty most urgently requested to make peace at any price, catastrophe inevitable!" But the PM and the powers of Tropicana, being embarrassed with the situation, were obliged to reply negatively to my request: "Impossible to conclude peace. If unavoidable, retreat in best order" as during the Turkish War of Independence.

I had struggled so hard and found my way to see the Prime Minister hoping that he, being head of government, would make me sail to the shore. I could see the eye of the storm coming but I was comfortable I had someone who could save me from drowning. In the close meeting I had with the PM, he advised me that I should not yield to Lena's request; that the situation would lead me to jail if I yielded. I had thought he would bring Lena to justice and even sanction her for the wrongdoing. But he had surrendered, insinuating that the roots of Lena were very deep in the system. I believe he felt it was difficult or even impossible to uproot her out of the cabinet. He advised me *to retreat in best order.* He quietly sat in his office with full powers bestowed upon him and watched as the King of Tropicana fired me. Then, and only then, did I know nothing was straightforward and nothing was objective in Tropicana. It was a rotten territory, and that it was certainly an error I had made to accept the offer to serve as the CEO of TRDI.

That morning, I was busy treating files in my office when my cell phone rang. I took the phone and saw that it was a call from the head of one of the research centers of the institute. The call was short, "CEO, what am I hearing?" I told him I did not know anything. Then he said, "in that case I should not be the one to give you this information." A few minutes later, my chief of the budget service stepped into my office and told me that there were groups of workers gathering out there discussing me. He did not want to tell me the subject of their discussions. I looked up to him and asked him what he thought could be the problem. He smiled and left my office. Some minutes later, my chief financial officer came in to discuss some files with me. As we discussed, someone called him out of my office and gave him breaking news. He excused himself from the discussion we were having and stepped out of my office. After about ten minutes he came back and broke the news to me. "CEO, you have been fired." I will go out and get Suzana, a member of the board to tell me if she had heard anything. He effectively called her, and confirmed the story that I had really been fired. "The information is carried in the *Tropicana Tribune* of this morning."

That same day I wrote two letters, carefully composed, one to the King for having given me a chance to head the largest and most important research institute in the entire region. I made sure the letter got to him. I had been told by the Speaker of the National Assembly that if I wanted to be sure the King received a document I had to give it to the King's *Chef de Camp* (his principal chief of staff). I wrote the second letter to the chairman of the board of the Tropicana Rural Development Institute for having given me guidance and administrative support during my tenure as CEO. His constant advice had been certainly important in making me survive for twenty months. When I handed the letter to him he smiled and told me "Good luck. Do not bother. The King has certainly seen what has happened. He knew about the fight"

My third child, Magdo, was visiting me and she stepped into my office just to receive the bad news. She started lamenting. I consoled her that it was not the end of life. What was certain was that at least the burden I had been carrying for twenty months was now over. I had suffered serious torture for the past twenty months. This was the time to rest, and think of how life would be in the coming years, if God gave me life. It was the time to live a life without insults from a boss. This was now the time that fingers would no longer be pointed to my eyes. I was free at last. Just as I was talking to my daughter the phone rang. That was my wife, Hannah. She was calling to tell me I had been replaced. "I am coming to help you pack your personal belongings out of your office. Never mind, have courage, we have to forge ahead. We shall pick up the ashes and proceed. Life must continue." I heaved a huge sigh of relief as I saw the big smile on her face. She hugged me and told me to keep hope alive. She told me the struggle had been too much for me; it was now time for me to rest and live a normal life and give support to my family. My family needed me. I had loaned out my life to Government and this was now the time to take it back for the benefit of my family. That was very consoling.

When I had finished packing my personal belongings in the office, I told my chief of cabinet and the secretary to take off for the day; our reign was now over. I called my driver to place my service car at the entrance of the office to go home. As I went down the stairs to get into the car, two military officers (gendarmes) intercepted me on the way. "Mr CEO. I hope you know you have been replaced." Yes, I know, I replied. "Please do not take a pin out of your office. It has to be closed now until your predecessor is installed in his functions." A scientist, head of the research center which was nearest the headquarters, an ugly looking *"moliki"* fellow had called them and told them that I was busy emptying my office, taking away government property because I had been fired. The military officers, behaving like dunces were taking the law in their hands, by rushing to get me out of my office even without the instructions of their boss.

I got into my car and was about to drive home when the head of the military police, accompanied by the district officer of our area stopped me. "Mr CEO, we hear you have been replaced. Never mind, go back to your office and work until the new person is inaugurated." But I did not have the strength to go back and sit on that seat which I was never going to use again. I took off the day, went back home, settled in my veranda and began reflecting on how tedious the twenty-month journey had been.

Some days later, as I sat receiving workers who came to condole with me I started reflecting over the time I had spent in TRDI and the stories I had heard about Lena. I thought of the many things I had heard she had done as a minister. I had heard she had been very disrespectful to the PM. I had even learnt that she would boycott several cabinet meetings called by him. I said to myself that she was an impossible person and that it was nice that we had been separated; the *divorce* was certainly a good one. I had to mend the remnants and start a new life.

The second story that comes to my mind and which I affectionately like to recount with regard to the way I was treated by Lena is that of the Turkish War of Independence led by Mustafa Kemal. The Turkish War of Independence was fought from 19 May 1919 to 24 July 1923. It was a series of military campaigns waged by the Turkish National Movement, led by Mustafa Kemal Ataturk, a high-ranking officer in World War I. He became the leader of the Turkish National Movement, after parts of the Ottoman Empire were occupied and partitioned following Turkey's defeat in World War I. The military campaigns were directed against Greece in the west, Armenia in the east, France in the south, and Britain and Italy in Constantinople (now Istanbul). These campaigns led to the creation of the Republic of Turkey.

The Ottoman Empire had been a state that controlled much of Southeastern Europe, Western Asia, and Northern Africa between the

14th and early 20th centuries. It had been founded at the end of the 13th century by the Turkoman tribal leader, Osman I. After 1354, the Ottomans crossed into Europe and with the conquest of the Balkans, was transformed into a transcontinental empire.

Mustafa Kemal Atatürk, given the name Atatürk in 1934 (meaning "Father of the Turks"), in recognition of the role he had played in building the modern Turkish Republic, was a Turkish field marshal, statesman and the founder of the Republic of Turkey. He had served as its first president from 1923 until his death in 1938. He had undertaken sweeping progressive reforms which modernized Turkey into a secular, industrial nation in Europe. Due to his military and political accomplishments, Atatürk was regarded as one of the most important political leaders of the 20th century.

Atatürk had become prominent in Europe for his role in securing the victory of the Ottoman Turkish in the Battle of Gallipoli in 1915 during World War I. Following the defeat and dissolution of the Ottoman Empire, he led the Turkish National Movement, which resisted mainland Turkey's partition among the victorious Allied powers. Establishing a provisional government in the present-day Turkish capital Ankara (known in English at the time as Angora), he defeated the forces sent by the Allies, thus emerging victorious from what later became known as the Turkish War of Independence. He subsequently proceeded to abolish the Ottoman Empire and proclaimed the foundation of the Turkish Republic in its place. In addition to these accomplishments, Kemal Ataturk was remembered by many for his firmness and bravery. In one of his encounters he sent people to the battleground. His forces were facing serious casualties. The head of the forces he had sent to the field realized that his army was being destroyed by opposing forces. Embarrassed by the situation, he wanted to save the situation and sent a telegram to Mustafa Kemal: *"Marshal, where is the defence line?"* But Kemal replied, *"There is no defence line. There is a defence area which is the whole country. Not an inch of it is to be given up until it is wet with Turkish blood.*

As the president of the newly formed Turkish Republic, Atatürk initiated a rigorous program of political, economic, and cultural reforms whose aim was to build a modern, progressive and secular country. He made primary education free and compulsory, opening thousands of new schools all over the country, introducing the Latin-based Turkish alphabet which replaced the old Ottoman Turkish alphabet. He gave Turkish women equal civil and political rights such as voting rights in local elections and full universal suffrage. He carried out a policy of *Turkification*, which tried to create a homogeneous and unified nation. Kemal Ataturk became so important that in 1981, the centennial of his birth, his memory was honoured by the United Nations and UNESCO, which declared it *The Atatürk Year in the World* and adopted the Resolution on the Ataturk Centennial, describing him as "the leader of the first struggle given against colonialism and imperialism" and a "remarkable promoter of the sense of understanding between peoples and durable peace between the nations of the world and that he worked all his life for the development of harmony and cooperation between peoples without distinction." Atatürk was since commemorated by many memorials, and several places were named in his honor in Turkey and throughout the world.

Lena was aiming to be as powerful as Mustafa Kemal. She wanted to conquer all the research institute directors of the institutions under the supervisory authority of the Ministry of Rural Development Investigations. She wanted to be known as the Minister who would do everything to have fired any director who went against her policy of grabbing. But unlike Kemal, she was so full of greed that instead of building a strong Ministry with innovated institutions, she wanted to amass all the fortune she could from those institutes and from everywhere in the poorly controlled Federal Republic of Tropicana. She succeeded in making herself rich and she is still there amassing wealth in a country where several people cannot boast of having one square meal in a day. Many remember her only for the wealth she has accumulated over the years and the terribly fetish means she has used to acquire them and achieve her goals. Recently, she was under investigation by the Supreme State Audit for swindling funds acquired by the Government for saving lives affected by the viral pandemic. God alone knows what decision will be taken against her. As usual she would count on her roots in the King's Palace for a cover up. But how long that cover up would go for someone who is never satisfied with wealth is a matter difficult to predict.

I dreamt I wrote a memo which turned out to be viral. It was titled: "Greed, ethnicity, tribalism and administrative power: a post-mortem of Lena's Institute." In it I outlined the greed in Lena, the wealth she had accumulated for the time she had been there, her ethnic tendencies in the institutes and her tribalistic feelings during her reign as Minister. The memo reached the King's palace, and in one of my trips abroad some months later I was privileged to be given a copy of the document. Journalists had carried out an exhaustive analysis about it and it became not only an interesting analysis of corruption in the Federal Republic of Tropicana, but was now considered a major contribution to financial management of people of power in Tropical Africa. I laughed. At least my memo had had an impact, if nothing else.

CHAPTER 12

Managing funds, personnel and research

. . . .

RESEARCH MANAGERS MANAGE FUNDS, EMPLOYEES AND RESEARCH activities. As the means of acquiring funds increased in some research institutes government backed up from providing sufficient funds for research, in favor of the military, public health and education. But expectations among investors and regulators also grew, requiring several partners to require institutions to develop new strategies and efficiencies in assembling, managing, and reporting on pooled funds received than ever before. Once a relatively simple task, fund administration had become a resource-intensive and complex activity requiring a higher and greater expertise, and more sophisticated technologies than ever before even with the meager funds provided by the Government. In the past decade before I was made CEO, the private capital industry had changed, and grown dramatically including increased regulatory scrutiny, heightened investor expectations for accountability, rising administrative costs resulting from audit and control, and broader compliance obligations.

Initially, our agricultural research institute was required to produce results for growers and the industry and nothing else. The institute could not engage in any activity that could bring profit to its coffers. An experiment would be harvested and after data collection, the harvest would be abandoned in the field to rot. But as time went on it was found that the products from research trials could at least be consumed by workers or sold to make some money for the institute. There were pros and cons to this. Those supporting the use of research products by the institute argued that the funds generated could supplement the meager funds being sent by government. Those against that insisted that the funds generated could be mismanaged by scientists whose products were being sold. They felt that if that had to be done, the funds generated had to be accounted for in the same rigorous manner government funds were controlled. Those against the idea also argued that research products could be toxic to consumers and livestock and would entail law suits, creating an additional burden to the institute. The story was recounted one time of a cassava harvest in which roots were collected by field workers and sold to a passer-by who fed them to his pigs in his piggery. The pigs were all killed after they consumed the raw roots. It became a big scandal that the talk was that research cassava had killed peoples' pigs. It was too late when the pig farmer was told that cassava roots contained two cyanogenic glucosides (linamarin and lotaustralin) which were easily converted to hydrocyanic acid (HCN) after hydrolysis. The pigs had been killed by HCN. Therefore the roots ought to have been boiled to remove the HCN since that acid was easily removed by heat. Glucosides (which are molecules in which a sugar is bound to another functional group via a glycosidic bond) normally play numerous important roles in living organisms. Many plants store chemicals in the form of inactive glycosides. Although hydrocyanic acid is a violent poison, oral intake of cyanogenic glucosides for example via foods, such as raw cassava roots especially in primitive diets is not necessarily toxic particularly in the short term. It is the hydrolysis of the glycosides by the digestive tract or by the liver which leads to a slow release of hydrocyanic acid. Even that is readily detoxified by the body.

Cyanogenic glycosides are substrates for the enzyme myrosinase producing thiocyanate, a chemical that can inhibit thyroid function. Cyanogenic glycosides have amino acid–derived aglycones, compounds remaining after the glycosyl group on a glycoside is replaced by a hydrogen atom. They are often considered to be a safety concern in medicinal plants. For example, the aglycone of a cardiac glycoside would be a steroid molecule. Cyanogenic glucosides have always been considered to be mostly a safety concern in medicinal plants. The concerns about these glycosides have been that these compounds interfere with iodine organification and thus can cause or promote goiter and hypothyroidism in the long-run. Unfortunately, there are a variety of introduced plants that contain cyanogenic glycosides, which yield hydrogen cyanide upon hydrolysis. Not only cattle can be affected by them. Ruminants are particularly susceptible to toxicosis from these plants, because the rumen flora produces large amounts of β-glucosidase, an enzyme which hydrolyses the glycosides to hydrogen cyanide (HCN). Many foods also have cyanogenic glycosides in them. There are approximately 25 cyanogenic glycosides known which contain cyanogenic glycosides found in the edible parts of plants such as amygdalin (in almonds); dhurrin (in sorghum); linamarin (in cassava and lima beans), lotaustralin (in cassava and lima beans); prunasin (in stone fruit); and taxiphyllin (in bamboo shoots), all eaten by humans and sometimes fed to livestock. Therefore, although so much negative propaganda had been made of research cassava killing farmers' pigs, it happened only because the roots were not boiled. Cassava roots had never been a killer.

As I was supposed to manage research, so also did I have to manage the personnel working for the research. It was my role to prioritize employee safety and wellbeing. I was supposed to enhance productivity with a single connected experience, and use all modern techniques to manage employee devices. But I lacked IT devices such as attendance clocking machines to tract late-comers and absentees, items which were common in workplaces in developed countries.

I had to be innovative in managing physical locations by providing employees with a safer environment, which would safeguard and support employee safety and wellbeing in those locations. To do this I had planned to establish health centers in each remote station and the headquarters to ensure the health of employees. I had the huge task of engaging research teams of diverse disciplines at work at those remote locations and onsite. These all required perfect internet connections which had to be permanent over a long period of time. It was my duty also to support the flow of work wherever it happened remotely and onsite, a massive task given the distance that had to be covered if I had to do constant supervision. To do this I had to ensure that everyone stayed connected, productive, and secure. This was to ensure that the institution quickly responded to the needs of government, the growers and the industry we served. Progress had to be communicated to the press to make sure that the population was aware of what we were doing.

And as circumstances changed, new innovations in communication of research results had to be developed.

I needed to understand the key principles which needed to confidently bring employees back to the workplace and how customizable, pre-built sclutions could help. I also had to utilize a turnkey solution allowing for the Institute's continuity, and support the health of employees and their families, as well as understanding the key workforce transformation scenarios as time went on so as to get the most from both onsite and remote physical locations. These all had to do with enhancing productivity of the institute.

In spite of all the efforts I had put, I faced a lot of stress in managing the Institute especially the funds which were sent to me to run the Institute. The first budget I received was the running cost budget. This was fairly easy to use because the funds were credited to our account in the central treasury and they came with a letter of notification which stipulated precisely what that money could be used for. The letter of notification indicated six budgetary lines – bills for electricity, water, and telephone, out-of-station allowances, salaries of locally (institute) recruited staff as well as allowances paid to appointed staff of the institute including the CEO. The running cost budget came in six instalments, each coming after the previous instalment had been accounted for. The stress in executing that budget came from the fact that since those funds came directly to the account of the institute, many eyes were on them. It was as if this was liquid cash put in the pocket or private safe of the CEO. The Minister could make any request from those funds and expect to be satisfied, otherwise the CEO would be accused of insubordination. On the other hand, if I made the slightest error in using the funds away from the stipulated budgetary lines, even if the expenditure was for the institute, that was considered embezzlement and could lead me to jail. The unfortunate thing was that my Minister considered those funds as liquid cash enjoyed by the CEO and because of that she made frequent requests from them even though she knew how implicating misuse of the money could be.

The second funding was for the infrastructure budget. This budget was for the construction and maintenance of staff houses, purchase of capital equipment and tools – computer supplies, field equipment and other capital materials. The procedure for using this was that contractors would compete for bids published by the Institute, the bid winners make their supplies or implement their contracts and be paid from the institute account directly by the treasury of the country. Those funds never came to the institute. The stress I had here was that I had to ensure every now and then that the work for which the contractors had been given was well done before the payment could be authorized. However, it was not that easy to oversee those jobs. Contractors were interested in making the most profit so they would do the work barely optimally and think of corrupting the CEO to sign off their payments in the treasury.

Another stressful situation I faced was regarding the retirement of staff. The policy in the country was that the retirement age was 55 for senior staff and 50 years for lower employees. I would send scientists for higher degree training, they would come back with their doctorate degrees only to find out that there were letters awaiting them from the Ministry of Public Service informing them that they had been sent on retirement. This was frustrating to me. The stress here was that if any of such staff members was heading a project, he would leave the institute and the project would fail because there would be no project head to direct the activities to the end. The institute lost several people and some projects in that situation.

A major stress I faced as CEO was not only in acquiring but in the accounting of research funds. Of the four kinds of funds available for research funds received by the institute for research activities conducted within regional networks could be problematic to account for. The funds obtained from international research projects and funds from expatriate research in the institute were usually simpler but could be very complicated if the money was used for lines other than those approved lines. Of these the most stressful were government subventions for scientific research. The procedure for obtaining these funds was that I would start by creating a regional programs committee in each agro-ecological zone. This committee was made up of various stakeholders – farmer organizations, the civil society, representatives from technical ministries (agriculture, livestock, and forestry) and scientists in the region. They would identify the field constraints brought by growers and translate these into researchable issues. These research issues would then be forwarded to the headquarters of the institute where they would be collated and evaluated by a national programs committee. After their evaluation, they would then be examined and approved by a scientific committee (of eminent scientists) created by the CEO. The results of that examination would then be sent to the Ministry of Rural Development Investigations to be forwarded to the national assembly to vote the research budget of the institute.

The procedure was not over yet. The Ministry of the Treasury would now discretionally decide to credit the research account as funds were received by the government from its tax revenues. The stress here was that research was considered to be of very low priority and sometimes the year would end when less than half of the approved budget by the National Assembly had reached the institute. This would affect several research operations which depended on those funds.

But that was just the beginning of the process. Once funds had been received managing of the various scientific research projects often required a variety of organizational and leadership skills. It was generally assumed that scientists would naturally acquire these skills over time due to experiences with failed experiments, planning a research question, and writing manuscripts. However, when I took over as CEO I was forced to remind scientists in the first meeting I held at the headquarters with the heads of research centers that there were six steps in conducting scientific research. The very first was to define the problem. The second step was to formulate a hypothesis. Then the third was to design the experiment. After that the experiment was implemented in the field and data would be collected, and this had to be done meticulously. This was then followed by a good statistical analysis of the data. The final step was the drawing of conclusions. If this had been properly done the scientist would observe useful trends which could be communicated to the public or documented in a scientific paper. The chiefs of centers listened very attentively. I urged them to remind their scientists of those steps and to ensure that they were properly implemented.

In spite of the fact that the bulk of the work to identify what activities had to be performed had been done by the regional programs committees in each agro-ecological zone, I was forced to remind them how they had to plan and conduct a scientific experiment no matter its nature. I told them that designing a scientific experiment involved careful and exhaustive planning as to how the scientist was going to execute the trial in the field or laboratory, and how to carefully collect their data. It could be likened to the making a good plan for the construction of a house, the more time that the architect spent on making modifications during the planning phase, the less adjustments the builder would make in the final structure. Often, the nature of the research question influenced how the scientific research had to be conducted and how the data had to be collected. For example, for a research project in the social sciences where information was needed from peoples' opinions on the newly developed technology, researching people's opinions naturally required conducting surveys and implementing structured or semi-structured questionnaires. In an on-farm trial a proper selection of growers and making an attempt to "uniformize" the field plots could be crucial in the collection of data and the eventual results that could be obtained.

I showed that the best way to do research was first to begin with identifying a problem to solve. Usually the constraints identified by the regional programs committees could be quite vague. Thoroughly researching a topic and identifying gaps in knowledge was the best place to start with the research. It is from there that the scientist could properly design their experiments, perform them, gather and analyze their data, and eventually submit their work to the public of send their articles for publication. Therefore what the scientist had to do in the process was to record the data properly from beginning to the end and complete the tasks required in the conduct of these experiments.

Funds that were received from research networks in the region or from international organizations were a lot easier to manage because they came directly to the institute. The CEO just had to open a separate account in a commercial bank with the project head and institute accountant as signatories. Such research activities were smoothly executed and the CEO only had to supervise the dishing out of funds as were needed by the coordinator of the project.

Funds were also received for expatriate scientists working in various programs in the institute. These funds were managed directly by the organizations which sent the scientists. In such cases the organizations recruited a chief of party to control their scientists, oversee their activities and then manage their funds. The Institute had no hands in their management. In fact in some cases the chiefs of party were just like CEOs managing both their funds and their scientists. The only issue was that some research projects would be finalized and sometimes even published without the Institute knowing that the work had been concluded. In such instances they would not be seen to contribute to the growth of scientists of the Institute. What a pity!

CHAPTER 13

Managing medical challenges

• •

NOW RETIRING IN MY PRIVATE HOME IN THE CAPITAL OF THE COUNTRY after a hectic stay as CEO of TRDI, I was resting in my sitting room one day when a friend Paul came to see me. When the guard ushered him in, we sat in the veranda and started chatting on a variety of issues, from childhood memories to adulthood professional life. The conversation led him to ask me how I was feeling as far as my health was concerned because he knew I had gone through a lot of stress that may have caused some harm to my health. I replied him that certainly the many stresses had caused a lot of harm to my health. I told him about my blood pressure which had been constant at 120/80 over most of my scientific life but which abruptly started to increase from 138/82 when I became CEO. I told him that as CEO I had several difficult decisions to take for the twenty months I was there, adding that I still believed that most of the stress came from my relations with my Minister although a little few were also from disloyal officers who were working with me.

He wanted to know how high blood pressure could be related to the kind of work I had been doing. I replied that the only probable cause of the increase of my blood pressure could only be from an unfavourable work environment. We then joked over the issue of aging which could also be playing its tole and affecting me at this point of my life.

I told him that, as far as I could recount from my church lessons, the Biblical perspective on aging was that aging was a universal part of life often associating growing old with gaining wisdom. For example, in the book of Proverbs 16:31 it is said that, "Gray hair is a crown of glory; it is gained in a righteous life." The Bible also reminds us that even if we live a relatively long life, life on earth is short: For you are a mist that appears for a little time and then vanishes" (James 4:14). Now talking as a preacher, I told him that eternal life was partly spent on Earth and the rest in Heaven. And that varied with individuals. Some could spend most of it on Earth and just a little bit of it in Heaven. Others could spend only a short part of that Eternal life on Earth but most of it in Heaven. All depended on the decision God had taken on that individual.

I went on to give him an analogy of the automobile and the aging process. When you buy a brand new SUV, you can make long distances comfortably with it. But after a short time, you would need to change the oil and its oil filter. It won't take too long again to change the brake pads. You take the van to the service center and they change them and bury the worn out pads. Then after a few other years, the dash board would start indicating overheating showing that the thermostat was telling you that the radiator had developed a leak. Then you would take the van to a service center and the radiator would be replaced, burying the old one. You may drive well and smoothly for some time again, may be five years or so and then have to change the transmission system. And then, the engine may start worrying to the point that you would want to have it replaced. That was the aging process in a man-made thing.

That is how the human body too is. Under unfavourable working conditions, hypertension could set in. The blood pressure is high when the force of blood pushing against the walls of your arteries which carry blood from your heart to other parts of your body is high. Hypertension could be easy to treat but could also be considered a serious medical condition because people with the condition have a higher risk for heart disease and other medical problems than people with normal blood pressure. The condition could even lead to other complications as kidney damage. About four months as CEO I started seeing the signs and symptoms of hypertension such as early morning headaches, irregular heart rhythms, vision changes, and buzzing in the ears, although generally most people with hypertension are unaware of the problem because it may have no warning signs or symptoms. For this reason, I started seeing a family doctor who put me on antihypertensive medication and began measuring my blood pressure regularly. The pill bottles started increasing in number, as more ailments were diagnosed.

I then recounted to him how another friend in a similar administrative position like me was feeling when he saw a doctor and was suddenly diagnosed with hypoglycaemia, an endocrine disorder that caused blood glucose to rise above its normal pre-prandial level of between 70-140 mg of glucose per decilitre of blood. I explained that in that condition normally your body does not use insulin properly. The condition called insulin resistance, makes cells of the body such as the muscles, liver and fat cells fail to respond to insulin even when the levels are high. In Type II diabetes the body either produces insufficient amounts of insulin to meet the body's demands or it may be that insulin resistance has developed. It was unfortunate that when you had Type II diabetes, the condition, being an endocrine disease, affected other organs of the body and could even lead to more serious health complications.

I told him that the progression of health challenges during aging was also related to the kind of activity you were engaged in. Even before becoming CEO I had been diagnosed with an intervertebral disc prolapse between the 5th lumber vertebra and the 1st sacral vertebra, which the doctors said was as a result of my constant trips to unpaved roads to research sites. A spinal disc herniation, commonly referred to as a slipped disc, could happen when unbalanced mechanical pressures substantially deformed the *anulus fibrosus*, allowing part of the nucleus to obtrude. It is the compression of nerves by the obtruded anulus which causes the excruciating pain felt when you have a slipped disc. Anatomically there is one disc between each pair of vertebrae. There are 23 discs in the human spine: 6 in the neck (cervical) region, 12 in the middle back (thoracic) region, and 5 in the lower back (lumbar) region. Any one could give way at any time. Discs are named by the vertebral body above and below. For example, in my case, the disc between the fifth lumbar and first sacral vertebrae which was defective was designated "L5-S1.The intervertebral fibrocartilage which lies between adjacent vertebrae in the vertebral column forms a joint (a symphysis) in each disc which allows slight movement of the vertebrae, acting as a ligament to hold the vertebrae together, and thus functioning as a shock absorber for the spine. A defected disc could be treated by complete removal or conservatively by traction to increase the intervertebral space.

To make him understand what I was telling him about the spinal injury, I told him that an intervertebral disc consists of an outer fibrous ring, the *anulus fibrosus*, which surrounds an inner gel-like center, the *nucleus pulposus.* The *anulus fibrosus* consists of several layers (laminae) of <u>fibrocartilage</u> made of collagen. The fibrous intervertebral disc contains the *nucleus pulposus* and this helps to distribute pressure evenly across the disc, preventing the development of stress concentrations which could cause damage to the underlying vertebrae. The nucleus pulposus contains loose fibers suspended in a mucoprotein gel. Under normal conditions the nucleus of the disc acts as a shock absorber, absorbing the impact of the body's activities such as lifting and pushing of objects and keeping the two vertebrae separated. But if the annulus fibrosus was torn as a result of trauma, the nucleus pulposes would protrude and compress any nerve root such as that of the sciatic nerve and cause pain all along the leg which is supplied by that nerve.

For four full months I suffered from physical stress from the prolapsed disc. I could not even walk. The treatment I received in the National Center for the Rehabilitation of the Handicapped involved traction, massage and exercise, but it was too slow. At one time I nearly gave up the slow conservative treatment to go and have a discectomy. Discectomy is the surgical procedure to remove the damaged portion of a herniated disk in your spine. A herniated disk can irritate or compress nearby nerves. A discectomy is most effective for treating pain that radiates down your arms or legs. The procedure is less helpful for treating actual back pain or neck pain. Most people who have back pain or neck pain find relief with more-conservative treatment. I was lucky that my slipped disc gradually healed from conservation treatment but the doctor cautioned that I could have a recurrence of the problem at any time if I misused my spine by weight lifting objects in inappropriate positions or if I drove in vehicles with poor spring systems. I did everything to avoid that and bought myself comfortable automobiles even though I knew that would provoke attraction from my bosses also.

I had sustained an ankle injury in one of my trips to the University of Ghana where I had gone to examine my doctoral students in the West Africa Center for Crop Improvement. Surgery had been performed in the reference hospital in the economic capital of Tropicana. The operation had led to a bone infection (osteomyelitis). Osteomyelitis is an infection in a bone. Infections can reach a bone by traveling through the bloodstream or spreading from nearby tissue. Infections can also begin in the bone itself if an injury exposes the bone to germs. People with chronic health conditions, such as diabetes or kidney failure, could be more at risk of developing osteomyelitis.

To have better treatment I had made a trip to the Memorial Hospital of the University of North Carolina at Chapel Hill where corrective surgery was done by a nice vascular surgeon, Dr Luigi Pascarella, and the ulcer was treated until it was healed by a team consisting of Dr Alex Keagy, Kelly Sluss and Morgan Wamblo. But during the 2-month stay in the hospital other health challenges had been diagnosed, namely a heart problem and eventually a kidney problem.

Apart from the osteomyelitis, the first disorder which was diagnosed when I was admitted in the Memorial Hospital was congestive heart failure. This disorder occurs when the heart muscle doesn't pump blood as well as it should. When this happens, blood often backs up and fluid can build up in the lungs, causing shortness of breath. Certain heart conditions, such as narrowed arteries in the heart (coronary artery disease) or high blood pressure gradually leave the heart too weak or stiff to fill and pump blood properly. Proper treatment can improve the signs and symptoms of heart failure and may help some people live longer. Lifestyle changes — such as losing weight, exercising, reducing intake of salt (sodium) in your diet and managing stress — can improve your quality of life. However, heart failure can be life-threatening. People with heart failure may have severe symptoms, and some may even need a heart transplant.

My prolonged hospitalization accompanied by heavy doses of antibiotics to treat the osteomyelitis that had resulted from my ankle surgery logically led to end-stage renal disease. End-stage kidney disease occurs when the gradual loss of kidney function (that is, chronic kidney disease) reaches an advanced state in which the kidneys are no longer able to work as they should to meet the body's needs of filtering wastes and excess fluids from the blood. What could follow is dialysis where an artificial kidney is made to do the work that the kidneys had been doing.

That reminds me about what a journalist friend called Charlie had told me. He said he had told his family to preserve his liver in a special place after his death, because he believed that his liver was really special.

He could drink all the liquor around and still feel normal. That strain on the liver did not appear to do him any visible harm. Weighing around 3 pounds in adulthood (roughly the size of a football) your liver is your body's largest solid organ. It removes toxins from the body's blood supply, maintains healthy blood sugar levels, regulates blood clotting, and performs hundreds of other vital functions. It is vital to the body's metabolic functions and immune system. Without a functioning liver, a person cannot survive.

When my visitor friend was curious to know about why there were vast differences in the way humans responded to environmental stress, I gave him an analogy using trees in the forest. I told him jokishly that humans were actually manufactured from different kinds of wood in the forest. One example was President Jimmy Carter who in his 97th birthday just celebrated recently was still looking strong and kicking. Using the analogy of different species of woods in the forest I told him that some people had been manufactured with bubinga, others with iroko, others with mahogany while others still were manufactured with white wood.

The Bubinga tree (*Guibourtia* spp) is an extremely large tree, found in Central Africa. It can grow upwards of 150 feet in height, with long, clear trunks 3 to 6 feet in diameter. It is extremely strong, exceeding nearly every other species, making it near resistant to splitting. Due to its hardness and toughness, bubinga is often used in high-end furniture, acoustic and electric guitars and for high-end manual woodworking tools. When used for construction there is little worry that the wood will dent, split, or break. Probably those who live longer than 90 like President Jimmy Carter were those manufactured with bubinga.

Iroko (*Milicia* spp.) is a large, very durable hardwood tree from the west coast of tropical Africa that can live up to 500 years. The wood is used for a variety of purposes including the construction of pews, boat-building, domestic flooring, furniture and outdoor gates. It is also believed to have healing properties. I would say those living between 85 and 89 were made with iroko.

Mahogany *(Swietenia spp)* is a straight-grained, reddish-brown tropical hardwood timber, indigenous to the Americas and part of the pantropical chinaberry family, Meliaceae. Mahogany is a commercially important lumber prized for its beauty, durability, and color, and used for paneling and for making furniture, boats, musical instruments and other items. I would place those living from 80 to 84 in the category made with mahogany.

Whitewood, classified as softwood, actually refers to wood that comes from the tulip tree (*Liriodendron tulipifera*) and sometimes colloquially called the American tulip tree, tulip poplar, fiddle-tree, or yellow poplar. It varies in color from creamy white to pale straw with occasional contrasting orange/brown growth rings. White Pine, especially White birch is one of the most versatile of woods and it is used in cabinet making and in building and furniture making. Those individuals who do not live up to eighty years are probably made from white wood.

My conclusion was that if an individual was lucky to have been manufactured with hardwood he would find himself staying longer than another who had been made with whitewood. He laughed but I think the message had gone through.

CHAPTER 14

Tropicana Bureau of Investigations

· ·

A MAJOR STRESSOR I HAD WHEN I BECAME CEO WAS MY DEALING WITH the Tropicana Bureau of Investigations (TBI). This agency had been created a long time ago as an agency of the Tropicana government that dealt with internal security and counter-intelligence. Although its main job was to protect the government from terrorist attack and foreign intelligence operations, the TBI extended its activities by spending a huge part of its time protecting the laws in the constitution, especially the combat of public corruption at all levels. It also investigated violent crimes and white-collar crimes (such as bribery for personal financial gain) within the country. It also investigated fraud and embezzlement, as well as civil rights of citizens mostly civil servants in government. The TBI then became the top law enforcement agency of the Federal Republic of Tropicana. Through its work, several Ministers and CEO were sent to jail.

When my problems with Lena had reached their peak, she sent confidential petitions all over the country to find faults in me so that she could eventually get rid of me. That is how, on her instructions, I got to be known by the TBI.

One evening I had a phone call from the Director of the TBI. He introduced himself and told me he wanted to talk to me about a hot issue that concerned me. He told me it was highly confidential and that I had to make sure that there was no one in my office to hear what he was about to discuss with me. I became frightened. I had never had anything to do with the TBI. I did not even know who the Director was and what his functions were. I was wondering what he really had to do with me. He had a brief chat with me during which he gave me an appointment to come to his office at 1:00 am the following morning. I wondered why he wanted to see me that late. At 1:00 am people would normally be deeply asleep.

When I reached my home I told my wife that I wanted to discuss something with her which was highly confidential. "I have received a phone call from the director of the TBI. Frankly, I have done nothing wrong to warrant a meeting with the TBI. The only problem I have with a member of government is the problem of 700,000 USD which I had with Lena. I would be going to see the TBI director at 1:00 am. If anything happened to me she should know that it had been done in that office."

I told my driver to get ready and that he was going to take me to a certain office very very early that morning. He was surprised with the late appointment. I instructed him to go down to the filling station and fill the tank with gas and be ready. He also told his wife that he was going out with me very early that morning and insisting that if anything happened to him and me she should contact my wife, who had information regarding where we were going.

At 12:30 am we left the house and twenty minutes later we were in the office. The office building was in a hugely fenced premises with a solid gate. Entry into the compound was strictly forbidden except you were ushered into the premises by a guard in the place. The driver had to park out of the gate when we reached there. There was a small parking lot outside the fence where non-office vehicles could park. There was a gentleman by the gate waiting for me. We did the last prayer with my driver in the car, and I told him a final goodbye because I did not know what was going to happen with me inside that compound.

The gateman led me to a small conference room that could contain about thirty people at a time. I spent about thirty minutes there alone then another gentleman came in and led me into another room; it was slightly smaller than the first office. I spent another thirty-five minutes there then another officer took me to another office, a much smaller one. Here he verified information about my identity to be sure I was the person the director really wanted to see. After getting the information he wanted he left me and went back, I suppose, to his office. I was there alone for another one hour when another gentleman came in and took me. He led me through several corridors until we reached a solid metal door. Here, he used a code to open the door. He then led me to another office and gave me a seat. My heart was throbbing. I was now in real distress because I concluded that that was the end of my life. I thought of my wife, how peaceful a life we had lived before I was made CEO. We had lived a relatively happy life without the problems I was having with the post of CEO. I thought of my few investments in town and wondered who was going to have the interest to complete them. Then I thought of my extended family which depended so much on me for their sustenance. So many things came to my mind. I thought of my children and wondered who was going to give them the care and love I had been giving them. Now they were going to be raised by a single parent. What a massive task for my wife alone! Then I thought of what was going on in the mind of my wife as she lay on the bed in the house without me. Was she already thinking I had been murdered? If I had been killed, had I been shot. And was I now just bleeding profusely? Or had I just been poisoned in the office of the director. In which mortuary would she start looking for me early that morning?

After some forty-five minutes in that office, a huge man with a rigidly waxed moustache stepped into the door with a big folder. He greeted me, "good morning, how are you doing?" I greeted back politely, my heart beating like a drum. Then he started interrogating me. "Are you the CEO of the TRDI? How do you like your job? How many budgets do you operate in your Institute? How do you use the government funds which are in your keeping? What kind of relationship do you have with your board chairman? How is your relationship with your Minister?"

I tried to answer all the questions I could answer and gave him all the information I could give. Why was he asking whether I liked my job? What did he want to do with that kind of information? So many questions lingered in my mind. He took notes as I spoke, and asked more questions where he needed precision. He stepped out of the office for some time and left me alone. I thought he was going to get a soldier I had met as I entered the first office. Perhaps that was the person he was calling to come and *eliminate* me. I became even very worried until a few minutes later when I saw him come back alone into the office where he had left me. I watched closely; he did not come with a soldier, neither did he have a gun. I heaved a sigh of relief. Now I started thinking of what he was going to do as he examined the folder he had, page after page.

Then in his heavy voice, he told me the reason he had invited me so late. He told me that the kind of work they were doing was such that the information they gathered was very confidential. It went straight to the King. The persons who had ushered me into that office only knew he wanted to see me but no one knew what the subject of the encounter was. He told me the folder he was consulting concerned me. "Your Minister has accused you of embezzlement," he said. "She has sent in a report that a certain sum of money in the amount of 700,000 USD which was meant for the humanitarian activities of the Queen had been used up by you. And that despite the many letters she had written to you to transfer the funds, you had failed to remit the money just because you had used up the money for yourself." He added that other accusations she had levied against me were insubordination, non respect of hierarchy, my inability to respect her, my calling her that she was a prostitute and that she was going out with young men much younger than her.

Then he told me to defend myself from all accusations which the member of government had made against me. I went on to explain to him that I could not insult my Minister and whether or not she was going out with men was not my business; that was her private life. I told him that the accusation about insubordination was simply because of the 700,000 USD she had asked me to give her which I was not prepared to give because I did not have authoritzation from my board nor from the Minister-Secretary of the Treasury to effect that transfer. I went on to explain that I had been given budgetary lines from the Minister of the Treasury for any funds my Institute received from government, and that those funds had to be spent only according to a *letter of notification* which accompanied the funds. I concluded that as far as I was concerned the notification letter was my Bible and I faithfully executed the prescription given in that letter.

He listened very attentively and after I had finished speaking he told me that the file had been closed and that he was satisfied with the explanations I had given and was now ready to transmit his report to the King's palace. He told me to go back home and continue with my work.

I was led out of that office by another gentleman who passed with me from one corridor to the other until I was outside the building. I kept looking back if someone else was following me with a short gun, because until I got into my SUV I was not sure my life was safe. My driver welcomed me back when he saw me enter the van and immediately started the vehicle. He drove off and in the next twenty minutes I was back home. It was already morning, about 5:00 am. I had spent the whole night talking with the security instead of sleeping. I was too tired to recount a thing to my wife. I went straight to bed and slept till late in the afternoon. I got up from sleep only when my board chairman got me up with a phone call. He told me he was in the office but he had not seen my car in the CEO's parking space, and was wondering what had happened to me. I told him I was not feeling well and I had sent for my doctor to come and consult me in the house. The story ended there.

Two weeks after that interrogation, I was sleeping in my home when the guards called me that there was a group of four people who wanted to see me very badly. They told me that they felt I was already deep asleep as it was 11:30 pm. But that since the people insisted on seeing me, they took the risk to get me up from bed. I instructed them to control them and usher them to my patio in the waiting veranda where I usually received casual visitors. I took off my pyjamas and put on a shirt and pair of trousers and came out to see them.

They introduced themselves as members of the Tropicana Territorial Security Agency (TTSA). I had never heard of the TTSA before for the past thirty-four years that I had been a civil servant in the Federal Republic of Tropicana. They said that the TTSA was an independent federal government agency which was responsible for providing national security intelligence to the various branches of government. They said the information they collected was to protect both the citizens and the government. The intelligence information they gathered was to provide tactical and strategic business so as to pre-emp threats to citizens and national security objectives. The activities and analysis of situations they gathered were to keep the republic safe.

Then they came to the crux of the matter. They told me the reason they had come so late was not to disturb me from my sleep but to give me vital information which was meant to protect me. That the information was highly confidential the reason they did not call me before they came. And that they came so late so that they would be sure no one saw them or even heard what they wanted to tell me. They told me that their wish was that I would keep the instructions they were going to give me to myself and abide by everything they were going to say.

"Your Minister is not in good terms with you. She has written so many letters to the King to replace you but the King is taking his time to act. So she has decided to act. Information which has reached us is that she wants to pay tugs to eliminate you. And it won't be long from now. It is our duty to protect the citizens of this country, and would certainly not want to see you killed because of one reason or the other. We do not know the details of her problems with you but what concerns us is that we want your life to be saved. From now and henceforth, when you are in town, never be in your car alone. Secondly, do whatever you had to do and return to your home before it is dark. Tugs prefer operating in the dark, when no one can identify them. Instruct your guards five minutes before you get to the house so that the gate is opened before your car reaches there. That way you will not have to wait even one minute for the gate to be opened before you get in. Tugs seize the fastest opportunity to act, and after their mission, they disappear. Do not go to drinking places because you do not know the team she has hired to do the act. Do not go to public ceremonies except meetings which are well guarded by the security."

I listened very attentively as they spoke. There were quite a good number of restrictions I had been given. I asked myself why I should live under such conditions. I had virtually become a prisoner in house arrest, although I was not really behind bars. Was that going to continue for long? What was sure was that I was not going to yield to Lena's request of 700,000 USD. What was also true was that I needed my freedom more than anything else. The jail was not for me. I would yield to any request from my boss as long as it was not implicating to me and get me in jail. I told myself that I was a Christian and that the requests of Lena were immoral and I could not succumb to them.

All along, Lena had made several requests. All had to do with money and property: sell government houses to fhrer relatives, give her money to repair her house in the village, give her money to make her contribution for the enthronement of their village chief, and other lousy things. I had tried my best to avoid her many temptations because from the beginning I had taken a vow not to misuse government money entrusted to me. I was going to stay with my vow. I had been brought up in a home where I could not boast of affluence. To say the least I had been raised in abject poverty. Now I had worked my way to becoming the CEO of TRDI. I had enough to feed my family and send my kids to school. I did not need to be very rich with money taken from government. I knew I would continue to live in the situation that the TTSA had recommended as long I did not yield to Lena's request. I knew she would keep pursuing me till I yielded. And since I would not yield, she would continue hating me, I would be in her bad books and probably she would keep pursuing me till she got the worst out of me.

The guys from TTSA finished speaking and took off. They did not ask a dime from me for giving me such vital information. For once I had a group of security people furnishing such important information for nothing. I was surprised.

I went back to bed but could not sleep again till morning. I kept thinking about what the people had told me. I finally disclosed the death threat to my wife. She got up from bed and asked me if those were not fake people who had come to disturb me. I told her that I believed they were authentic people because they finished talking to me and left immediately. They did not ask me for any tip, even fuel for the vehicle that had brought them to see me. I told her that I told one of the guards to see them off in a way to protect them and that on his return he told me the people parked their car about half a mile away so he could not accompany them right to where their car was. I told her I believed that was also indicative of the fact that they were genuine people.

My wife took her computer and googled the TTSA. She found out that their main function was to ensure the security of the territory and whoever lived in it. It was their job to protect me just as it was to protect a government Minister who was undergoing dead threats. Another of the duties was to advice the King about the source of threats which high officers of the State were facing. TTSA had a fairly large budget for their activities, as well as the technology to gather intelligence information very efficiently and in record time. They also had a team of experts who were trained to carry out analysis of the investigative information they brought back each day from the field. We now began to understand why they were not interested in any tip I could give them for providing me with information of that nature.

One month later, I had to make a trip out of the country to secure funding for an international research project. The project was on vegetable research. I was glad to make that trip because I had not been to Tanzania, an East African country, before. I had finished preparing the documents the organization had sent to me to prepare. I was very excited to make the trip because I was also going to meet some friends I had known in other international meetings. Also, the meeting was going to take me out of the routine of working too hard with government files and all kinds of financial files from contractors. I planned to take a day after the signing meeting to explore the town, much of which I had only heard of from reading books and listening to people. I would have the chance to see the so much-talked-of Mount Kilimanjaro, a popular dormant volcano in Tanzania, the highest mountain in Africa and the highest free-standing mountain (not being part of a mountain range) with its three cones – Kibo, Mawenzi and Shira - in the world with an altitude of 5,895 metres (19,341 feet) above sea-level.

That morning I got into the car and my driver took me to the airport. My driver had a policy of leaving the airport only after my aircraft had taken off. After I had finished the departure formalities and checked in I proceeded to the immigration. The police who I met in the counter looked at me and asked me a question, "are you the CEO of TRDI?" I said yes. He told me I could not make the trip. I asked him why I could not travel. He replied that my Minister had issued a travel ban, and being a member of government, they were bound to respect the instructions she had given. I immediately showed them my mission order duly signed by my board chairman. The police took his time to read through the mission order and found that it was regular and recognized the signature of the board chairman of TRDI a specimen of which was in their files. He left me and went and consulted his boss to ask what he thought could be done about the situation. He came back after twenty minutes.

"The document you have is genuine but we cannot let you travel." I was so embarrassed that I decided to call my board chairman on the phone to tell him what had happened. He told me that I should just obey and return to the office.

The following day I went to town and booked to see the Prime Minister. I had a letter of protest with me which I left with his director of cabinet. In the letter I was complaining that I was going out to look for money in an international research project and I was banned from travelling by my Minister after I had obtained a legitimate mission order from my board chairman authorizing the trip.

The Prime Minister had received my protest and sent it to one able director to investigate. In the Prime Minister's office there was an investigation service whose only job was to look into administrative problems of that nature. The service had all the government texts regarding top officers of government. They also had investigators who were sent out to the field to collect additional information to verify if the information in the protest was founded and accurate. They had lawyers to answer any legal questions that could arise from their investigation.

One month after I submitted my protest, a facsimile came to my office. It was from the Prime Minister's office. It read thus, "the travel ban of the CEO of Tropicana has been lifted. Only the board chairman of the TRDI has the ability to issue a travel ban of his CEO, and this could be done only if that trip conflicted with a major government gathering such as one in which the King was presiding."

My board chairman, who had received a copy of the fax, called me to discuss the matter with me. He was happy that his authority had been recognized as the only personality who could ban me from travelling. He was a nice person and he knew he could never ban my travelling as long as it was for the good of the Institute. He also knew that I could not just make a request to travel if the matter was not important enough to bring benefit to my Institute because the work load of the CEO alone was heavy enough to prevent me from travelling just for fun. At the time when resources were limited for the conduct of research, any opportunity the Institute had to bring in money was useful. That was a big victory for me although I had missed the opportunity of travelling to bring in the vegetable project in my Institute.

The next week the Indonesians invited me to come and give them my expertise on their oil palm germplasm which they had collected from Cameroon to build up their oil palm industry. My board chairman was glad to issue me a mission order to travel. He did it and I went. My Minister heard I had travelled and notified the Minister of National Security that I had fled the country because I had embezzled government funds. The Minister of National Security set up a commission to investigate the matter. The commission was headed by the director of frontier police. My Minister in her letter to the Minister of National Security had informed him that most likely the director of frontier police had received a handsome tip from me to have allowed me to travel out of the country. The director of frontier police told his Minister that I had regular papers to permit me to travel and did not see any reason why he could prevent me from travelling. He told his Minister that I was going to return, he was sure.

One week after my evaluation work in Indonesia, I returned to the country. The director of frontier police went and informed his Minister that I had returned to the country as he had told him. That story also ended there.

CHAPTER 15

Tropicana Supreme Audit Agency

· ·

THE NEXT MAJOR FRUSTRATING ENCOUNTER I HAD WAS MY DEALINGS
with the Tropicana Supreme Audit Agency, a branch of the Ministry of
the Supreme State Audit. The major role of that agency was to ensure
that the primary ideals of rigour and moralisation with regard to
government funds were followed by any government officer entrusted
with managing government funds. Through verification missions
carried within annual verification programs the Ministry of Supreme
State Audit is partner to public managers; it advises and gives support
to management. The services of Supreme State Control contribute to the
modernisation of the system for the external audit of the administration
and public enterprises, as well as professional bodies benefiting from
state grants. In their role as watchdogs of good administrative and
financial accounting management and performance of state structures,
these structures restore the authority of the state and maintain its
sovereignty.

With the Supreme State Audit, the Federal Republic of Tropicana
intends to win a threefold battle: the moralisation of the behaviour of
managers and public book-keepers, the good management of public
affairs and the fight against corruption, a gangrene to public life in
developing countries. Unfortunately, throughout the time I was in
government I realized that some of these managers happened to have
people in high places who could protect them in the event a sanctionable
offense was committed. This made them appear to be immune to
sanctions each time they embezzled funds or committed similar crimes.

Each time they were out on the field, the members of the mobile
mission team of the Supreme State Audit had a free hand vis-à-vis the
administrations and institutions that they are called upon to audit. They
were invested with all the powers of investigation and in the course

of their investigations, the members of the audit team could not be subjected to measures of detention without the consent of the King. The way things were organized was such that these audit measures were found to be not only at the highest level of public management but were also related in some way to the technical units charged with internal audit in the various ministries, institutions and public enterprises. The overall intention was to guarantee good economic and social management in the country. The goal of every audit mission was to ensure that the government preserved its economic gains, guaranteed the success of reforms undertaken and encouraged new investments. The objective was also to create more wealth and bring in more jobs in the country.

This was the ideological foundation of the new deal administration of the Federal Republic of Tropicana. The government had undertaken to encourage transparency in the management of public funds in particular and State affairs in general. The Ministry was responsible for enforcing proper financial management stipulated by the law of the land, and at the same time combat corruption, embezzlement, laxity in managing government funds and to fight all the malfunctions existing in public life in the country.

In order to make that the different measures which that Ministry of Supreme State Audit was taking were effective, the government had taken the irreversible step of political and economic reforms in order to reassure and gain the trust of the population, development partners as well as investors (local and foreign) of sustainable human and social development in the country. All culprits found really guilty of fraud and embezzlement accusations would be fully investigated and immediately sent to jail. There were all kinds of members of government in jail. In fact, the private press used to make jokes that there was a whole ministerial cabinet team, including a head of government in the central jails of the administrative and economic capitals of the country. Others used to comment that those guys could even plan a *coup d'etat* against the King with all the funds they had accumulated from embezzling government funds over the years. Some people even said that those high level criminals were kept in a high-security jail because government wanted them only to interact among themselves and not with the outside world. We even heard that some of those criminals, involved in very high crimes, were kept in a special part of the jail where there were bright lights shining on people's faces twenty hours a day and that they believed that whenever those guys were released from jail, they would already be blind.

A story was recounted to me about a group which made a trip to a nearby country to make plans of succession. At the borders they succeeded in buying their ways through the security of both countries and made their way into a small village in that country. The security officials of that country were aware that they were there and having a closed meeting but did not do anything because they had been bought over by the team. After their deliberations they made a big party among themselves because they were happy with the deliberations and decisions they had reached. Then they made their way to another neighboring country to concretize their decisions. Here they were spotted by the security of that country also. The group was so rich that they bought over the security of that country also with the money they had brought along. I was told that the convoy of vehicles they had brought along was conveniently guarded from place to place and from one hotel to the other. In the end of their *mission* they took different routes to get back into the country to implement the decisions they had taken. We were told that the only reason they did not succeed to execute their decisions on that trip was because two of their group members were fighting for the two most lucrative positions in the cabinet they had formed. Unfortunately, because of a leak-out their plan failed. The King considered their action treasonable, and sent them straight to jail. The jail was already too full that the government had to build new structures, properly protected to accommodate them.

The King counted very much on the information he received from the Ministry of Supreme State Audit. He usually used the recommendations they made in the measures he took for the attainment of the objectives he had set to keep the government machinery working, and especially in the execution, controlling and overseeing of the judicious use of public funds, goods and services. Because of the important role that Ministry was playing, the members in the department for the Control of Public Finances had been endowed with the legal, financial, human and material means necessary to carry out their mission. During the conduct of their duties they could not receive tips or favours of any type from the institutions they went to audit. They were responsible for protecting all forms of public prosperity. They had the powers to recommend sanctions to those managers and public book-keepers guilty of misappropriation and misuse.

A story that was recounted to me by an influential member of the Supreme State Audit was that the principles were there but sometimes they would not be followed by cabinet members who felt they had strong roots in the King's Palace that nothing could be done to them if they were found faulty. The fellow who recounted to me had been an old acquaintance in high school. She told me she would make a report about a cabinet member who judged herself to be *immune* to sanctions and send it to the King's Palace but nothing would be done to them. She found out such cabinet members had been taking government resources to buy over people in King's Palace who mattered.

However, in the past five years there had been an overhauling of that Ministry. so many high-level officers of government, the unfortunate ones, had been jailed. There had been a request from prisons administrators to fortify the high-security prisons which were erected for high-security jails. Those too were already so full that the government had put aside additional funds to put up new structures to house them in the administrative and economic cities of the country. To ensure that culprits were all punished, in the overhauled system the service of the State Auditors was now put directly under the direct authority of the King, There was now a *Chef de Camp* who was now charged with channelling all embezzlement reports straight to the King. Such reports did not have to pass through the Director of Civil Cabinet as before. This improved the situation and the many recommendations they made from their work in the field became firm and could not be contested. Hence the decisions taken by the King on such individuals who had been found to have defaulted were final.

It is now time to recount the many encounters I had with them. One morning just as I was settling down to start the day's work, my chief of cabinet came into my office and told me there was a team from the King's Palace which wanted to see me. I told her to let them in. The team, which had been screened by the security, was headed by a lady. The head of the team came in and greeted me. I gave her a seat. She told me that as part of their routine work with parastatal organizations, the King had sent them to control the Institute's financial activities. She said that usually they took about one month to audit an institution and had to be in the locale for that period of time. So they needed a conference room with sufficient space to accommodate eight people. She said they also needed a photocopier for their work. To do their audit I had to guarantee that they would have full access to all our financial files. I also had to ensure that the financial services were not sent on vacation during the time the auditors were in our campus because they would work with the chief financial officer and any of his staff members as the need arose.

I sent for the chief financial officer. When he came I gave him instructions to prepare a conference room for them and put a photocopier at their disposal. The next day they started work. They had a check list which showed the kind of information they wanted to get from our Institute. Basically they wanted to know how funds from government had been spent in the past three years. They wanted to know if there had been irregularities in spending and in the accounting for the funds. Most importantly they wanted to know how payments were being disbursed to contractors and other people who did business with us. The way they worked was that if they found any *dirty* faulty file and they could ascertain that it involved my predecessor, they would involve him or her to the campus to give the required explanation. I listened attentively and promised them that I would cooperate fully with them and do whatever I had to do to facilitate their work.

Apparently my Minister, Lena BigStuff, had sent a letter to the King that I had misused government money for personal gain. The most recent event which she felt I had benefitted from was from the expenditures of the agricultural show which had just taken place in neighbouring Ebolowa. Many CEO's were suspected to have benefitted from the many and diverse expenses during the event, because quite a good bit of money had been allotted for the preparation and holding of the event. Funds were spent to install field plots, to purchase field equipment, refurbish apartments and houses to provide accommodation for scientists, technicians and support staff. Funds were also supposed to be used to refurbish the house which the Minister was going to inhabit during the one-week event.

The auditors went through all the folders, file after file. Sometimes they would need information which only I could provide and would come into my office and interview me. Other times, they would need documents or information from the finance service and would either get them from the chief financial officer or invite personnel from that service to give the information. They worked like that for one full month. Contrary to what they had thought before they came to our Institute, all the financial irregularities were found to weigh on the shoulders of the Minister of Rural Development Investigations, Lena BigStuff.

The Audit team booked ten appointments to see the Minister but she would not receive them. The auditors were getting worried that their mission was coming to an end without filling the gaps of information which the books showed could only be given by the Minister. Frustrated by that, they made a note that the Minister who was withholding important information about some files had not been accessible. They had to do that so as to bring the work to a close.

At the end of their exercise, they wrote their report and were ready to quit our premises and go back to the King's palace to present their report. As a custom, they had to give me, the host CEO an overview of their findings. They were glad to report to me that my financial management was sound. That they had found no irregularities in my management and that everything they had found which was abnormal was instead weighing on Lena BigStuff who had refused to receive them and give them the information they required from her.

I had been told confidentially by one of the auditors that the Minister's main adviser who was the director general of administrative affairs had advised her not to receive the auditors; she had ministerial immunity to refuse auditors she did not want to receive. That was the main reason that during their one-month stay they had not been able to talk to her in spite of the many appointments they had made to do so.

The Minister, according to my informant even bragged that they could not *get* her even if she had decided to receive them.

One of the crucial pieces of information which they wanted her to defend herself about was that the accounting books in the Ministry of Rural Development showed that she had signed out funds for the agricultural show from the Ministry of Rural Development to purchase items for our research Institute but nothing had been delivered to the Institute. That was crucial because 100% of the funds destined for TRDI had been signed out by the Minister but there wasn't a single document to account for what she claimed she had spent. They wanted her to give two pieces of information: why she signed out the funds in the first place given that TRDI had financial autonomy and was required to manage its own funds directly, and secondly she had to provide papers accounting for the different items she claimed she had acquired with the money. They also wanted to know two issues which were hanging in the air: how she had managed to collect 700,000 USD from my predecessor for humanitarian activities of the Queen, and how she had in her keeping a brand new Toyota SUV bought with resources of TRDI. Since she refused to receive them they could not get this information. There were also vehicles belonging to the Institute which she had confiscated for her own use and for the use of the Ministry. Some of them still had the logo of TRDI and were found carrying out private errands by her family members in the bushes many hundreds of kilometres from the Institute headquarters. The audit team was concerned about one other Toyota Land Cruiser SUV which the CEO before my predecessor had bought for her with Institute money. This was irregular, given that the Ministry had a budget of its own for vehicle purchase. Those two landcruisers, amounting to some 400,000 USD needed to be accounted for. The auditors started now understanding why the Minister had refused to receive them to offer any explanation. All those irregularities went into their report which they finally submitted to the King without hearing from her.

The entire one month when they stayed in our premises was quite stressful to me as CEO. It disrupted the rhythm of my work because they kept coming into my office from time to time to ask one thing after the other. The team found it very irregular that Lena had made a serious report against me for not having transferred 700,000 USD to her private account. The letter which they had sent to the King and which the team had in their file showed that that amount had been embezzled by me. The team had the information first-hand from me and why I could not make the transfer. They confirmed that I was right and that the issue, if I had complied, would have created a big *hole* in my account in the Treasury which would have been impossible for me to account for. I would have been already in jail.

The agricultural show had come and gone. All of us in the Institute were happy that we had been praised by the King for a job well done. Our plots had been recognized by the King for their cleanliness, and for the explanations I had given to his convoy as being so informative. The King who had been scheduled by the protocol to spend 45 minutes in our plots ended up spending two hours visiting them. One funny thing which happened just before the King's visit was that Lena BigStuff sent me word through one of our colleagues that I should not make an attempt to shake hands with the King. My board chairman heard that message and asked me, "is it here that your Minister wants to cancel the decree which appointed you?" Anyway, the director of civil cabinet of the King had played his normal diplomacy and avoided chaos from taking place in the place until the King came and left.

The team from the audit agency was expecting that the King would do something in the form of sanctions to Lena BigStuff. The crimes were countless: agricultural show money, Institute vehicles confiscated, 700,000 USD transferred under pressure by my predecessor and many other things which were meant to implicate the CEOs who had been there in TRDI since she was appointed Minister. What is surprising is that until today, nothing has happened. She is still there.

Another thing that happened during the agricultural show period was the reaction of the Governor of that region when I was making a supervisory trip to ensure the plots in the agricultural show village were tidy. One morning during my stay in Ebolowa I received a phone call from my room in our research station. The person who was on the phone was the Governor inviting me to his home for breakfast the following morning. When I reached the Governor's residence that morning he offered me a nice breakfast and we ate together. Then he asked me a question, "what problems do you have with your Minister? I ask you this question because she keeps talking very badly about you." I replied that I did not have anything with her except that she had given me instructions in which she wanted me to do something irregular (transfer of a sum of money from a safe place in the government Treasury to a private commercial account), which I refused to do. "No wonder, I knew there was something really wrong; now I know the cause of the problem." The story ended there. But many people were noting her reaction and insults towards me, and were bound to wonder the kind of problem which was between the two of us that warranted that kind of hostility. But as a subordinate, I kept quiet and stomached all the hostility and insults.

The regional officer of the Tropicana Bureau of Investigations heard the way and manner my Minister was talking about me in one of her official trips during which the Minister was supposed to carry out an evaluation before the agricultural show event. He figured that there was something really wrong between us and, as an investigator, wanted to know what was going on. He succeeded in getting my phone number and when he reached his office he called me and invited me to come to his office as soon as possible. After I had visited my plots I found my way to his office. He asked me the same question which the Governor had asked me, "what do you have with your Minister that she insults you like that? I find that abnormal that a high official of government is being insulted by another high official in this manner." He insisted that I should tell him everything and nothing but the truth. If there was any document I could give him about my problems with her he would like to have it for his report. I was now in cold water and needed not fear the coldness in it so I recounted the story of the 700,000 USD and handed him the folder I had prepared with all the letters she had written to me in that regard as well as the replies I had given to her for each letter. He was glad to hear all that and to get those documents. He told me that the next day he would send his report directly to the King. But eight months later I was fired as CEO of TRDI.

An acquaintance who worked in the King's Palace heard of my problems with the Minister and came to confide in me as to why Lena BigStuff was so bold in doing what she was doing to me. The main reason behind this whole thing, he said, was because Lena was the one who had offered to take full care of the Queen's mother. She would give her chunks of dollars for everything she wanted to do. So the Queen was happy with her and ready to protect her every step of the way. That is why she was doing all forms of embezzlement of government funds from the research institutes and nothing was done to her. I was not surprised with that piece of information. Everyone needed to have that kind of support to be able to do what she was doing.

From the political side, Lena also had a strong *protecteur*. This fellow was very rich and influential and had major investments in the country. He was also a big employer in his private enterprise. He was also friendly and close to the King. This individual was from the same ethnic group as Lena and was actually the one who had introduced Lena to the King to be made Minister. Lena counted also on him because as long as the guy was alive, Lena would get any protection that was needed and could do anything in government and get by with it. You could see the massive support Lena had from the two ends. She was bound to be naughty as she was.

CHAPTER 16

King Palace Protocol

. . . .

I HAD BEEN IN THE CEO JOB FOR SEVEN MONTHS WHEN I STARTED receiving visitors who claimed they were members of the protocol of the King. They all appeared to be authentic and people sent by the King to see me. Sometimes, they would come with documents, supposedly sent by the King which bore the dry seal of the King. Other times they would come with badges showing that they were from the King's Palace. Some of them would come with flashy cars and SUVs to see me in the campus and claim to be assisting me with information which would help me in managing the Institute.

I had read that the protocol of the King was a powerful arm of the Office of his Chief of Staff. The main job of the protocol service was to establish the Order of Precedence of the Federal Republic of Tropicana. Its activities were also tightly associated with the Ministry of Foreign Affairs and External Relations. The protocol service was responsible for organizing visits by heads of state to the Federal Republic of Tropicana. That service was also responsible for receiving high-profile visitors of foreign governments or their highest representatives in Tropicana. It was also responsible for missions abroad by the members of the Cabinet of the King. The Office of the Chief of Protocol coordinated the many visits each year by foreign leaders, foreign ministers and other high-ranking foreign dignitaries to the country. Tropicana was not the only country with a Chief of Protocol. In some countries that service had more duties than in others.

My reading about that service showed that the order of precedence was only used to indicate ceremonial protocol. It had no legal standing and did not reflect the order of priority stipulated by the constitution of the country. According to the Constitution that service was an advisory set of procedures maintained by the Chief of Protocol which listed the ceremonial order for domestic and foreign government officials including military and civilian officials at diplomatic, ceremonial, and social events within the country. The list was used to mitigate miscommunication and embarrassment in diplomacy, and offered a distinct and concrete order for ceremonies. Often the order was used to advise diplomatic and ceremonial event planners on seating charts and the order of introduction of former presidents, vice presidents, retired Supreme Court justices, first ladies, and secretaries of state. As a result of what I read about that service I was able to give its members direct access to my cabinet and could be admitted to see me whenever they came to have a talk with me in my office. The guards were aware of that.

The first person who introduced himself as a member of the protocol of the King was a gentleman called Andrew Yabassi. He had been brought to my office first by my former chief financial officer (CFO), Aloysius Mbamala. When the guy came into my office he told me he was a close member of the King's protocol. He said he was the one the King often sent ahead each time he was to make a trip within the country or abroad. He said his duty in those missions was to make sure that the place was safe for the King's visit. He indicated that he was a commissioner of police by training but that he was not wearing uniforms because of the confidential nature of his duties. He added that he was also sent from time to time to any Minister who indicated he or she had problems in their administration. That was why he was sent to Lena BigStuff to assist her with administrative problems she was facing ever since she was appointed to head the Ministry of Rural Development Investigations.

After he had finished talking about himself and the role he was playing he and the chief financial officer left. An hour later the CFO came in to tell me that I should be very careful with Andrew Yabassi. He was very powerful and he believed he was a member of the secret service of the King. He cautioned that in addition to all that he had told me he was the right arm of the King and could *make and unmake*; he could recommend the dismissal of a CEO if he was not satisfied with his work, and could on the other hand also help a CEO if he was having administrative difficulties in managing his institution. He concluded that, because of the delicate nature of his work, his family was being lodged in France by the State, and would always go and see his family every now and then on government expenses.

I counted very much on my CFO because I had much trust in him. Every bit of information he gave me I considered to be very useful. I believed he could not tell me a lie, and that he was merely guiding me in my work. After all, he had been a friend before I was appointed CEO.

When the CFO left my office, I had a frightful image of Andrew in my heart. I asked myself so many questions: How did Andrew Yabassi get into that kind of job? How did he get so close to the King to the level that he could unseat a CEO? And why did he have to be the one the King sent to help Lena BigStuff in her administrative problems? I certainly had to be careful with that kind of person.

Because of the information I had received about Andrew, I gave him easy access to my office. I made sure I gave firm instructions to my chief of cabinet to allow the Security in my cabinet to give him easy access to come in and see me each time he presented himself. I did this because I felt he would want to see me only if he had some good information which could help my administration of the Institute. Because of his functions I also carefully chose my words each time he came in to discuss something with me.

One morning, at about 10:00 am, Andrew came to see me. I had barely done one month in my CEO job. He told me he had been sent by the Minister, Lena BigStuff. When I opened the letter he had brought to me, I read that the Minister was telling me to transfer 700,000 USD to a certain account in a commercial bank in town, and that had to be done immediately. I thanked him for the letter and told him that I would find time to see the Minister the following day, and he left. As he left I made an appointment to see the Minister. The next day when I saw the Minister to ask her the procedure for making such transfer, she told me it was easy. All I had to do was instruct the Central Treasury to discount that amount from my Institute's account in the Treasury and have it credited to the account she had given me which was in a commercial bank in town. She assured me that that was the way they operated in government. Members of government were from time to time given certain assignments by the Queen. They had to execute them without asking her any questions as to how they were going to execute them or where they were supposed to get the funds to implement the actions. She told me that all confidential hand-carried messages from then on were going to be delivered by Andrew Yabassi, adding that that was his job.

One month later, Andrew came in to see me and brought me another letter. He told me that the Minister's request was urgent and that he wanted an answer to take back. I told him as I was new in the job I was having real difficulty seeing how I could account for a large sum like that. I told him that what I had found out in the short time I had been CEO was that routinely funds I received from government came with a letter of notification which spelt out the budgetary lines I had to use in spending the money. I told him that I had looked at all financial instruction papers in my keeping but had not seen any one giving me information as to the way and manner I could account for that money. He left and went and told the Minister.

The third time he came to my office he told me verbally that the Minister wanted that money urgently; time was running out for the things the Queen wanted her to do with the money. When I told him that it would be impossible for me to account for the money if I made the transfer, he replied, "Mr CEO, it sounds like you are trying to make a *bras de fer* with the Minister," meaning that I was unnecessarily wanting to offer resistance to a member of government. I replied that I was not offering any resistance. All I was trying to do was to do things which I was allowed by law to do, and that as long as I could not account for government funds correctly I did not see how I could spend them.

The fourth time Andrew came to see me with that same request I decided to be firm in my reply. "Mr Yabassi, I would prefer that you do not come to my office any longer if you are coming with that request. I would find my own way of settling the problem." He left and never came back to see me again. My investigation later showed that Andrew had been insisting so much for me to make that transfer because he had been actually benefiting from the funds collected in that manner from the seven research institutes. The reason that particular matter was one of urgency was because he himself had an urgent use for his own share of the money. One of his urgent financial needs was to acquire funds to buy a new car for his girlfriend who had made a road accident as she was driving from the economic capital to the administrative capital. It was terrible to know that. I did not know whether to believe it or not.

Two months later, I had a call from someone who said she was an employee in the King's Palace. She said she had something to show me. I was returning from a trip in one of my stations. I arranged and stopped by to see her in her home. She pulled out a letter from her bedroom and showed me. It was a photocopy of a letter written by my Minister telling the King to fire me for insubordination. The lady said that the reason she had shown me the letter was so that I could start preparing my response because the King could contact me through his cabinet to respond to the accusation. I could feel stress building up in my system. I had not yet done a year in my dream job and now my Minister was requesting that I should be fired. What a pity!

Two months later, two guys, claiming to come from the King's Palace came to my office to see me. They told me that the King had seen the letter from my Minister requesting that I should be fired from my job but told me not to be worried. They would do everything within their powers to prevent that from happening. As they left, they asked if I did not have any fuel vouchers to give them for the trip they had just done. I told them that I would have given them fuel for their return but that I had not bought fuel yet for the trimester. I made no promise. They left and I did not see them again until after one month. They came into my office again and showed a copy of another letter which my Minister had written again to the King requesting that I had become too insubordinate and arrogant that she could not work with me, and wanted me to be replaced immediately, or my signature revoked temporarily while awaiting a permanent replacement of me. As they left my office, they asked for some fuel to enable them return well, adding that even if I did not have fuel, I could give them some dollars to fuel their car as they returned home. I gave them the same excuse that I had not bought fuel and did not have any money with me which I could share with them. They reluctantly left my office.

Two weeks had elapsed when I had a call in my cell phone. When I picked up my cell phone I realized that the call had come from a foreign number. I took a diary I had and verified from which country the call was coming. I did not know who for Heaven's sake was calling me from Switzerland. "Mr CEO, I am the chief of the protocol service of the King. I am calling you from Switzerland. I want you to come to Geneva tomorrow. The King has instructed me to tell you that you should be accompanied in the trip by a certain Joseph Monda. He was supposed to be presently doing some work in the north of the country. I am instructing you to get a one-way ticket for him to Geneva – just a one-way ticket. Tell him to come and get it in your office and you both should board the same Swissair flight tomorrow night to reach Geneva the following morning. My service would be waiting for you guys. It is a very confidential trip. I have made all arrangements with the Swiss Embassy and you will be given entry visas at the airport." I suddenly realized how important I had become as a CEO. But what was the whole idea behind that trip? Was I going to be appointed to a higher position like that of a cabinet minister? Why did I have to be accompanied by Joseph Monda? Who was he? Was he a member of the King's cabinet? I had so much going on in my head.

I told the so-called chief of protocol that buying the ticket for Joseph Monda was not so much of a problem, but the issue at stake at that moment was how I could make an international trip without a mission order from my board chairman. He replied, "the King's request is tantamount to a command. You do not need a mission order from your board chairman. He does not need to know anything about the trip."

I returned home that evening and started making calls to locate Joseph Monda. Many questions were lingering in my mind. "Why Joseph Monda? What was the subject of the mission? Why was it so urgent that I could not even inform my board chairman who was my direct boss?" Then I finally got Joseph on the phone, I could determine that effectively he was answering from the north of the country as he described the exact location in which he was found. I went on to determine his identity, what he was doing for a living and whether he had any information regarding the trip. All he told me was that he had been called also by the Chief of Protocol of the King and felt the trip was for our own good. It could be that the two of us were being proposed for senior government positions like Ministers. He recounted to me that from his evaluation of the circumstances he was top in his region of origin in the King's cabinet list for appointments. Other than that he had no more information as to why the chief of protocol was asking him to come to Switzerland. He concluded his chat by telling me that he had contacted the local airline and obtained a quote for the cost of the air ticket and gave me a means to send the money for it.

What I found strange was that the chief of protocol had requested that I should get but a one-way ticket to Joseph Monda. Secondly, he said I should prepare the ticket for the Swiss trip and invite Joseph Monda to come and collect it from my office, without any background information about the trip. Another thing that surprised me was that when I finally got in touch with him Joseph appeared to know more about what the trip was all about than me. I could certainly not use government funds to purchase such a ticket because the file would have to pass through the financial controller of the Institute, and without any information about the file giving the purpose of the trip, approval would not be given by the financial controller of the Institute to purchase it.

The whole issue was fishy. Yes I had contacted his number in Switzerland through the various communications we had had and was sure I was being invited there. Yes, I had contacted Joseph Monda in the North and he would be coming to see me. But those other questions were not clear in my mind. I was the ultimate decision-maker. It was my destiny that was at stake.

I decided to shelf the transaction no matter what gain I was going to have from it. I did not buy the tickets. I decided, instead to carry out a little investigation. I called again the Swiss number which the chief of protocol was calling me with. It went through. The chief of protocol was asking me if we were already in Geneva. I told him I was still at home recovering from an upset stomach. I added that I had been in contact with Joseph Monda and we were making plans to leave that night.

After several attempts to reconcile facts relating to that trip, I called Andrew Yabassi to find out if he knew anything about the Swiss trip. He came immediately. When he started telling me how things happen in the King's palace, he told me that the chief of protocol was his personal friend and colleague and that it was certainly a true mission adding that he had been too busy with another assignment that he had not been given that particular assignment. He urged me to execute the instructions. As he was finishing to talk to me his cell phone rang and he claimed it was coming from the Ministry of Rural Development Investigations. So he left and went back to the Ministry.

I was already sick of a matter like that which appeared too difficult for me to understand. I had packed my bag and was ready for the trip. But, after hearing what Andrew Yabassi had told me I gave the matter a second thought. I went home, thought of the matter for one full hour, and last minute I told myself that I would not make the trip. One hour before the planned departure time, Joseph Monda gave me a call. "Mr CEO I have not yet received the ticket to join you in your workplace. Could you please send me some money through *Mobile Money* so I can join you to start the trip tomorrow? The trip from the north to your place is 400 USD?" I responded that I would send the money with my driver to send it in the next thirty minutes.

I assembled all the facts in my head and concluded that the trip was not authentic. But how could I be contacting some officer from Switzerland who was responding from a Swiss number? I called my nephew-in-law who was an engineer in the national communication company to tell me whether it was possible to have a Swiss phone number in the Federal Republic of Tropicana. He told me yes, adding that people who use such foreign numbers were 419 (fake) people and that I should be extremely careful with such people; they could be dupers. I cancelled the trip and refrained from contacting the chief of protocol again. That ended the story.

That had been a set-up by a network of fake protocol people among which was Andrew Yabassi. I later came to realize that they made such contacts, collected money and shared it among themselves. I was going to meet such people in my job as CEO every now and then and their goal was to make personal gain from government managers who were in positions to dish out money without meticulous verification of the circumstances just because they wanted to keep their jobs.

The Minister called me one morning when I had just reached the office and gave me certain instructions again. The first was that I should give Andrew Yabassi 4000 USD to buy an air ticket to travel to France to see his family. I was not sure whether that was a private loan between us or an official disbursement from the Institute account. I did not want to ask her questions over the phone because Andrew had accused me earlier about wanting to offer resistance with a member of government. I went to the bank that afternoon and took 4000 USD from my personal bank account and called Andrew and handed the money to him.

The next day, the Minister called me again but this time she was telling me that they were enthroning their village chief and she had been contacted to make her own contribution for the ceremony. She was calling me to assist her in her contribution. I asked her how much she wanted from me. She told me she needed 40,000 USD. That was a large sum which I could not get from my personal account and give to her. I could not get if from the Institute account because I did not see from what budgetary line that was going to be accounted from. So I went to her office and excused myself why I could not give her the money. She stayed quiet. I could tell she was angry because she was not succeeding in squeezing anything from me. But there was nothing I could do about it.

One week later, word reached us that her office had caught fire. I got into my car and we rushed to see the damage that had been caused. When I reached her office I sympathized with her on what had happened. She turned to me and told me quietly that she hoped my Institute was going to assist in the repairs of the office as well as replace the burnt furniture. The estimate the contractor had given for all that was 200,000 USD for the repairs and the new furniture for the office. She turned to me and said she expected to have the money the following day.

Of course, I could not satisfy her demand because I could not just account for it. And my board chairman would not authorize the approval of that kind of expenditure because such funds had not been budgeted a priori. She was very angry, but although she could not openly show her feelings, that just added to the animosity she had against me. According to her, I had refused her funds several times on diverse problems that had happened to her. These were signs of disrespect for her. A week later, she invited me to a meeting in the Ministry. During the meeting she vowed that she was going to do everything, even using *her body*, to get rid of me. I stayed quiet until the meeting was over. That was the kind of life I lived as CEO of TRDI.

CHAPTER 17

Tropicana Psychiatric Evaluation Agency

It was a sunny morning in August. The sun blinds of the windows were drawn over my office windows. When I looked out, I realized that hardly a soul was stirring. The only animation was shown by a few vehicles from the neighbouring IITA research station passing by to take workers to the fields. In a lazy absent-minded way I thought to myself why the place was so quiet. Then suddenly a knock came on the door. My chief of cabinet came to announce a team of four officers who badly wanted to see me. When I authorized her to usher them in, they came into the office and sat down. Their leader introduced the group as members of the Tropicana Psychiatric Evaluation Agency.

They told me that their job was to conduct a psychiatric evaluation of top government officials who were not behaving according to the norms of the republic. They added that they needed to conduct a mental health evaluation of my emotional status, as well as my psychological and behavioral health in general. Their goal was to provide a diagnosis and assess the status of me to be sure there was nothing especially wrong with me. I was surprised.

I knew what psychiatry was. In my university days I had learnt that psychiatry was the branch of medicine focused on the diagnosis, treatment and prevention of mental, emotional and behavioral disorders and that a psychiatrist was a medical doctor with an MD or DO degree from a medical school who had specialized in mental health and was thus qualified to assess both the mental and physical aspects of psychological problems, including substance use disorders. I asked myself the question: why did these people feel I was a mental patient? Had I told my attending physicians that I had a mental problem which made them feel I should be examined by a psychiatrist? When did my mental problem start that my family was not aware of it? Did I have a history of drug abuse? Before I became CEO I had free time and I could drink a bottle or two of beer, but now in my new assignment I was too busy to find time to drink. For the short time they introduced themselves to me and what they were about to do I kept asking myself internally what the real issue was. But since they had a warrant from the King's Palace showing that government had sent them to evaluate me I yielded.

I was ready to comply in all ways because I had proof that they were all medical doctors: two psychiatrists and two family doctors with sound training in psychology. The psychiatrists were there to assess my physical history, behavioral and cognitive histories and make recommendations to the King for ongoing intervention. The medical doctors in the team could prescribe appropriate medications for the management for my condition if they found anything wrong with me.

They told me that from the information they had, something appeared to be wrong with me. As they were arranging their equipment I kept thinking about people who had had radical ideas which could merit this kind of evaluation. Kwame Nkrumah of Ghana and Sekou Toure of Guinea Conakry had been considered to be too radical to think of a pan-African State – a United States of Africa. They had been considered abnormal by imperialists who fought against a unified Africa.

Kwame Nkrumah, was born in Nkroful a town in the southwest part of the British colony of the Gold Coast, present day Ghana, located along the Gulf of Guinea and the Atlantic Ocean. He had received training in the famous Achimota College, probably where he had started nursing this idea of pan-Africanism. He is known for being the father of Pan-Africanism. He led his country to independence from Britain in 1957 and was a powerful voice for African nationalism. African nationalism at the time referred to political ideologies, which reigned within Sub-Saharan Africa during the 19th and 20th centuries towards the end of the period when colonized African states were fighting to get their independence from colonial rule. These ideologies were based on the idea of national self-determination, the creation of nation states and the fact that there was an exploitation of the African continent. Imperialists considered extremists of these ideologies to be abnormal and hence too radical because they emerged as a major obstacle to European colonial rule during that period. (These ideas had in the late 1780s been manifested in other countries like the United States when freed slaves decided to establish their own churches in response to racial segregation in white churches.) To get rid of Nkrumah, colonialists apparently plotted, as the stories are told, to have him overthrown by a military coup some nine years after independence using the pretext that his rule had grown to be dictatorial.

Ahmed Sekou Toure, born on January 9th 1922, was a Guinean politician and a Pan-Africanist who also played a key role in the African independence movement. His disciplined organizing and activism were a decisive factor in the fusion of the trade union movement with his political party, the Democratic Party of Guinea (PDG). As the first President of Guinea, he led the country to gain its independence from France in 1958. In a message sent to Tanzania at the 6th Pan-Africanist Congress, he gave a strong argument destroying the intellectual myths of reactionaries by making it clear that Pan-Africanism had to be henceforth the class struggle in Africa to be held by any reasonable African. His ideas and those of Nkrumah would later be taken over by an American like Kwame Ture whose independent thought and action on Pan Africanism, as well as revolutionary theories and culture had actually been taken from the activities of people he had physical contact with like Osageyfo Kwame Nkruma, Ahmed Sekou Toure, Amilcar Cabral and others.

These characters were reasoning ahead of their time, foreseeing the vast natural resources which the continent of Africa had and which it could use to develop itself if the various African countries decided to fight as a united force and were ready to become a single nation. Imperialists certainly found such people to be abnormal.

On the other side of the coin were people like Field Marshal Idi Amin Dada, the third President of Uganda. He shook the world in different ways and was most infamous for his treacherous regime. He was known for his smile, but a military dictator who in 1971 had succeeded in overthrowing President Milton Obote, ruling Uganda with an iron fist for eight long years. Those who had celebrated the general's military coup had had no idea how violent and tyrannical the next decade was going to be. Idi Amin became known as the "Butcher of Uganda" for his brutal, despotic rule and for his gross abuse of human rights. His rule as the President of Uganda in the 1970s had been considered by many as perhaps the most notorious of Africa's post-independence dictators, imprisoning or killing at least 100,000 of his opponents. Although he was ousted in 1979 by Ugandan nationalists, after which he went into exile in Libya and later in Saudi Arabia, he was a figure who would be remembered by many in Africa.

These are the kinds of people who, being considered to have eccentric behaviors could be subjected to psychiatric evaluations, not an innocent person who through hard work had worked his way to become a CEO of a research institute.

The psychiatric evaluators said that they could not tell that I was normal except they conducted that evaluation. They said that, based on what my supervisory authority had told them they felt something had gone wrong with me ever since I was named CEO because my Minister had told them I was finding certain things abnormal which other people were finding normal. For instance, I was of the belief that using government funds for the Queen's humanitarian activities was abnormal whereas that was important for the stability and functioning of the State.

I listened very attentively and let them conduct their evaluation. I let them do what they intended to do. They connected all kinds of wires on my head and led these to a machine which they had brought along with them. Then they started questioning me on all kinds of things. The core aspects of the evaluation were taking my history, documenting the history of the problem, taking a family history, taking a developmental history, performing a mental status exam and performing a physical exam. Having run their medical assessment of me as a psychiatric health patient, they then focused on explaining everything there was to know on the pharmaceutical and biological treatments that they felt would be appropriate if at all they diagnosed any mental health disorder in me.

The other two team members were psychologists; they were also medical doctors but had doctorate degrees in psychology and their job was to assess my mental health through another psychological evaluation which focused on the behavioral, psychological, and sociological aspects of my mental health status with the goal of providing a comprehensive behavioral analysis of my presenting problems. They did all what they had to do and made a printout of their findings. They then left my office and told me they would be in touch with me at a later time. I found myself in a terrible situation where all kinds of evaluations had to be done on me because I found it abnormal to steal money which could lead me to jail.

CHAPTER 18

Hiring and firing

· ·

As CEO I BELIEVED THAT HAVING THE RIGHT EMPLOYEE IN EACH position was a crucial component of running a successful Institute. It was therefore important for the CEO I had become to incorporate in my management the best strategies for hiring and retaining employees.

I had to adopt certain guidelines for hiring personnel. Hiring, I soon realized, was normally an exciting time for the Institute, and learnt that there were several steps I had to follow to make sure that I was legally compliant and that I was hiring the best individual for each position. I was obliged to check for legal compliance in the hiring process. Although this was in the Procedure's Manual of the Institute, I had to make sure that I consulted legal experts before I took a final hiring decision. This was important because I did not want to go against legal provisions for personnel benefits and other advantages. For instance, the Procedure's Manual stated that during the interviews, I did not have to, and it was also illegal to ask for an applicant's marital status, birth date or religious affiliation. These were not required and they could be considered as basis for discrimination of a candidate.

The second guideline was to clearly explain the position to the candidates. Many candidates, unfortunately, don't have a clear idea of what they would be doing until they actually started a job. But as CEO I had the obligation to precisely explain what skills were necessary and what the job entailed. These were important to stress in the job description and during the interview process.

The third guideline was to conduct effective interviews. For these interviews I planned to use expatriate scientists in the Institute who were neutral and would not be influenced by the problem of ethnicity in the selection of qualified candidates. I realized that it was just as important to focus on factors such as temperament of candidates as it was to ask about specific job-related skills for the particular position. It was also important to let the candidate ask questions about the job. This way I would judge how much they had researched about our Institute and how they viewed our specific industry.

Fourthly, I often times considered hiring within the Institute. While many small institutions may lack an adequate pool of applicants to consider for every job position, I realized that my Institute was large and among 1200 employees I had genes for every trait I wanted; it was often a good idea therefore to hire internally if that was possible. For instance it made more sense to promote a chief of bureau in the budget service to the position of chief budget officer because of the accrued experience he had acquired over the years. Promoting a current employee usually saved the Institute money. In addition, the Institute would also have an individual who had already adapted to the work environment.

I also had to adopt guidelines for firing personnel. Many of those guidelines were stated in the Procedures Manual of the Institute, but my plan was to refrain from firing as much as possible because terminating an employee could be an emotional experience for both employee and employer. I realized that it was important to follow a specific procedure if I really had to fire an individual. He ought to have committed a serious crime and for this I needed to keep extensive documentation to back my decision. It was absolutely crucial that every significant incident involving an employee was well documented. If there were adequate reasons for deciding to fire an employee, I told myself that there needed to be sufficient documentation to prove it.

Secondly, I had to follow policies in the Procedures Manual to back my decision to terminate a defaulting employee. I had been advised, and that was also in the Procedures Manual, that the termination of employees needed to be carried out in the same way, although crimes could differ. Treating employees differently would open up potential lawsuits against the Institute. I decided that the legal service in Human Resources had to be always consulted before a decision to terminate an individual was taken.

As CEO I was supposed to follow the law at all times before deciding on terminating the appointment of a worker. Of course temporary workers who had been recruited without signing a contract could be fired at any time, but those who were recruited after they had signed a contract could only be terminated for reasons stated in the contract.

Finally, I was always advised by the legal service of Human resources to have witnesses who would back me in the event I wanted to terminate the appointment of a worker. This, they said was important to avoid potential lawsuits. I found out that it was always a good idea to have another individual present when I was in the process of terminating an employee. Consistently following procedures could make the process run more smoothly and help reduce any potential legal complications that could arise. These guidelines helped me more effectively hire employees, and if there was need to do so fire defaulting employees in the Institute.

In spite of these guidelines, when I was named CEO of the Tropicana Rural Development Institute I decided to adopt the Sony system of management, what I liked to call the Sony Principle. I was listening to a documentary one evening and heard someone interviewing the CEO of Sony Corporation. He asked him why the company was so successful in its business. The CEO replied that it was because the corporation had a high retention rate for its personnel. He explained that it takes a while to screen people before they are hired. Once hired, the people start developing an interest in their work and this leads to accruing experience over time. This experience is crucially important for the growth and success of the company. He said that he realized the usefulness of their experience very early and decided that retaining workers with a lot of experience was more important for the success of the production and sale of their products than changing people every now and then. He indicated that his own principle was that whenever the company was fairing well, he gave a raise to the workers. And whenever the company was in financial difficulty, he convinced workers to accept salary cuts instead of firing them. I thought that was very meaningful.

Sony is considered the most innovative company in the world. Although Japan's respected technology industry has gone through difficult times at some stages of its development it has still emerged as a stronger company, in part on the strength of its success in product categories, in part because of its high worker retention policy, although also because of its emphasis on customer satisfaction which leads to higher customer retention also. Sony has been so successful in customer satisfaction partly owing to the effectiveness of the characteristics of the corporate culture of connecting the company with its target customers, considering its organizational culture as synonymous to customer satisfaction. Through a strong organizational culture adopted by the company and Sony's operations of customer satisfaction, the corporation maximizes its workers' effectiveness in satisfying customers' preferences and expectations. This emphasis on customer satisfaction makes satisfied customers more likely to purchase from the company again and this indirectly leads to higher customer retention. Also the organizational culture has had a positive impact on Sony's employees, and its characteristics of reliability, credibility and cordiality have been exercised not only toward customers but also between employees. This cultural condition has resulted in improving employee morale and organizational effectiveness.

As a new CEO wanting to introduce innovation in my Institute, I knew that I could copy the many advantages which the CEO of Sony had adopted but drop those which were not going to improve my visibility of the Institute. For instance, Sony feels it should listen to its clients and make any improvements to its products based on what the customers want. However, the main disadvantage of this is a limited focus on innovation. Since the company focuses on what customers want, there is a lack of incentive and institutionalized support for innovation through new ideas; this discourages employees from developing new ideas simply because corporate focus is to satisfy customers' specific demands.

The kind of corporation I was heading was concerned mainly with the production of services, in some ways different from Sony which produced services and products. In that respect the two were different. However, in many respects the principles in TRDI could be similar. However, I had decided that I would do everything to try to retain my appointed officials in the Institute. Firstly, I would continue to benefit from the experience they were gaining in the institution. Secondly, it would install stability among the personnel. There is nothing as detrimental to an institution as getting rid of workers who are experienced, hardworking and conscientious in their work. But I knew there would be circumstances during which I would have to deviate from my institutional culture of retaining officials of the Institute.

As a new CEO, I called a meeting with the officers in the headquarters and told them about the culture I had adopted in managing the Institute, and what I expected from them. First, I would want them to be reliable. I would want each person to be stable in his post and make a positive contribution to the Institute's goals and objectives. Reliability of employees meant that they had to consider the viewpoints of our clients (the farmers and the agro-industries), and address their expectations. The characteristic of reliability was even more important for those working in the field, such as the directors of the technical departments, as well as the directors of the research centers and research stations who were developing agricultural technologies for the benefit of the farmers and the agro-industrial companies. Reliability on the work would increase customer satisfaction by ensuring that workers were capable of addressing customers' needs and inquiries about the many products, techniques and technologies which the research was producing. Then and then only would our institution's output be able to match market demand.

The second thing I expected from them was that they had to be credible. To be credible researchers had to be knowledgeable and skillful. This would make them admired by clients. Researchers would also be able to satisfy customers that way. Faking data which had not been properly tested would lead to failure and not give a good image to the Institute. I cautioned that the heads of research structures should organize training programs with their researchers based on the perspectives and feedback of clients to improve standards and procedures; these would reinforce the institutional culture through a credible and informed workforce.

The third thing I expected from them was cordiality. The voice of customers and their expectations from the research were very important for the success of the research institute. Personnel cordiality would make clients feel welcome to the Institute to inform them about the kinds of field problems they were facing. If technologies were developed based on farmers'needs they would be very easily adopted. Because of this, they had to create warm and friendly relations between them the workers and researchers on one hand and customers (farmers and agro-industries) on the other.

I concluded my presentation by telling personnel that a word to a wise was sufficient (*a bon entendeur, salut*). And they were dispersed.

I expected the presentation to form the culture of the Institute as we began working together. However, as I later learnt, some personnel, especially those in the headquarters, had adopted weird ways of behaving, especially to make personal gains for themselves, and to those the talk appeared to have entered a deaf's ear. I noticed this one afternoon just about five months after I had taken over as CEO. My cabinet was made up of the chief of cabinet, a secretary, and a chief of the mail service. I decided to be especially stricter on these three mainly because their loyalty was vital to the success of my work. The head of the mail service was the custodian of the key to the mail box of the Institute and received all the mail that came to the Institute. I had warned him that all mail that came in my personal name, had to be brought to me directly; I had to open them myself or by someone I had designated to do so. I had a private mail box for personal mail, but many times official mail of extreme importance, especially hand-carried mail, would be sent in my name, not in the name of the CEO. Such mail had to be opened by me alone.

One morning, the head of the mail service, who I had met there in the Institute and who he had been brought in there by my predecessor, brought a mail which had been sent by the King's Palace. It had been hand-carried (*a message porté*). He handed it to me and I thanked him for it. I kept it on one side, and planned to open it a few minutes later. My predecessor was a personal friend of mine and so I judged that his choice for the mail service chief had been a good one. I believed that he would be loyal to me. So I had planned to keep him. But something happened that made me change my mind.

I looked at the big khaki envelope containing the mail he had brought to me. The letter inside I could determine had been sent by the King. I looked at the other side of the envelope; there were stamps on the sealed part of the envelope, two wet stamps on the sides and a dry seal stamp in the middle. The seal the King used was a dry seal, an embossed emblem used as evidence of authenticity. It was a kind of seal in which the impression it made on paper resulted from the greater pressure on the paper. Sealing a document was equivalent to the signature of the King (owner of the seal). In this envelope the purpose was to authenticate the document inside, which as I later found out was also embossed with the dry seal. The wet stamps, which used liquid medium were red-inked rubber stamps commonly used in official letters.

Close observation of the envelope gave me the impression that it had been opened before it was glued again. The two halves of each of the red stamps were slightly displaced so also was the seal at the pointed edge where the V-shaped closing flap touched the envelope as it was closed. I made notes about all these, and opened the envelope to examine its contents. It was a letter, marked *strictly confidential,* which the King was sending to me asking about different correspondences that my Minister had sent to me regarding the transfer of 700,000 USD from the government Treasury to her private account.

The next day before I had even sent my reply, a phone call came from the King's Palace during which an informant was telling me to meet with him urgently somewhere in town. When we met, he told me my Minister had sent a letter to the King defending herself regarding letters she had sent to me about money transfer. I set up a small confidential commission to investigate the leakage of the information. The results were clear: the chief of the mail service was the culprit who had leaked out the information. This confirmed my suspicion that he had opened the letter the King had sent to me, probably copied it and *sold out* a copy to the Minister, who now had it to write defending herself. This was gross disloyalty. I fired him.

Two weeks later, the chief financial officer came to my officer and told me that the head of the budget service appeared not to be loyal to me. He added that the guy had been very close to my predecessor and was likely to be disloyal to me because he could be leaking out information to him. He was recommending that the guy be replaced by someone else, especially one who had a degree in accounting or business administration. I told him to identify three people with that profile of qualification and experience and bring the short list to me. The next day he brought me the list, with his preferred candidate on the top of the list. I named the individual, Robert Boyomo, to the post. He came in to thank me for appointing him to the post. That particular position was a lucrative one. The chief of the budgetary serve was in direct contact with contractors and suppliers of the Institute. He was the one preparing their files for payment so he could be motivated by those contractors by giving him tips every now and then to speed up the preparation of their files for payment. Of course this means that if he was dishonest he could shelf a payment file until a contractor came to give him a tip.

The new budget officer started up well but after barely two months I started noticing irregularities in his work. There was constant leakage of information about the fueling of the Institute account in the Treasury. Each time the Institute account in the Treasury received funds from the Ministry of the Treasury, the Minister knew that even before me. She would make requests and would even tell me that the Institute had sufficient funds to cover her requests.

The investigation I carried out showed that Robert was related to Andrew Yabassi, the emissary and the friend of the Minister. They were from the same ethnic group. So there was an efficient and vicious cycle, (a superhighway) of information flow between Robert, Andrew and Minister. And my CFO was well informed in what they were doing but did not let me know he was involved. I called Robert to my office and advised him that he had to change very fast because I was not satisfied with the way information was leaving his office and going to town. He apologized for that, but the situation did not change. One Friday evening, I fired him. I named him finance officer in a remote research station so that he could at least continue to receive the allowance of a chief of service.

I realized I had been induced in error to fire the former budget officer from his post when actually he had been doing his job. That evening I named the former budget officer back to the post of chief of the budget service and he continued to work loyally till I left the Institute. I had learnt a lesson never to act very quickly before I had finalized my investigations on a subject.

It was my intention to continue to work with the chief of cabinet who I met there when I was appointed CEO. However, I found out after just four months that she was feeling quite uncomfortable working with me because she too had been brought there by my predecessor. So I called her one day and told her I would still want her to serve me in another capacity in a position comparable to that she had occupied. So that evening after talking to her I named her chief of the technology liaison service of the Institute. She was very happy that I did not fire her but merely changed her to another position. She came to my office and thanked me for that.

In administration you learn by the mistakes you make. From then on I changed officers of the Institute usually only after the position became vacant (through death or departure on retirement) or if the fault the individual had committed was very serious to contain.

CHAPTER 19

Conflict of beliefs

. . . .

I MAKE AN EVALUATION OF THE KIND OF LIFE I HAD LIVED FOR THE twenty months I took the job of CEO. I see that there was a serious conflict of beliefs between me and Lena BigStuff. That conflict, to say the least, amounted to a kind of civilization struggle between Lena and me. In Bismarck's Prussia, a struggle of this nature was known an *Kulturkampf.*

Kulturkampf was a cultural struggle, a conflict that took place from 1872 to 1878 between the government of the Kingdom of Prussia led by Otto von Bismarck and the Roman Catholic Church led by Pope Pius IX whose main issues were clerical control of education and ecclesiastical appointments. A unique feature of *Kulturkampf,* compared to other struggles at the time between the state and the Catholic Church in other countries, was Prussia's anti-Polish component. The term *Kulturkampf,* could be sometimes used to describe any conflict between secular and religious authorities or deeply opposing values and beliefs between two groups of people. My Minister, Lena BigStuff, had many beliefs which she wanted me to know. First, she deeply thought that she had to have full control of the Research Institutes placed under the supervisory authority of her Ministry of Rural Development Investigations. Secondly, she thought that the CEO of the Tropicana Rural Development Institute ought to serve more like a figure head; he did not have to conduct any new research in his Institute, stressing that there were enough research results which just needed to be transferred to the farmers. Thirdly, she believed that the funds the TRDI was receiving from government had to be transferred to her to use in keeping herself in power by buying over the political and administrative people who needed to make her stay as Minister forever. I wonder why the King of Tropicana had not just named Lena the Minister and the CEO of the research institutes at the same time so that she could officially control the institutes as well as the ministry.

I had different beliefs. I had been a researcher all my life. I had conducted a lot of research to help the farmers of Tropicana. I knew the many constraints which farmers were facing in their production. I had needed the opportunity to contribute even more in solving these constraints. Now as CEO of a research institute, I had the chance to do just that. As CEO I could safely solicit funding from outside grants to supplement government funds and direct any research I felt was necessary. The Federal Republic of Tropicana needed my extensive experience as a researcher to solve its rural development problems. The country needed the experience I had acquired through visits to other research institutes in the region and in other parts of the world during which I had learnt so many things about the way things were done in other countries. I had learnt how to manage with transparency. I had known from what I saw in developed countries that I needed to be strict with any budget I received for my institute. I had also learnt that I had to manage personnel to achieve the goals of the Institute by setting an example myself. That volume of information needed to be used now for the benefit of the country.

As an individual, there were several things I had to do. I had to strengthen the five technical departments of the TRDI, and occupy the 1200 workers as well as the 300 scientists to churn out results from burning issues in their various departments for the benefit of the country of Tropicana. I knew there were boundless deserts and plains and illimitable dark forests of ignorance just awaiting the axe and plough of the devoted researcher to yield rich crops of golden wonderful knowledge.

I thought of the department of forestry and environmental sciences of the TRDI and the many challenges that lay ahead of it with current issues such as climate change adaptation and mitigation. Climate change had become a major issue all over the world, among developed countries like the USA, and in other economies like China and developing countries. I had read that climate change in China was having major effects on its economy, society and the environment. China had been reported to be the largest emitter of carbon dioxide, through an energy infrastructure heavily focused on fossil fuels and coal. Other industries in that country, such as a large construction industry and industrial manufacturing contribute heavily to carbon emissions. In the on-going debate, the Chinese argue that, like other developing countries, their carbon emissions were considerably less than countries like the United States: as of 2016, they were the 51st most per capita emitter. The Chinese brandish data to show that higher-income countries have outsourced emissions-intensive industries to China. Chinese home activities as well as those outsourced from developed industrial countries have made China to be suffering from the negative effects of global warming in agriculture, forestry and water resources, and this trend is expected to continue. As a result the Chinese government is taking some measures to increase renewable energy to replace coal and fossile fuel to mitigate those efforts. The government is also using other decarbonization efforts, and is vowing to be carbon neutral by 2060 by adopting "more vigorous policies and measures.

Many of the environmental issues include both global warming driven by human-induced emissions of greenhouse gases and the resulting large-scale shifts in weather patterns. It was now known that humans have, undoubtedly, had an unprecedented impact, through the activities of man in agriculture, forestry exploitation and fossil fuel use, on the climate system of the earth. All these activities have caused change on a global scale, affecting everyone. I had made it a major commitment to address this issue by putting my forestry and environmental scientists to study the effects of carbon dioxide, the largest driver of warming and the emission of that gas and other gases that create a greenhouse effect. I wanted them to study the effects of methane, burning fossil fuel from our automobiles, the production of coal, oil and natural gas during the production and consumption of energy, as well as the contributions from agriculture, deforestation and manufacturing. I needed them to study the human cause of climate change. I had a burning desire for my researchers to study the effect of temperature rise as it was accelerated by climate feedbacks, as well as the role of increased water vapour and changes to land and ocean carbon sinks in the whole context of climate change. I had followed in the news about temperature rise on land and that it was about twice the global average increase, and that it led to desert expansion and more common heat waves and wildfires. This needed to be investigated by my researchers to provide practical recommendations that could assist government in formulating its policies on the matter.

I had noticed that in recent times warmer temperatures were increasing rates of evaporation, causing more intense storms and weather extremes. These had impacts on ecosystems which included the relocation or extinction of many animal species as their environment changed. My greatest worry was that my grandchildren would grow up not to know many animals found in our zoological gardens as our generation had been privileged to see. High temperatures had also had an immediate effect on coral reefs and mountains but we needed to know how this was occurring, so that we could formulate scientific recommendations to government on what could be done. Climate change had been known to threaten people of many countries with food insecurity and water scarcity. It had also provoked flooding, infectious diseases, extreme heat, economic losses and displacement in some countries. These human impacts had led the world institutions like the World Health Organization calling climate change the greatest threat to global wealth in the 21st century. I was scared to know that even if efforts to minimize future warming were successful, some effects would continue for centuries, including rising sea levels, rising ocean temperatures, and ocean acidification. There were certainly enormous challenges that faced researchers in the forest and environment sector.

I thought of the many constraints of food crops. In roots and tubers, there were still unsolved problems on cassava mosaic disease, cassava root rot, cassava root and tuber scale, and the hardening problems of some cassava varieties. The cassava root and tuber scale (*Stictococcus vayssierei*) was now not only attacking cassava but several crops and weeds also. Its spread to multiple hosts was awful and had to be dreaded. Yam farmers still continued to face the problems with the greater yam beetle (*Heterolygus meles*), and the hardening problem of the trifoliate yam (*Dioscorea dumetorum*). Staking had always been the second most important constraint of yams, and was more crucial for yam farmers in the savanna regions of our country where substantial hectarages of yam are cultivated. Growers were waiting for solutions from the research.

The sweet potato weevil (*Cylas spp*) and the sweet potato virus disease were still menaces to sweet potato growers, who still cannot harvest their crop after four months because the root would be infested by weevils. Sweet potato, a short cycle crop, could be developed to produce non-sweet types that could be very useful in the flour and bakery industry. Irish potato growers were still worried by the prevalence and severity of the late blight (*Phytophthora infestans*) and the foliar bacterial wilt (*Pseudomonas salanacearum*). They needed answers from the research.

Cereal growers were not free from constraints in their farms. For maize, despite several centuries of research effort, there was still the menace of the maize stalk borer (*Busseola fusca*). There were gaps in management efforts to reduce infestation. Farmers were still facing the problems of soil acidity and aluminium toxicity and needed maize varieties in the forest region that could be grown with little sensitivity to these soil conditions. Upland rice farmers still needed more varieties to grow in home gardens just as other crops were grown. Wheat and barley farmers wanted genotypes they could grow comfortably to make their contributions to reductions in wheat flour imports from developed countries.

I thought of the many challenges of grain legumes. Bruchids (*Bruchus* spp.) were still a major problem in cowpea, an important protein source in the country. Farmers continue to complain that the insect pest is more serious in cowpeas especially during storage. The rosette viral disease and poor pod filling were still major constraints in the cultivation of groundnut (*Arachis hypogaea*), for which solutions had not been found. The common bean (*Phaseolus* spp.), grown all over the country still needed varieties with high yields and good palatability. Our food technologists were still struggling to develop food forms that would increase the shelf lives of harvested grains.

Sugarcane (*Saccharum officinarum*), the main sugar-producing crop in the country was facing serious problems of stem rotting and adaptability of varieties to various ecologies. Also researchers still needed to provide information about crop management of the crop.

Tobacco, (*Nicotiana tabacum*), a highly addictive plant for users was still being grown but attempts had been made to produce varieties with low nicotine content that would make it less addictive and less harmful to health. I had planned to make arrangements with the Ministry of Public Health so we could fight the many health hazards –high blood pressure, heart disease, increased risk of heart attack, increased risk of early delivery when used by pregnant women and still birth - all caused by cigarettes. I had learnt that cigarette smoking could cause lung cancer, chronic bronchitis and emphysema. I had also read that smoking had been linked to leukemia, cataracts, Type II diabetes and pneumonia. I knew that smoking was a habit which had been adopted by a large part of the population across the nation. It was an opportunity now to assist in doing something about it.

There were too many field constraints as well as post-harvest technology issues that needed investigation. Furthermore, research, the way I knew it, was continuous because constraints kept coming up when you least expected them. I knew that was why a whole research institute had been created by the government, and that was why government was paying salaries of some 1200 employees to develop solutions to its many development constraints.

My Minister, Lena BigStuff, had adopted the dogma of Ministerial infallibility, very much like the dogma of Papal infallibility in Bismarck's Prussia. Papal infallibility was a dogma of the Roman Catholic Church which stated that the Pope was infallible in whatever he did and wanted to do. This doctrine was defined dogmatically at the First Vatican Council of 1869–1870 in the document *Pastor aeternus* but had been defended before that, existing already in medieval theology and being the majority opinion at the time of the Counter-Reformation.

According to the dogma of Ministerial Infallibility, Lena BigStuff felt she was infallible in whatever she wanted to do as a Minister. She could give instructions to the CEOs of research institutes and they were bound to execute them. She could use the funds kept in their Institutes and no one had the right to question that. Whatever she said as Minister was right and could not be challenged. If she induced a CEO in error and he was jailed, that was fine with her, as long as that could keep her in power.

Her doctrine of Ministerial infallibility was one of Ministerial supremacy which relied on one of the cornerstones of Tropicana dogma. She was the ruling agent and she was the only one who could decide on what had to be accepted as formal belief and was the mode of functioning of research. Any other way of management by a CEO other than the dogma of Lena BigStuff infallibility, was considered mass resistance (*bras de fer*) to a member of government, and this was not acceptable at all as long as she lived.

On paper, there was an influence of new philosophies and ideologies, such as rigour and moralization, nationalism, secularism, liberalism and positivism. Under those philosophies, the role of the Ministry on research institutes had to be grossly enhanced to reflect what the Kingdom of Tropicana expected Ministers to do. The Minister of the Treasury who was the other supervisory authority of TRDI, and who was supposed to supervise financial management of the Institute, was never intervening in the management of TRDI. The only time I heard from him was when he sent me the letter of notification informing me that he had sent money to the TRDI Treasury account.

From the recommendations of the auditors, the Ministry of the Supreme State Audit had tried to strip the Ministry of secular powers and to let the duties of the Ministry to be restricted to the activities of the Ministry, and not the research institutes which was endowed with autonomous management. She resisted this development, which it portrayed as an attack on her powers and an attempt to prevent the maintaining and strengthening of her strong role in the Ministry and its institutes. It had been made clear that TRDI was an autonomous institution and had to be left alone to carry out its activities. But Lena did not want to relax her grip on TRDI, which was a major source of her earnings. She still wanted to be in command and to assert her supremacy. In view of her opposition to the enlightenment and seemingly liberal reforms of the institutes to enforce the conduct of research activities, these dogmas of the Ministry expressed insistence on Ministerial primacy, which angered several people of the general population, in the research institutes, in government and even in the Kingdom. But there was nothing they could do to avert the situation. Lena had her roots, and those roots were getting deeper and deeper into fertile grounds as time passed by.

This conflict of beliefs continued throughout the twenty months I was CEO. The CEOs of some research institutes, in order to keep their jobs, yielded to the doctrine of Lena BigStuff infallibility and gave her as much money as she wanted even if that meant the crumbling of their institutions. Others aligned with her and hated me for not adhering to her instructions, after all that was the way government was run. I was ostracized. But I told myself that I would continue to do what was right. I knew the consequences that would befall me but I preferred that to happen instead of going to jail where I would not see my wife and children again. I knew that from what I had heard, I certainly did not want to be in the place of political prisoners and high-level prisoners who would be freed from jail only to find themselves condemned in health; many simply died shortly after. Did I want that to happen to me? Certainly, not! I had lived a free life. I had not been brought up in wealth and affluence. But, amidst a humble upbringing, I had worked my way up to becoming a CEO. I had done national work and I had been appreciated for it. I had worked for several institutions in the region and I was known for my active participation in regional activities and networks. I told myself that I could just continue working for the region in several other capacities, if Lena succeeded in getting rid of me. My mind was prepared and although I liked my job, and the contribution I could make with that title, I convinced myself that it could not be the end of the world.

I remembered the communication between the captain who was sent to war and the Turkish leader, Mustapha Kemal Ataturk. When the captain realized that he was sustaining too many casualties, he sent a telegram to his boss: "Master, your Majesty most urgently requested to make peace at any price; catastrophe inevitable." And the reply that came from Kemal, "Impossible to conclude peace; if unavoidable, retreat in best order." The Turkish leader, Mustapha Kemal Ataturk whose troops had been sent to the war front and his commander realized that things were rough and his forces were incurring too many casualties sent word to Kemal. He felt he had to restrict the remaining soldiers to secure the most important part of national territory. To do this he sent a telegram to his leader: "Master: Where is the defence line?" Mustapha Kemal answered: "There is no defence line; there is a defence area which is the whole country. Not an inch of it is to be given up until it is wet with Turkish blood."

But who could I turn to. I could not turn to the King to urgently conclude peace between Lena and me at any price, because the catastrophe was inevitable. Other agents of government such as the Supreme State Audit had done that, yet there was no response. Officers in high places in the King's palace had assured me they would intervene on my behalf, but there had been no result. I had been left alone to bear my cross. My mind was now inflamed like pre-World War II Europe which in 1939 was like a tinder box ready to burst into the flames of war at the slightest spark. Serbia's annexation of Bosnia provided that spark. My blood pressure started increasing. It had been stable for years from 120 systolic and 80 diastolic to 135/85. I had lost appetite because even the best meals I liked could not be appreciated by me. I was in utter stress. I did not know where to go.

In many respects I had become like Captain Alfred Dreyfus, a young French Jewish Officer who in 1896 was condemned by court Marshall to a life sentence in Devil's Island for offering to sell French military secrets to the Germans. Much of Dreyfus's accusation was the result of anti-Semitism. In like manner, the accusation I was having from Lena BigStuff which she painted all over the country was partly because I was from a minority ethnic group and she knew she could do anything to me and would not have any person to defend me. I could not afford to have a bulletproof shield to protect me either. This was the kind of life I was condemned to live until she finally had her way and got me fired.

CHAPTER 20

Post -Traumatic Stress

WHEN I LOST MY POSITION AS CEO, SO MANY THINGS CAME INTO MY mind. I thought of how punctual I had been to work. I had wanted to set an example that if I was preaching to workers to be punctual to work I should start by first being punctual. In the Tropicana administration the order of arrival to work was this: The cleaners came to work at 6:30 am to prepare the place for work. The other workers who did not have administrative positions came to work at 7:00 am. The chiefs of bureau and chiefs of services came to work at 7:30 am. Directors came to work at 8.00 am, and the CEO came to work at 9:00 am. I did not follow that order. I came to work at 7:15 am. I would get up at 6.00 am, get a bath, eat my breakfast and at 7:10 am I was in the car and in five minutes I would be in my office. Workers were not happy with that because, with my early arrival in the office, I was able to see all those who were coming late to work. But because we did not have punch machines to tell when workers came to work, I decided not to be too strict with the workers on that matter because they could also defend themselves that they had problems catching taxicabs to get to work on time. All I did was to be early at work so that the workers would feel guilty if they did not emulate my early arrival to work.

I had spent a good bit of my personal money for Institute activities. It was sad to remember how much of my personal money I had put in to improve the infrastructure in the Institute. I was in a way not reasonable enough to know how government money could be used in reimbursing individuals. I did spend my money to do Institute work because the procedure in securing money quickly to solve Institute problems was very long. The policy set by government, I came to understand, was that all expenses had to have been approved by the board of administration before any spending could be done with Institute money. For instance, when I took up the post as CEO, I noticed that drivers were not stable.

They would leave the campus and go to a nearby snack to get a drink. If a scientist wanted the driver, he would reply in his phone that he was rushing his sick child to the hospital. There would be no way to track his exact where-about. I decided to build an office, as a matter of urgency, for the drivers, so as to be able to track where the drivers could be found at any time. I considered this to be an urgent expenditure which could be easily justified when I submitted the receipts for the expenditure. That was not possible. I lost that money.

But the normal administrative procedure was that in spite of the urgency, a file had to be prepared comprising estimates given by an authorized contractor. That file would be submitted to the board of administration which in a budget session would approve it. The approval would authorize the CEO to spend Institute funds for the office building. That would just be the beginning of the process. Then the budget officer would prepare a file and send it to the chief financial officer who would visa it and send it to the financial controller. The financial controller would visa it before sending it to the CEO for a final signature authorizing the expenditure before the construction work could be done. Then, the accountant would prepare a check or bank transfer to pay the contractor to build the office. This was good for the control and protection of government money. But frankly I found this too long if any urgent improvement of this nature had to be achieved. So I would deep my hands in my pocket and spend my money, have the office building put up very quickly, and expect to be reimbursed later after the normal procedure had been followed by the finance staff. I was making a mistake which I only came to realize when I had left the place since I failed to be reimbursed for any of such expenses.

I did all this because I loved my job and wanted to make a difference in the institute which I was now heading. I believed I was going to be evaluated at any time based on the number of new things I had done, and how innovative I had been to do them. But as far as administration was concerned I was doing the right thing but not doing it the right way. It was wrong to spend my private funds to pre-finance a government operation. I was never reimbursed for the money I spent for that contrary to what I had thought. This was a major stressor I had after I was replaced in my job. I had heard of post-traumatic stress. This was much like it and it was at its peak.

I had known post-traumatic stress disorder (PTSD), to be a mental health condition that's triggered by a terrifying event. In my case the trauma had been caused by my removal from a post in which people thought I was doing really well. In fact, the rumors which went around were that for once Tropicana Rural Development Institute had really had a CEO who was interested in making a different in the place. The symptoms of the stress I had when I was removed included such feelings like flashbacks, nightmares and severe anxiety. I also had uncontrollable thoughts about the event that I had suddenly been replaced at a time when I was at the peak of my activities as CEO, at a time that I was enjoying all what I was doing as contribution in the development of the country. I had great difficulty trying to adjust and cope with the new situation that I was not there to continue the reforms I had started. I knew from my evaluation that the person who had replaced me would never have the interest in improving the place the way I had planned.

What was striking was that my symptoms actually started within one month of my trauma of removal from office, and continued for several years later. Until now, whenever I think of it, it is like I am dreaming. These symptoms have caused significant problems in my social life. When I think of accepting a job of high responsibility I feel uncomfortable about what again would happen to me. I have found it extremely difficult to proceed with activities which were one time normal. The post-traumatic stress tends to interfere with my ability to go about my normal daily tasks. I have intrusive memories, avoidance tendencies, negative changes in thinking, my mood, changes in physical and emotional conditions and the way I generally look at things. Everything appears negative to me. I feel that whatever I do again in life, no matter how well I do it will be considered inadequate. It will boil down to being useless.

Since then, (it has already been ten years) I have tended to have intrusive thoughts such as repeated memories about things in an involuntary way. Sometimes I have distressing dreams, and even in those dreams I dream of other dreadful events. I think of friends who had passed away and how they would come and help in building up the place I had left. Other times I think so deeply about the efforts I put in my job that I find a fresh trauma piercing my heart as if the event only happened yesterday.

In the first year since I lost that job I hated being reminded of the event. I tended to avoid hearing anything about TRDI and how it was functioning. One day, I think it was about 4:00 pm. My guard came into my sitting room when I was relaxing and told me that a group of people had come to see me. Some junior colleagues of TRDI had come to tell me how bad the Institute was now run by my successor. They said no research was being done, the scientists had just organized themselves in gossiping cliques to chat about their frustrations brought about by the current management. Even the scientific journal I had created was no longer functioning. I listened to them but that discussion did not appear to please me. At some stage I avoided just seeing people from TRDI. Since I left the place I have never entered the campus and have avoided it altogether. My mind just tells me that I should resist talking about what happened in those twenty months with Lena BigStuff and how I feel about the treatment she gave me.

Even now friends tell me my mood has changed since I was replaced in that job. They even feel my cognition abilities have reduced somewhat. I personally feel I am unable to remember important aspects of the job, and keep only thinking of the bad meetings and insults I had from Lena, and the slandering from my predecessor. I keep telling myself that no one can be trusted in this world because I had never expected that the person I was confiding in was going to be the one to blackmail me in front of Lena, simply because he wanted my job. There is an ongoing fear, horror, anger, guilt and shame. When I want to keep myself busy, my mind instead goes off the rails. I personally do not have any interest in activities which I previously enjoyed. Even my real estate business that I really enjoyed because I liked seeing builders do my work, has turned out to be sour. My mind makes me feel detached from friends and those things which we used to discuss which used to please and satisfy me so much. I used to find time to do jogging to keep fit, but now the interest in outdoor activities like that had gone. I used to like videography and making compact discs from videos I had taken. That also was no longer of interest to me. I had been asking myself if life was going to continue like that.

In all these I remain indebted to my family which has played a wonderful role in bringing me together again. My wife told me the ashes would be gathered and life would go ahead. Even during meals, we keep reviewing the problems I had had with Lena over a twenty-month period, the many insults she had given me and how every meeting I attended in the ministry became a scene for showing how incompetent I was, and how I had finally been saved from going to jail. During our chats my wife kept telling me that I had worked so hard throughout my upbringing and my during my schooling, and that I had done my best in my professional career that it was time to rest and not bother about Lena and her problems. Sometimes during rest we would think of the day when my successor was inaugurated, how my wife accompanied me to the ceremonial grounds. We went over the lousy speech Lena made giving the impression to all who attended the event that appointments of the CEO were the prerogative of the King, and that the King had taken his decision to replace the CEO and was urging the new person to be respectful to hierarchy as he had been chosen by the King to head the prestigious research institute. Then we would remember the colourful speech she had made when I was being inaugurated in that position twenty months earlier.

I also had a lot of comfort from many of my workers of TRDI. Throughout the first one month following my trauma, many of my workers came to my home and gave me words of comfort. They all indicated that the trauma was since long awaited, and said that it was even wonderful that it took twenty months to happen because they had been aware of the struggle between Lena and me. They praised me for a job well done, adding that it was admirable to see someone who stood by his words and beliefs, one who did not mind losing a big job like that of CEO because his conscience told him he could not do the wrong thing to satisfy a Minister. They said that I was very brave because the way the storm was coming I would have been in jail. Everything they said was true. It was just amazing that they had been keeping stock of the pressures I was having from Lena, and the famous 700,000 US dollars she was asking me to give. It had become a major scandal in the country.

The story was well known and had spread viral but I did not know that because I was not talking about it to people. I thanked each group that came to condole with me very heartily and I thought to myself that it was now time to think of other things to do to make my life interesting.

About one week after I was removed, I received a long letter from a friend from Sierra Leone, giving me consolation for what had happened. In his letter he told me that he had foreseen the change ever since he learnt that at the start of that job Lena had warned me, the CEO, that she did not want me to carry out any research in my Institute because TRDI had enough results to give the farmers; according to the Minister all that was needed was to transfer those results to farmers. The friend told me that that was when I had to know that in essence what Lena was telling me was to prepare my mind that the funds I was receiving from government for the Institute had to be transferred to her to carry out her political adventures and keep herself in power.

Letters poured from many parts of the region all sympathizing with me. They were sorry for the country because they all had had a lot of confidence in it. Then some mentioned how the same kind of politics had been done to cause the re-location of the ISTRC-AB symposium from the Federal Republic of Tropicana to Nigeria. Others consoled me by saying that unfortunately the continent had several resources to make it even become more developed than countries like the USA but that with people like Lena, whose major objective of governing was to amass wealth, the continent would continue to be underdeveloped, in spite of all the preaching that was being done about rigour and moralization.

Many friends and colleagues who had participated in various research networks with me advised me not to bother at all, stating that the region was interested in my experience and expertise. They indicated that I had done quite much for the region and that I now had even more opportunities to do so and work for the benefit of the region.

When I had composed myself somewhat I started doing my consultancies in the region again. The first place that invited me was the West Africa Center for Crop Improvement in Ghana. It was nice to meet colleagues I had not seen for quite some time, and to make a contribution in graduating new PhDs in plant breeding. I enjoyed the assignment because the students were glad to have a mentor who was guiding them positively in their path of becoming scientists.

Although many people I had met earlier had been exposed to traumatic events like the one I had experienced what differed from the symptoms I was experiencing was the degree of the effects of the trauma as well as how early or how late those symptoms appeared following the event. For instance, a senior colleague working in an international center was sent to identify and receive corpses of scientists who had died in a plane crash on their way to a meeting in that center. For quite some time following the event, he kept dreaming about the horror of seeing those dead colleagues and he kept having frequent hallucinations about the whole idea of seeing dead people he had known and interacted with for long in his working life with the center. I believe that until now, he still has symptoms of post-stress of the event.

In my case, I had a combination of acute stress, social adjustment and disinhibited social engagement because I was just completely cut off from friendly company. I even hated to receive phone calls from friends who found my life too moody to contain because they had been quite intimate to me. I guess my acute stress was because my trauma started immediately and continued days after I was replaced. I had distress and tended to have problems with the way I was carrying out activities in my daily life. For some ten years or so I was thinking about the event, and each time something strange happened, my mind went back to what had happened to me several years back. For instance, a year ago, news reached me that a nephew –in-law had been shot in Maryland. It hurt me so much that I started thinking of the bad memories I thought I had forgotten when I was replaced in my job. It was as if I was the one who had been shot. I could hardly sleep for the one month that followed. A few days ago when a memorial service was being organized to remember the anniversary of the shooting of the guy, my mind went back to memories about the trauma I had had several years ago. Now I had come to realize that it will be a continuous feeling each time something bad happened in my family.

I have had a lot of adjustment to do. My mind has been conditioned to feel that I still have more adjustment to do to make my daily life good. But I continue to respond to the stressful event that occurred to me ten years ago. Now I see that the trauma was more severe and more intense than what I reasonably expected things to be. Whenever I think of my professional life my mind goes to sadness and hopelessness and I tend to withdraw from people in that Institute who were one time friendly to me. Sometimes I even have headaches and palpitations in my heart. But more traumatic events keep piling up to make the situation even worse. For instance, in June and July 2020 my niece Serah Etonde Bissong, the third child of my late elder sister passed away suddenly after a brief (2-day) fever. She had worked hard to have training in nursing and midwifery and had made tremendous progress in her work in the country, only to die abruptly from a fever. I wept all day thinking that would bring her back. It hurt me so much because till today I do not know what happened to her to cause her sudden demise. Early in 2020 when I visited the country, Etonde had brought me a lot of cooked food which I ate for one full week, and we had a long and fruitful conversation about her plans to build a home so that her husband and her children would have a more comfortable place to live in. Then she died. All those plans could not be implemented. That stressed me so much. I would only think of what would happen to the two innocent girls – Princess and Princessa – who she had left behind, and where her husband would start from there.

But as if that was not enough, just one week after her death, my grand nephew who was also my namesake, died almost abruptly from a cardiac problem which had been diagnosed barely three months earlier. At a tender age of twenty, Jacob Mbua Efome Njie left this world. So my stress continued to reign in my system. Till now I do not know whether it is worth the trouble struggling to go to school and making a career because all this effort could just end abruptly one day.

I have comforted myself that a stressor could be a single event (such as a romantic breakup), but could also be a chain of sad events that could befall an individual. The stress could also be just one event with a cumulative effect. Such a stressor could be recurring or continuous (such as an ongoing painful illness with increasing disability such as a slipped disc or a slowly advancing neoplasm). Stressors may affect a single individual, an entire family, or a larger group or community (for example, in the case of a natural disaster which causes several parts of a country to suffer). I had had my own share of stresses which followed my initial trauma of being removed from office. I try now to be in a position to console others in the family and in the community.

CHAPTER 21

Tropicana versus Me

· ·

WHEN I WAS NAMED CEO OF TROPICANA RURAL DEVELOPMENT Institute, the individual who was named to assist me was a gentleman from the northern part of the country. I thought it was a good match because I had known him for quite some time and so I thought we were going to be compatible in running the institute. I also felt that he would bring to the administration the experience he had gained from heading one of the remote research centers of the institute.

After our inauguration, we started work as a team which was determined to make a difference in running the institute. He told me one thing which impressed me and which made me have confidence in him, "My father is a *lamido* (a chief) in our village of origin. He has warned me that an assistant is an assistant; his role is to help his boss as much as possible. So as you are going down to the capital, remember to be obedient to your boss and you should give him as much assistance in his work as possible." I thought that was reasonable counsel his father had given him. Whether what he was telling me was true was a different story. But I believed him.

So I opened up to him, telling him how we would operate together to run the Institute smoothly. I told him that if there were any benefits we were being given as leaders of that Institute, we would share them well and that he should trust me in what I was telling him. During the first month of our reign things were good and we were happy doing the work that the State had entrusted in us. Then the bombshell came on the 3rd of the following month. That was when Lena BigStuff, our Minister, sent an emissary to deliver a letter personally addressed to me. When I read the letter, she was instructing me to transfer funds from a secure account in the Treasury to her private account in a commercial bank. I had found this instruction to be bizarre. I sent for my assistant and showed him the letter. I gave him my own impression about the request.

He also swore to me that it was an impossible thing to do, and that one time when he was head of the research center he had received visitors from the headquarters who were making a similar request. He said he did not yield to the request, but nothing happened to him even though from that time he had bad relations with the people who had made the request. I thought I had a good partner who was encouraging me to do the right thing.

I thought of the matter the whole night and decided that I would go and see her the next morning to tell her how implicating her request was. When I met her she was polite in receiving me thinking I had brought her good news about the transfer. I told her that from the Employee manual, for me to be able to make such a transfer I needed the authorization from either the board of administration or from the Minister-Secretary of the Treasury because the transaction carried the risk of taking funds from a secure place (the Treasury of the country) to an unsafe place (a private account in a commercial bank). After I finished explaining that to her, she scolded me and told me, "do you think you are strong enough to try to offer *resistance* to a member of cabinet?" I did not understand why she thought that was a matter of offering resistance to a member of cabinet's request. In my mind I was saying to myself whether I could just go ahead and kill someone simply because a member of cabinet had instructed me to do so.

It became increasingly strange to me because just a month before that letter reached me a cabinet member had been jailed because he had been convicted for misusing funds which had been received from an international agency for the fight against malaria. Also, at the time, another high-level officer had been convicted for swindling funds destined for the treatment of tuberculosis. So when a month after Lena's letter I saw her emissary coming again with another letter regarding the transfer of those funds I was astonished. I knew something was wrong with some people in that country. What was perhaps even embarrassing to me was that these cabinet members were comfortably using the name of the First Lady to commit these crimes. I imagined that the King was certainly aware because he must have been told by his closest collaborators about what was going on. Such firm instructions for CEOs to swindle money appeared too difficult to understand especially as they were given in writing. If such cabinet members were doing these things, could they not even fear what would happen in the event the security decided to make an investigation about those allegations?

The humanitarian work of the King's wife was certainly important but I knew that the King's wife did not lack funds to carry out any such activity. I felt embarrassed. Like others in the general population who were singing the song of embezzlement all over the place I did not know what to do. I went to the office of the board chairman and confided in him several times on the embarrassment I was having with the Minister-Secretary's request, and one instance when he called me to advise me I even showed him a copy of the most recent letter which the Minister had sent to me obliging me to make the transfer. As a former Minister, the board chairman appeared to know the games that were going on when some people found themselves in positions of authority. He was not surprised but he was astonished that it would happen to me just at the beginning of my job as CEO. He advised me not to yield to her request because that was very implicating; it could lead me to jail. He told me one time that he would be hurt if he had not told me the consequences of such actions. He had counseled several subordinates of his in the different cabinet positions he had held in government. He was doing the same to me and I had to take his suggestions seriously to be free from trouble and live a normal free life in the country.

I then remembered the third time that letter of transfer had reached me. That time Lena was actually threatening me that I would face the consequences if I did not yield to her request. When my board chairman discussed the letter with me he told me what he had told me before and advised me to make a copy of that correspondence and be ready to present it to the Security of the country if ever I was called up to defend myself. This was me in my first year as CEO facing threats from my Minister-Secretary who, instead of guiding me in my work, was wanting to get me into trouble. I discussed the issue with my wife. She also advised that I should not attempt to yield to Lena. She told me that there were several CEOs and Minister-Secretaries who were in jail because of lousy transactions like that, most of them using the name of the First Lady to commit their crimes. I picked up courage and decided not to go and discuss with her what I considered to be implicating in the whole affair – making a transfer of that nature without authorization from either the board nor from the Minister-Secretary of the Treasury of the State. And I stayed doing my work.

I had been in the job for about six months when I received a phone call from the Ministry. The call was coming from a lady who was working in the cabinet of the Minister-Secretary of Rural Development Investigations. She told me she wanted to talk to me very urgently on an issue which was worrying her. We arranged to meet in a secure place in town on a certain Friday. When I reached where she was waiting for me, I took her in my car to another place and she started a disturbing story. "Mr CEO, I had been worried with what I have been seeing in the past four months. Your assistant has been coming to see the Minister-Secretary frequently lately and when he goes inside her office he often spends a lot of time, sometimes up to one hour. I have been wondering what he has been discussing. It may be that they are discussing you. We all are aware that the Minister-Secretary has been asking you to give her money. Maybe that is the subject of their discussion. I wanted to alert you never to be disclosing intimate matters to him; he may not be as loyal to you as you think he is."

I was very embarrassed to hear her story. I thanked her and went back to the office. I pondered all day not knowing how to now take this fellow, my assistant, who I had thought was so truthful and loyal to me to the point where I felt comfortable discussing every work-related issue with him, including even problems I was having with the Minister. I thought of the advice to told me his father, the *lamido*, had given him regarding the way and manner he had to live with his boss who was me. Had my assistant been instructed to blackmail me? Had he been promised something in return the reason he was disclosing things about me? But why should someone appearing so honest be behaving like that? I asked myself all kinds of questions but could get no answers to them.

Three weeks later, after a meeting in the Ministry of Rural Development, a friend working in our Ministry, took me to the corner and told me he had something with which to confide in me. He told me it was very confidential. I listened very attentively. "Mr CEO, I believe there is a game going on between your assistant and our Minister-Secretary. They meet at least three times a week and I keep wondering what the subject of their frequent discussions could be. I have heard our Minister make cynical comments about you and how you feel you are *clean*. Be careful not to confide in your assistant any more. He may be a wolf in sheep's clothing, a green snake in green grass." I felt frustrated. This was the second time I was hearing this kind of thing about my assistant.

A board meeting of our Institute was holding. During the coffee break, the representative of the King's Palace in the board was chatting with the representative from the Prime Minister's Office about me, and told her that it appears I was having serious problems with my Minister. She added that these problems would continue until I was kicked out of the place, because the Minister had told her that I was not her own choice as the CEO of TRDI. The person she had preferred as CEO was my assistant, and was even surprised why the King chose me instead after all I was not very useful to the King because I was from a minority tribe and was not capable of bringing in a lot of votes in the event of an election. The representative from the Prime Minister's Office called me later at night and told me to meet her in her house at 8:00 pm. When I came to her house she recounted to me everything they had discussed with the representative from the King's Palace. She warned me that I should be extremely careful with my assistant. He was certainly not very loyal to me as I had been thinking. He could be framing stories about me just to get favors from the Minister-Secretary.

This was the third time I was hearing this about my assistant. Did I have to believe all what I was hearing about him? If so, how could I continue to work with him? I decided I would treat with him strictly on work-related files, nothing personal, and nothing about the Minister-Secretary. That is how things continued between us. I am sure he was surprised with the sudden change in my behavior.

In the next two months the Minister-Secretary of the Treasury made changes of financial controllers in State parastatal organizations, and our financial controller was replaced. The new person was someone, a certain *Likawo*, who had been sent there for a short time when I was not yet the CEO. He was friendly to me and I was happy that a friend had been sent to serve us as my financial controller. In fact when he was inaugurated, we greeted each other very warmly, and I felt that he was going to work well with me. One day, barely one week after his installation, he came to my office and told me he wanted to discuss the famous file concerning the transfer of funds from the Treasury to the Minister-Secretary's account in a private bank. I was surprised with his analysis. "You see, in such matters, what is important is *traceability*. As long as there is a written proof that it is a member of cabinet who had given you instructions to do such a thing, do it if you have a letter to that effect. That letter covers you." I was surprised with his sudden interest in my problems and the nature of his analysis of the situation. It was as if he had been properly briefed of the situation and was sent to TRDI mainly to solve that problem.

I compared what the financial controller was telling me with what the board chairman had told me and what was in the Employee Manual. It was like comparing night and day. Two days later, the emissary of our Minister-Secretary came to our campus and went straight to the office of the financial controller. I do not know what they discussed but what I learnt later was that they were from the same ethnic group, and his appointment to TRDI as financial controller had probably been influenced by our Minister-Secretary with a recommendation from her emissary, Andrew Yabassi. It appeared as if the financial controller had been promised something if only he succeeded in convincing me to effect the famous transfer of funds. That was the only possible explanation for the kind of intervention he had made barely a week of his taking office in TRDI. It appears as if his assignment in sending him to TRDI was to convince me to transfer the funds and that he had to do everything to convince me that there was no implication in doing that as long as I had a letter from the Minister-Secretary, an *authority*, making the request.

I now started to see the slandering and blackmail which had been going on by my assistant each time he went to see Lena. A friend of mine who had an administrative position in our Ministry met me one day and was telling me that he strongly believed there was high-level blackmail going on against me in the Ministry. He told me that several camps had emerged there, and those officers in the tribe of the Minister were all talking about me, and that even those employees from the tribe of my assistant who were in the ministry were not talking good of me. He cautioned that the multiple visits that my assistant made in the ministry were mainly to stir up his kinsmen in telling untruths about me to other workers who could have access to our Minister. Hence his conclusions were that he believed everyone in the chain of slandering was being promised something important in return for telling the Minister false information about me. The hatred of the Minister-Secretary towards me was increasing in leaps and bounds. My friend speculated that my assistant had certainly been promised something really important, something for his personal gain, for him to be talking about me in that manner.

One morning at about 11:00 am, my assistant came to my office and told me he wanted to go to the train station to meet some relatives who had come from the village by train. He excused himself and left. My mind told me to make a trip to town some fifteen minutes later. I went straight to the premises which housed the office of the Ministry-Secretary and packed my car in a parking space behind the office where the car was not visible. The friend came out and told me that, as usual, my assistant was having a *tête-a-tête* discussion with the Minister. I was there for another one hour and they were still having their private meeting. Then I confirmed that something fishy was going on. I needed to be very careful with him.

My board chairman was increasingly disturbed by the problems which were going on between my Minister-Secretary and me. He felt that all those problems were certainly affecting my work. He advised that I stay firm and focused on my work and not bother about what Lena was telling me to do. He had been a cabinet member for twenty years and knew that games of that nature were regularly played by some Minister-Secretaries. He noticed with sadness that such problems were occurring to me also and advised me to be avoiding attending her meetings. I could send my assistant to attend in my place.

Eight months in my position there was a meeting on seed multiplication. Lena invited me for the meeting and I sent my assistant to attend in my place. But Lena called me some minutes later insisting that I had to attend personally. I faked an excuse that I was having a running stomach and did not feel I could attend under such circumstances. She replied that there were restrooms in the Ministry which I could use, adding that the meeting was very important for my Institute and so I had to attend. I reluctantly entered my car and my driver drove me to the Ministry. After just a few minutes of discussing the seed issue, Lena digressed. She announced that the CEO of TRDI was claiming that he was very *clean* and *honest*, whereas if she sent Etame there he would still see dirt in his eye, referring to the Minister-Secretary of the Supreme State Audit in the King's palace. Then she continued with a series of insults to me, accusing me that I had told people that she was a prostitute because she was unmarried and yet was made Minister.

In the days of the former head of state, a female minister could only be named to that position if she was married. But things had changed with the new King. My accountant who was attending the meeting kept pressing my toe and whispering to me that I should not utter a word. But the stream of insults continued. I held my patience and did not say a word. I was just frustrated by the fact that so many other people from other Ministries and even the Prime Minister's office were attending the meeting and were hearing how a Minister was pouring all those insults on another top officer of government, a CEO of a research institute. They were embarrassed with the kind of rhetoric, in a government office and involving a high personality. I bowed my head and stayed quiet till the meeting was over. Without saying a word, even a goodbye, I jumped into my car and we drove back to the office. That evening was painful to me. I wondered if life was going to continue in that manner.

One evening, the emissary, Andrew Yabassi, came to my office and wanted me to go with him, on the instructions of Lena, to see Titi Liyai, a high officer in the Treasury Ministry. He said he wanted me to be assured by Liyai that the transaction of transferring the money the Minister had requested was a normal one. He claimed that Liyai was the person who, on the instructions of the Minister of Treasury, had created the Assistance Fund which the Minister was using to finance the humanitarian activities of the Queen. The objective of the visit was so that I get convinced that the transaction the Minister was asking me to do was legitimate and that I did not have to fear anything about it. We reached Liyai's office but he could not receive me. I stayed in the waiting room while Andrew Yabassi went in to see him. Andrew spent something close to two hours talking to him while I was idling around in his waiting room. When Andrew came out he gave me a flimsy excuse for Liyai's inability to receive me, adding that he had recommended that Andrew should take me to one fellow somewhere in town who had been the clerk who opened the Assistance Account for the Minister. That guy was going to assure me that the account was legitimate and that I did not have to fear. Hearing all that, I was already too tired to be moved from place to place to see all kinds of people. I entered my car and drove back to the office at 6:00 pm, to continue treating the many files which were awaiting me in the office. I had lost some three hours doing nothing, time too precious for a CEO.

Then I consoled myself with what a senior colleague had told me one time about slandering, blackmail and jealousy in the workplace. He told me that of all human vices, none was as destructive and wholly unprofitable as envy, adding that the vices of slandering and blackmail were so bad that they could involve bad threats of physical, mental or emotional harm that could hurt my health; that they could also hurt my family. He said that many times my assistant who was orchestrating all the stuff was certainly doing this for personal gain, and in my case, he was badly looking for my position. That the many promises from my Minister were leading him to say anything, manufacture any kind of lie, just to gain the favor of our Minister and lead her to get me fired. My colleague continued that blackmail could also be considered a form of extortion. She could be doing all these just to intimidate me for purposes of collecting Government money from me. In many countries or jurisdictions, blackmail was a statutory offense, often criminal, carrying punitive sanctions for convicted perpetrators. But in Tropicana, that was not really the case. If an individual had *deep roots* he or she could get by with blackmail to achieve their ends.

After the fourth letter came from the Ministry, I thought the matter was now more difficult for me to handle by myself. I needed to confide in some people in high places. The first person I thought of seeing to seek his advice on this matter was Hunter Stone, a gentleman who had good reputation in the country and who was working in the King's Palace as one of his advisers. I booked an appointment to see him and he received me on a certain Thursday. When I arrived the King's Palace, I was registered by the Security people at the main office in the entrance since the records showed that I was being expected by Hunter Stone. A minivan took me from where I parked my car to a parking lot close to his office.

As I entered his office he could tell I was going through a lot of stress. My face was filled with wrinkles. My lips were dry. As was usual with him, he greeted me with a lot of courtesy and gave me a seat. He listened to my story, and all he told me was, "Dr, you are my younger brother. All I can tell you now is just go back and do your work. The politicians will go but the technicians would remain. Many people know she is not a good person and we wonder why she is still there. I frankly do not know what I can do about a matter like this." I left his office, rather disappointed with his response, and returned to my office still pondering if I had done the right thing by confiding in him. I had not had the consolation I badly needed from him.

The next person I decided to see was the chief of cabinet of the King. In the Federal Republic of Tropicana, the chief of civil cabinet had the rank and prerogatives of a Minister-Secretary, and was appointed by the King. He was in charge of the King's residences and houses, among other duties which were many and diverse; on a regular basis he was in effect serving as the private secretary of the King, and being the closest person to the King, he held a very powerful position. And to see him was an almost insurmountable affair. Because of the wide array of duties (many of which were unspecified) he was assisted by two deputies all having the rank and prerogatives of Minister-Secretary, and by technical advisers, *Chargés des Missions and Attachés*. The King had other close collaborators such as the Minister of State Permanent Secretary General of the King's Palace responsible mainly for administrative issues in the country. He was assisted by two Deputy Permanent Secretaries.

Normally, the chief of cabinet was the principal secretary of the King. Every document that had to be signed by the King had to pass through the chief of cabinet who determined whether or not it could be submitted for the signature of the King. That tells you how powerful he was. Cabinet members made submissions on a range of important issues such as policy initiatives, the introduction of government legislation, financial appropriations and key appointments. The office of the chief of cabinet received and processed these submissions and if found appropriate, the chief of cabinet would visa them and submit them to the King for signature.

People who worked in the cabinet of the chief of the civil cabinet were trusted people. All of them were appointed by the King after the recommendation by the chief of civil cabinet. Because of the many confidential files which they treated, they were given a lot of benefits. They could be fired anytime the King heard something like releasing confidential information from the Palace. But every now and then, a few would leak out some information concerning a top officer in government who was in trouble. In return they hoped to have a small tip from that person for taking the risk to release that kind of crucial information.

I went through several steps to be given an appointment to see the chief of civil cabinet of the King. The day finally reached when he received me in his office. When I arrived I was first led by one of his employees to his waiting room. I sat in that comfortable waiting room and waited to be ushered in. I could see the staircase leading to the office of the King. I was now very close to power, the highest office in the Land. I was in the process of arranging my documents in the way I would present the information to him when he majestically walked out of his office to meet me. When he reached where I was sitting he greeted me politely and made a joke, "Mr CEO, why are you with so many papers and files as if you are going to attend a board meeting. Take it easy."

He led me into the office he used for receiving people, gave me a seat and listened to my story. At the end of my narration, he smiled and told me that the emissary of the Minister, Andrew Yabassi had really lied that he was working in the King's Palace and that he was the one who the King often sent to *survey* any place where the King wanted to go to. He had also lied to me that he was the one who could give recommendation to the King about any place the King wanted to visit before the King could make his trip to the place. He told me that even for international trips, only people in his immediate protocol could be sent to ensure the place was safe before the King could make a trip to those places. He ended by saying this: "the only people who are close to the King are the people you see on the TV moving with the King when he moves around.

No one should claim to be any closer to the King. What I would do is that one day I would invite you and your Minister to my home to discuss the problems you are facing because whatever the problems, you two are condemned to work together." That famous meeting in his home never held until I was fired.

One day I got a phone call in my office and a gentleman was calling me to tell me he had a very urgent message to give me. We met late that evening and he showed me a letter my Minister-Secretary had written to the King asking that I should be replaced because of *gross insubordination*, whatever that meant. But it showed how far my problems with her had gone. I knew I had been doing the right thing, and decided to fight it hard.

The next person I decided to see about my problem with the Minister was the Permanent Secretary at the King's Palace. He is someone I had known faintly and he had been a cabinet member for a long time. I thought he could assist me by giving me useful suggestions to the problem. After recounting the story of the problems I was having with my Minister, he called his assistant, the Permanent Secretary No. 2. When he came in the Permanent Secretary told him something that I had come to see him for. I found that very surprising and that worried me, "This is my homeboy. He has problems with his Minister *simply* because his Minister is asking him to give him *some small thing*, and he is refusing." I was startled first because such a high officer would consider that to be a normal transaction. Secondly because he called 700,000 US dollars a *small thing*. I knew I was in trouble, in real hot soup. If the Permanent Secretary in the King's Palace felt that the transaction was a normal thing, then who could I see again? I returned to my office and continued with my grief.

One week later the Minister called a meeting in her cabinet office. This meeting was attended by our board chairman also. After the meeting we went back to our research campus and the board chairman sent for me. When I entered his office he started analyzing the highlights of the meeting which we had just had. He said that he was most surprised with the conduct of the Minister throughout the meeting. First she announced during the meeting that she had written to the King to replace me. Such things were never made public in a meeting, until they happened. Secondly, she brought in her bodyguard, a *gendarme* officer, to protect her throughout the time the meeting was going on. How on earth could high officers of the state be having a meeting, discussing important State issues with their Minister, and a bodyguard is called in to stand by to protect the Minister? He told me he was very frustrated with that kind of behaviour. He concluded by telling me to be very careful with that kind of Minister. But how careful could I be? I just had to wait for the bomb to explode. Later, the board chairman had asked for an appointment to see the King. Probably it was to discuss my issue with the Minister. But the King appeared to have received the information about our problem. Whatever the case, he was now directly informed by my direct boss, and could do anything to arrest the situation if he liked to.

Lena sent more letters to the King insisting that I should be replaced. Each time she wrote, someone leaked out the information to me by giving me a copy. Of course Lena was now certain that I was not willing to make the transfer. Her greatest worry at this stage was that all these letters about my being fired were reaching the King but he was not taking any action. The King probably had his collaborators working on the file who would eventually get enough information to enable him make an informed decision. I believe the recommendations that his collaborators gave him was that in order not to bring an entire Institute to a halt, the best thing would be to separate the two people. It was a lot easier to get rid of me than the Minister-Secretary who, under the circumstances in Tropicana, could be removed only after a cabinet reshuffle. On that fateful morning I was informed that I had been replaced. It was not announced over the radio as it is often done because that time was election period and the King did not want to lose votes from my area of origin. If nothing else, my frustration was over. I would no longer be insulted in meetings. I would no longer be threatened to steal money from government coffers. I had lost a job for which I was very prepared, but I was now a free person. I had to do something else to keep life going.

CHAPTER 22

Post-mortem of TRDI

· ·

I HAD BEEN INFORMED BY A RELIABLE WORKER WHO I HAD GROOMED and who was occupying a high office in TRDI that the Institute was dead; it was only there by name. He had given me enough information to make me believe that any information I could receive about TRDI would only break my heart because in spite of the amount of effort I had put to redress a failing institute, things had gone worse after I had left. Not much was going on there in terms of technology development. I started wondering what could have happened to the Institute so abruptly after my departure. Just to satisfy myself, I felt I could carry out a post-mortem examination of TRDI.

A post-mortem (from Latin post mortem "after death") is an investigation of a corpse to determine the cause of death. It could also be an exercise which is carried out at the end of a project-solving scenario, which attempts to determine the cause of death in a work setting, where the individual or group examines the challenges and successes of the endeavor. First recorded in the year 1725 the objective of a post-mortem is intended to help people learn from past incidents. A post-mortem is easily done by examining a body after death, and can give reliable information to determine the cause of death. The examination typically involves blame-free analysis of an event after it has taken place. Post-mortems are of considerable importance the reason in almost half of all deaths each year in developed countries there is a post mortem examination. Post-mortem is synonymous to autopsy with the simple difference between them being that post-mortem is an examination conducted after the death of an individual whereas an autopsy is a dissection performed on a cadaver to find possible causes of death.

Although I was no longer in the Institute, I was interested in knowing what had happened to it immediately after it was known to have become inactive because, in a post-mortem exam the time difference between the time of death and the examination of the body, called the post-mortem interval (PMI), is a crucial period because the longer the PMI, the harder it would be to determine the cause of death. That is why pathologists have identified four stages after death: Pallor mortis, algor mortis, rigor mortis and livor mortis.

Pallor mortis (Latin: *pallor* "paleness", *mortis* "of death"), is the first stage of death. In this stage there is an after-death paleness that occurs in those with light/white skin. It is often measured with the help of an opto-electronical colour measurement device which is used to measure paleness of bodies. Algor mortis (Latin: *algor*—coldness; *mortis*—of death), is the second stage of death. It is characterized by a change in body temperature after death. First measured by the Scottish doctor, John Davy in 1839 and first used by the US physician and physiologist, Bennet Dowler in 1849, in this stage there is generally a steady decline in body temperature. This of course could be influenced by the ambient temperature such as it occurs in the hot desert where the cooler body acclimates to the warmer environment. Rigor mortis (Latin: *rigor* "stiffness", and *mortis* "of death"), also known as post-mortem rigidity, is the third stage and one of the recognizable signs of death, characterized by stiffening of the limbs of the corpse caused by chemical (mainly calcium) changes in the muscles after death. In humans, rigor mortis can occur as soon as four hours after death. Contrary to folklore and common belief, rigor mortis is not permanent and begins to pass within hours of onset. Typically, it lasts no longer than eight hours at "room temperature.

Livor mortis (Latin: *livor* – "bluish color", *mortis* – "of death"), or postmortem lividity is the fourth stage of death and one of the signs of death. It is characterized by a settling of the blood in the lower portion of the body after death, causing a purplish red discoloration of the skin. After death when the heart stops functioning and is no longer agitating the blood, heavy red blood cells sink through the serum by action of gravity. The blood travels faster in warmer conditions and slower in colder conditions. Livor mortis starts in 20–30 minutes, but is usually not observable by the human eye until two hours after death. The size of the patches increases in the next three to six hours, with maximum lividity occurring between eight and twelve hours after death. The blood pools into the interstitial tissues (extracellular tissues) of the body. The intensity of the color depends upon the amount of reduced haemoglobin in the blood. The discoloration does not occur in the areas of the body that are in contact with the ground or another object, in which capillaries are compressed.

A post-mortem examination should preferably be carried out within 24 hours after death. However it could be conducted within two to three working days of a person's death. Post-mortem examinations should be carried out by pathologists, medical experts who have been trained in and with expertise in diagnosing disease through looking at tissues and cells. They are able to decipher from the observation of body tissues the changes that could occur to them after death. The post-mortem examination of TRDI was conducted by the Supreme State Audit Agency, giving me doubts as to whether that agency was competent enough to determine all aspects that could have caused the death of TRDI – research implementation, financial management, personnel management, infrastructure and other aspects concerning the functioning of the Institute. The finding of the Agency was that Lena BigStuff should leave TRDI alone and should not interfere with the administration of that Institute because TRDI was an institution created by the government of Tropicana as an autonomous institution with a management of its own. But the other aspects of the running of the Institute had not just been neglected but ruined in such a way that the competence of Supreme State Audit was limited in deciphering all causes of the Institute's death.

When a person dies, his or her estate must go through probate, which is a process overseen by a probate court. If the decedent leaves a will directing how his or her property should be distributed after death, the probate court must determine if it should be admitted to probate and given legal effect. But with TRDI, since it was created by the King, only the King had to decide what to do with the patrimony of a dying institute, not Lena BigStuff, the Minister, as she had always claimed from her doctrine of ministerial infallibility.

Post-mortem care, which must be done out of respect anyway, is preparing a body for viewing after the patient has died, and may involve the process of closing the patient's eyes, putting on a clean gown by the nurse, and transporting the patient to a funeral home by a paramedical team. But with TRDI, Lena did not even want that last care to be given to the Institute, because being highly *budgetivorous*, she wanted to continue sucking the remaining juice out of the Institute until it was completely dry.

Whereas autopsy involves three levels – toxicology (that is pharmacology, chemical analysis), histology (analysis of body tissues), and microbiology (the complete analysis of the infection that may have caused the disease which led to the death) - as part of the whole internal examination, the post-mortem examination of the TRDI was done only in parts and has never given the population of Tropicana a holistic view of the situation.

In a dead body many things happen physically. A week after death, the skin blisters and the slightest touch could cause it to fall off. A month after death, looking bigger as the skin dries out, the hair, nails and teeth will fall out. In TRDI, as the skin was falling apart, every officer of the institution was just making the best out of the situation – amassing wealth and property and satisfying themselves with ethnic concerns.

Immediately after death it is advisable to keep the atmosphere around the deceased simple and peaceful, being careful not even to disturb or touch the body immediately after death. With TRDI, there was enormous turbulence as the CEO, Minister and even board chairman contested to make financial gain and social benefit out of the situation.

At least with a dead body, a hospice team works with the patient's family to support them as they deal with all the emotions and responsibilities involved, because a loved one has died, one of the most important aspects being to guide the patient and the family through the actual dying process, helping all concerned to recognize the signs of dying, what to expect, and how to prepare for the outcome along the way. But with the death of TRDI, everything came abruptly, no measures being taken to prepare the minds of the populations and those who had taken the pains to faithfully lead the institution before its fall, who could at least have made, or attempted to make efforts to come to its rescue or salvage the falling pieces.

As a result of the variability of the speculations (the different crops and animals being researched), an autopsy of the situation could better be conducted by Regional programs committees and validated by scientific committees who were capable of determining how much had taken place from the situation existing before the fall of the Institute. This of course, required enormous resources that could only be set aside if there was need to redress the situation. And if the King was interested in maintaining the Institute, he would have found it important and necessary to commit those funds to save the Institute.

The first thing to determine in the death of the TRDI was the output of agricultural research. When I was leaving the institute there were twenty-two research programs in TRDI, lodged in the various agro-ecological zones of the country, according to the importance of the activities of the research program in the zone. For instance, the root crops program stretched from the humid forest zone of the south to the moist savanna Adamaoua region of the country. There were scientists and facilities for them to carry out their research in all the regions. The cereals program (with research on maize and rice as the most important) stretched from the humid forest region to the soudano-sahelian region of the country. By contrast, the banana and plantain program as well as the oil palm, latex and stimulant crops (coffee, cocoa and tea) programs were only found in the humid forest, some stretching up to the western highlands at most. To carry out a good analysis of the state of affairs of agricultural research in TRDI, separate scientific committees, endowed with scientists of renown in the respective crop disciplines, needed to be created and given the responsibilities of dissecting the entire research of the country to determine what the causes of the malfunctioning of the various systems were.

In keeping with her doctrine of ministerial infallibility, Lena did not want any research activities to be conducted in TRDI, because according to her there were sufficient research results in the institutes that only needed dissemination to the users. Her doctrine insinuated that any funds received from any source by the institutes had to be transferred over to her, without any resistance at all, for her political gains, to bribe the powerful that mattered to keep her in power. But who could carry-out an autopsy of the research of the institute? No one was interested.

The Institute had started a new scientific journal, the *Cameroon Journal of Agricultural Science*, during the time I was working in the Institute. In fact, I was the founder of the journal, and was supported by the CEO of the Institute and the Minister at the time. It had taken so much effort on my part to organize and set up the functioning of the journal. It had taken much time even to get an International Standard Serial Number (ISSN), an eight-digit number assigned to many serial publications such as scientific journals, newspapers, magazines, annals, and series of books, for their identification. This made it easier to search for specific scientific articles in indexing databases and large data sets, for instance from the Internet.

The scientific journal had become as many are, an excellent means to convey research findings, latest discoveries and developments, and future research prospects to the public. It allowed scientific professionals not only in the country but also in the entire region to ensure that the information shared was accurate. The peer-review process also held each article up to a high standard and as a result, the manuscripts submitted and accepted by the journal were written with great care in an effort to clearly and effectively convey the findings of research initiatives.

The manuscripts submitted to the journal could include original research, re-analyses of research, reviews of literature in a specific area, proposals of new but untested theories, or opinion pieces. Thus, the journal enabled communication between scholars, formed the basis for the development of further ideas, and tracked emerging ideas in the many fields of science such as crop agronomy, livestock production and fisheries, forest and environmental sciences and agricultural economics. The journal had become quite reputable with great visibility and credibility for the researchers who published in it and even opened the way for further career opportunities. These factors made articles published in it to carry a lot of weight in the region.

Surprisingly, a journal which had been started to give more opportunities for local country scientists to publish the results of their research had become so popular that it was receiving even more scientifically informative and sound manuscripts from other institutions in the region.

But just at a time when so many research scientists all over Africa were becoming used to it as a scientific information medium, the journal disappeared with the sudden change of the leadership of the CEO. No one was interested in running it and even those who were interested could not afford to harness the time and effort to run a scientific journal. What a pity!

Just a few months after I left the Institute, there was a massive rush of recruitments. The first promoter of this was, as usual, Lena BigStuff. She felt that the obstacle had been taken away and that it was time to fill the place with people from her ethnic group. The new CEO let her have her way but for every Lena *moliki* who was brought in, he inserted a CEO *muza* also. Then the board chairman who had been quiet about such interventions also started filtering in people from his region. So the entire workforce was now made up of three regions – the west, the north and the east. There was now no consideration of the implication of these needless recruitments on the financial capacity of the Institute.

The CEO soon fell out with Lena BigStuff because of her frequent quest for money but also because of her many interventions for recruitments. To maintain himself in power, the CEO decided to make very powerful alliances with people who could help keep him in power. He remembered what had happened to me. I had been kicked out mainly because I did not have any people in high places who could defend or protect me. The first person he attracted himself to was the permanent secretary at the King's Palace. He provided him with land to make extensive plantations for himself. In addition, he provided him with field equipment for ploughing the land. It did not end there. He gave him the manpower to maintain the land, weed the fields and carry out the many field operations of fertilization and irrigation on the plots.

When Lena BigStuff wanted to get rid of him, she would send so many letters to the King's Palace complaining that he should be removed. She would present her regular motive of insubordination but those letters, passing through the permanent secretary were just thrashed away. He is still there, for ten years now. It is alleged that even his promotion to the grade of chief research officer had been influenced by that same permanent secretary. What a system! That is the way the system worked. I had to be part of it or get kicked out.

CHAPTER 23

Concluding remarks

• •

As a young researcher the life I had lived growing up in TRDI was filled with stresses. I had stresses from the heads of structures under which I worked, because we had just different perceptions of the way things had to go. There were also stresses when the time came to move to higher grades in the research. As I thought of getting promoted because I had met the prescribed requirements for advancement, my rivals did everything to stop me from growing. In addition, there were instances of instability in the administrative positions I occupied. I would get appointed to a position and my rivals would fight hard to have me dropped from the position. A time came when I was given the responsibility to be chief organizer of the ISTRC-AB symposium, an international event, when the Federal Republic of Tropicana was chosen to host the symposium. I had the greatest disappointment of my life when our symposium was re-located to a different venue simply because the file requesting funds for the event was not just transmitted to the King. This stressed me very much and over a long period of time.

Research in Tropicana hardly had sufficient funds for their activities. Because of this I found myself stressed most of the time but I managed to sail through that by making alliances with colleagues in the international research centers who came to my rescue as they shared their research activity resources every now and then so that I could be kept active and busy. This enabled me to continue improving my publication record which other colleagues in the Institute could not. In fact they found it strange that I kept publishing at a time when they were idle. Some even felt I was just publishing without working. This led to slandering in the workplace especially when it started appearing that I had been brought to the limelight and could easily be considered for higher positions in the headquarters of TRDI.

The CEO of TRDI would not stand the idea that I could one day succeed him. He did many nasty things to implicate me and get me out of the system, but that again did not work.

When I finally became CEO of TRDI, the stresses continued. I had to deal with project heads who had direct connections with the Minister and would see her anytime without passing through me. In TRDI, I had frustration continued with a CFO in whom I had a lot of trust. He did things that could have let me go to jail. Then came the organization of the agricultural show in Ebolowa, which required substantial amounts of funds. But my Minister would not want me to get access to the funds. I strained myself to borrow money from business friends until the event successfully came and passed. Again my Minister, unhappy with my success in the show, did everything to prevent me from being seen and appreciated by the King who was presiding over the occasion. Others intervened and that came to pass.

The Minister did many immoral things and expected me to get implicated and go to jail. But that did not work; I survived. But I ran into post-traumatic stress as I kept thinking about the many things that I had been subjected to do by the same Minister who ought to have been protecting me instead. All kinds of investigators from government agencies stressed me by visiting me and questioning me about mismanagement of funds but again I survived. I was even subjected to a psychiatric evaluation to determine if there was something not wrong with me that was making me refuse to do things which others found normal.

People, pretending to come from the King's palace, tried as much as they could to dupe me and get funds out of me. That again did not work. I kept managing to succeed in my tasks as a CEO.

Although my principle was to aim at high staff retention so as to capitalize on their experiences, occasions came when I had to hire and fire. Despite the many problems that I faced as a researcher, I had successes as a growing scientist and rose to the top of the research ladder of research professor. I had the opportunity to attend high profile scientific meetings all over the world which enabled me to listen to sound presentations given by high-quality experts on hot issues in science such as Barbara McClintock's transposable elements,

Bachmann's quantitative trait loci, Eberhart and Russell's regression analysis of genotype x environment interactions, and all kinds of issues that I had only seen in the literature. I was also able to rise to the top of the administrative ladder as a presidential appointee to the prestigious position of CEO of the largest research institute of the region, where I had to manage 1200 workers from 256 ethnic groups in the country as well as supervising expatriates from 10 nationalities. I learnt many lessons in the process. First, many expatriate scientists preferred to be left alone so that their outputs would be judged only by the organizations from which they came. Others even wanted to keep occupying technical positions in the Institute although the Institute was never involved in evaluating their scientific growth.

In spite of all these I could still show a positive balance sheet as a scientist not only in the country but in the region as a whole, with many contributions in the scientific literature from my work in TRDI and in the region. As research administrator I was appreciated for my work by many who were subjective enough to make a positive evaluation of me. I could say I was successful as a CEO. I could turn things around and make things happen. For once, I could get to make a difference in the way things were done, and could select the people I wanted to work with, instead of being told who my boss and workers would be. I could do something about the problems I often complained about and could get to make my own decisions and minimize doing things which I thought were stupid. I was able to do what I thought was right and could choose the chances which I was going to take in doing them. I could get to make decisions that I thought could make the world a better place, using my influence and resources available to me for my choice of initiative.

Now as chief executive, I was still able to attract some benefits which made my life more comfortable than before. As CEO, the most benefit I had was from travel. Nothing could be as relaxing as flying in a brand-new Airbus 380 aircraft on a first-class ticket for twelve hours. Comfortable stay in high-level hotels on trips provided me with the most luxurious conditions I ever had in my entire life. During long-distance transit I could only remember the warm comfort and soothing effect that a good massage gave me as I lay in a private room in the waiting lounge awaiting the continuing flight on another new Ethiad Airlines aircraft from Abu-Dhabi to Jakarta, Indonesia.

Also, as CEO I was not penniless, I had enough to take care of my bills and living costs and still take care of the needs of my extended family. I would receive executive compensation determined by the board of directors alongside with my salary as a civil servant. Extra benefits included allowances as chief executive, guards in my office, a free home, guards in my home and a functional house staff (including a cook and one worker to tidy the home). I also had Institute service vehicles (an SUV for long trips and a sedan car for in-town errands).

But for the two years I was CEO, my Minister, Lena BigStuff, and I had a serious conflict of beliefs. Our thoughts were moving on parallel lines all of the time. She wanted money which was under my control to use to keep herself in power. I wanted to use government funds to foster research activities and make an impact in the country and the region. At the end I realized that I could not last in my job because I had a *budgetivorous* Minister. I was fired.

I had been fired from my job as CEO but as I was relaxing in my home thinking of what to do with my life, the messenger came with a mail. A European institution was inviting me to attend an important meeting on research management which had been scheduled much earlier before I left the job of CEO. They knew that I was no longer the CEO but they needed my expertise and wanted me to be the one to attend.

I made my suitcase and was ready to make the trip in the next one week. I wanted to leave a handing over note to my successor so that he would start off well in his duties as CEO. Unfortunately, I had not had one when I took over as CEO. I dotted the i's and cut the t's in a document I had started a year earlier which summarized my experiences in the Institute. I scribbled a few more current lines while editing the booklet and the manuscript was ready for the press. I titled it: *Greed, ethnicity, tribalism and administrative power: a post-mortem of the Lena BigStuff Research Institute.* I placed one copy of the manuscript on the table of the CEO, and sent the other to the press.

The next day after my arrival in Europe, just when the meeting was about to begin, we were given a folder containing the working documents for the research management meeting. When I opened the folder one of the documents was a well printed glossy copy of *Greed, ethnicity, tribalism and administrative power: a post-mortem of the Lena BigStuff Research Institute*. Later, I was surprised to see that the booklet had been translated into two European languages and copies were already available in the shelves of the libraries of the institute which was hosting the meeting. The booklet seemed to have been really interesting to the point that it was also translated in a regional African language in which Lena BigStuff, the main character, was referred to as "*un echantillon ya pamba* (meaning *a worthless sample*). The popularity of the booklet, I was told later, was probably because it vividly documented the problems of research management in tropical Africa.

END